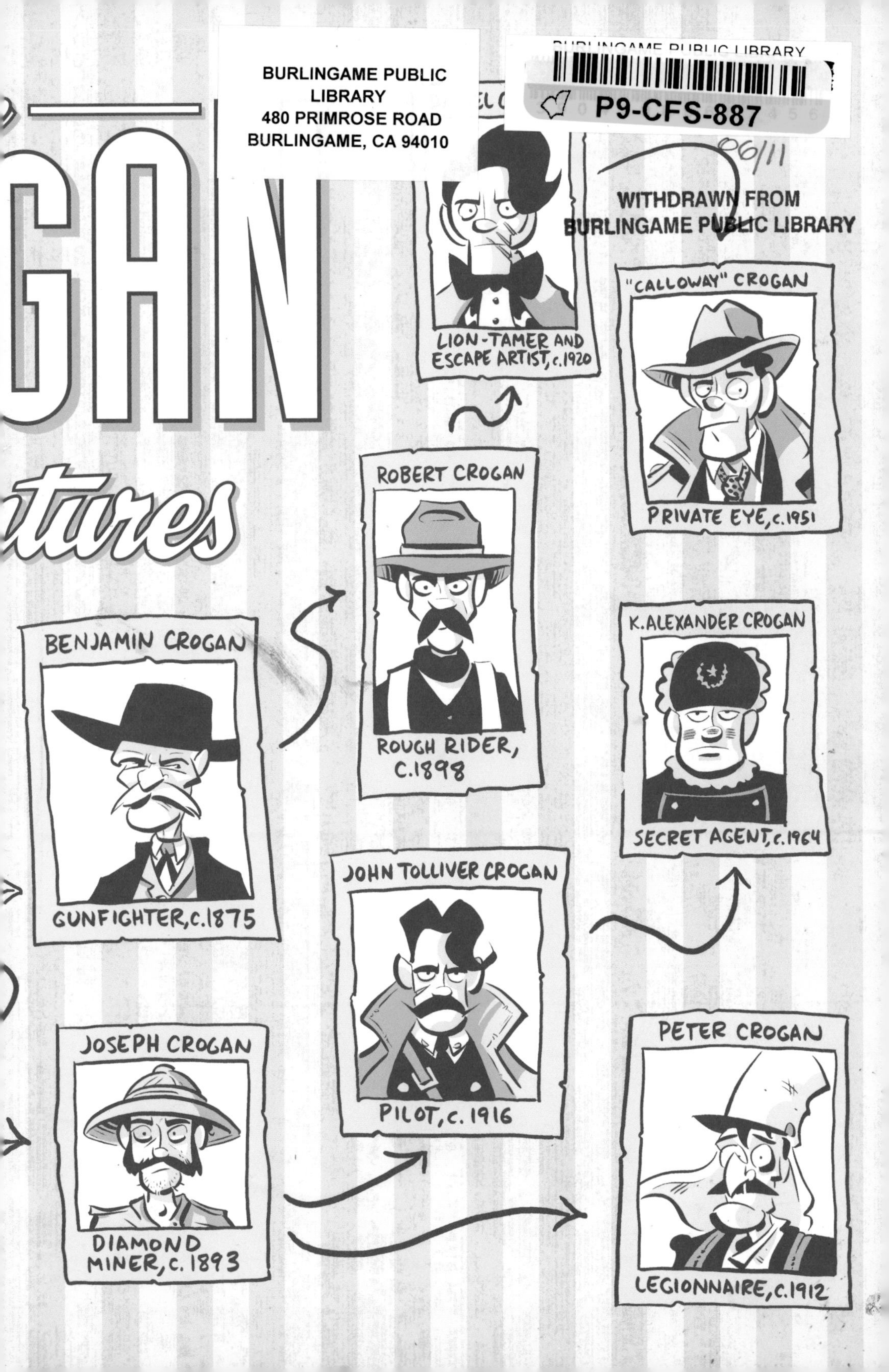
LION-TAMER AND ESCAPE ARTIST, c.1920
"CALLOWAY" CROGAN
PRIVATE EYE, c.1951
ROBERT CROGAN
ROUGH RIDER, C.1898
BENJAMIN CROGAN
GUNFIGHTER, c.1875
K. ALEXANDER CROGAN
SECRET AGENT, c.1964
JOHN TOLLIVER CROGAN
PILOT, c. 1916
JOSEPH CROGAN
DIAMOND MINER, c. 1893
PETER CROGAN
LEGIONNAIRE, c.1912

CROGAN'S™

VENGEANCE

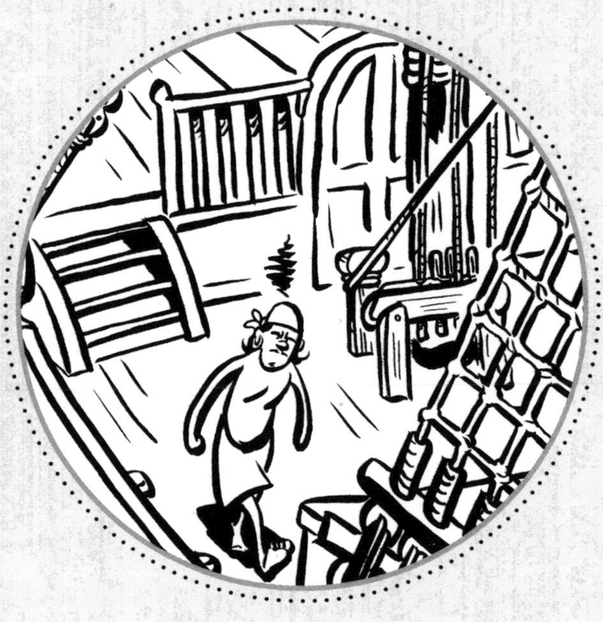

ONI PRESS

This book is for my father, whose love of history,
pirates, and comic strips was contagious.

....

CROGAN'S
VENGEANCE

by

Chris Schweizer

. . . .

book design by
Keith Wood

edited by
James Lucas Jones with **Jill Beaton**

ONI
PRESS

Published by Oni Press, Inc.

JOE NOZEMACK, publisher

JAMES LUCAS JONES, editor in chief

RANDAL C. JARRELL, managing editor

CORY CASONI, marketing director

JILL BEATON, assistant editor

DOUGLAS E. SHERWOOD, production assistant

ONI PRESS, INC.
1305 SE Martin Luther King Jr. Blvd.
Suite A
Portland, OR 97214
USA

www.onipress.com
www.curiousoldlibrary.com

First edition: October 2008
ISBN: 978-1-934964-06-4

3 5 7 9 10 8 6 4 2

Printed in China.

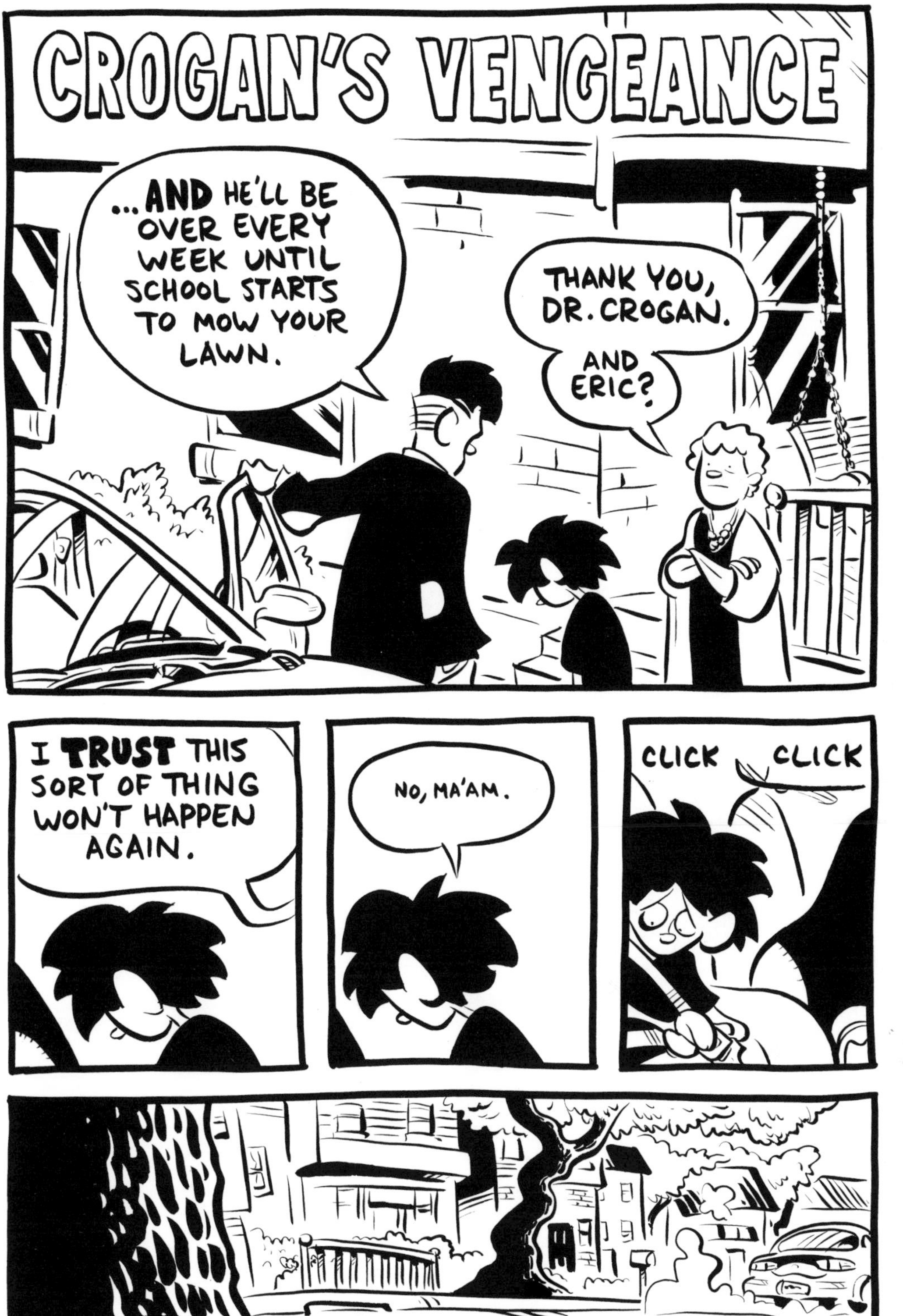
CROGAN'S VENGEANCE
...AND HE'LL BE OVER EVERY WEEK UNTIL SCHOOL STARTS TO MOW YOUR LAWN.
THANK YOU, DR. CROGAN.
AND ERIC?
I TRUST THIS SORT OF THING WON'T HAPPEN AGAIN.
NO, MA'AM.
CLICK CLICK

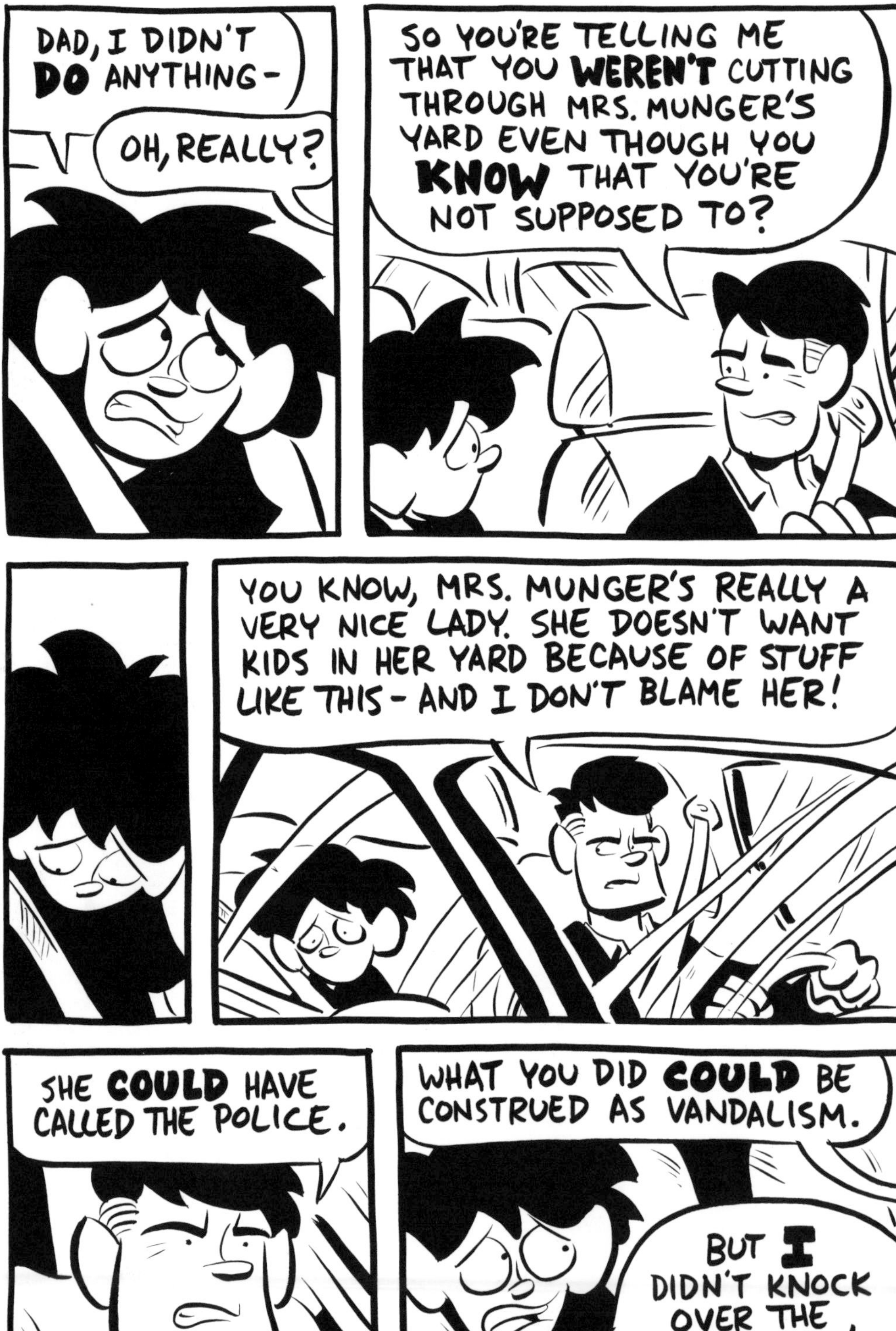
DAD, I DIDN'T **DO** ANYTHING-
OH, REALLY?
SO YOU'RE TELLING ME THAT YOU **WEREN'T** CUTTING THROUGH MRS. MUNGER'S YARD EVEN THOUGH YOU **KNOW** THAT YOU'RE NOT SUPPOSED TO?
YOU KNOW, MRS. MUNGER'S REALLY A VERY NICE LADY. SHE DOESN'T WANT KIDS IN HER YARD BECAUSE OF STUFF LIKE THIS - AND I DON'T BLAME HER!
SHE **COULD** HAVE CALLED THE POLICE.
WHAT YOU DID **COULD** BE CONSTRUED AS VANDALISM.
BUT **I** DIDN'T KNOCK OVER THE BIRDHOUSE!

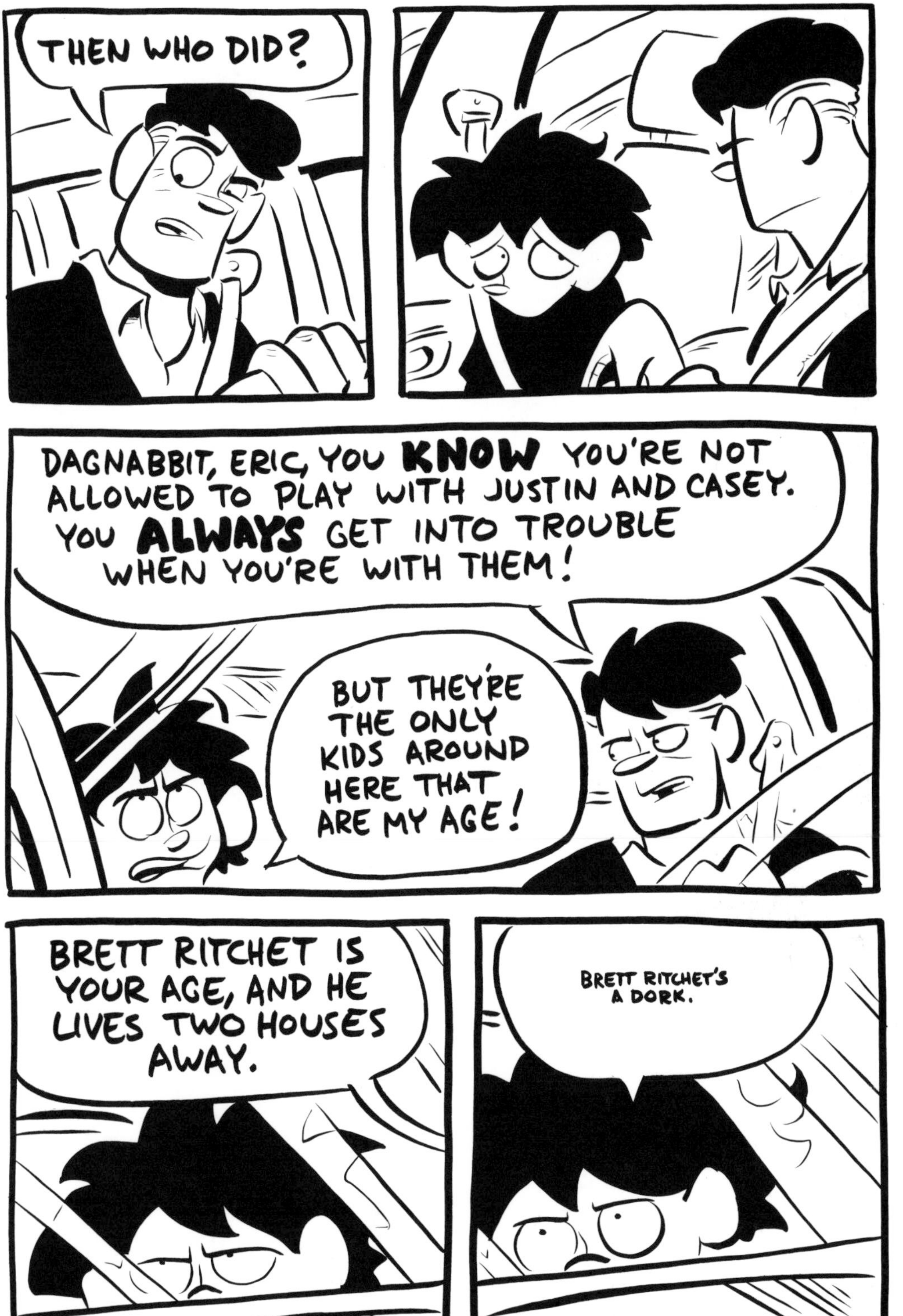
THEN WHO DID?
DAGNABBIT, ERIC, YOU **KNOW** YOU'RE NOT ALLOWED TO PLAY WITH JUSTIN AND CASEY. YOU **ALWAYS** GET INTO TROUBLE WHEN YOU'RE WITH THEM!
BUT THEY'RE THE ONLY KIDS AROUND HERE THAT ARE MY AGE!
BRETT RITCHET IS YOUR AGE, AND HE LIVES TWO HOUSES AWAY.
BRETT RITCHET'S A DORK.

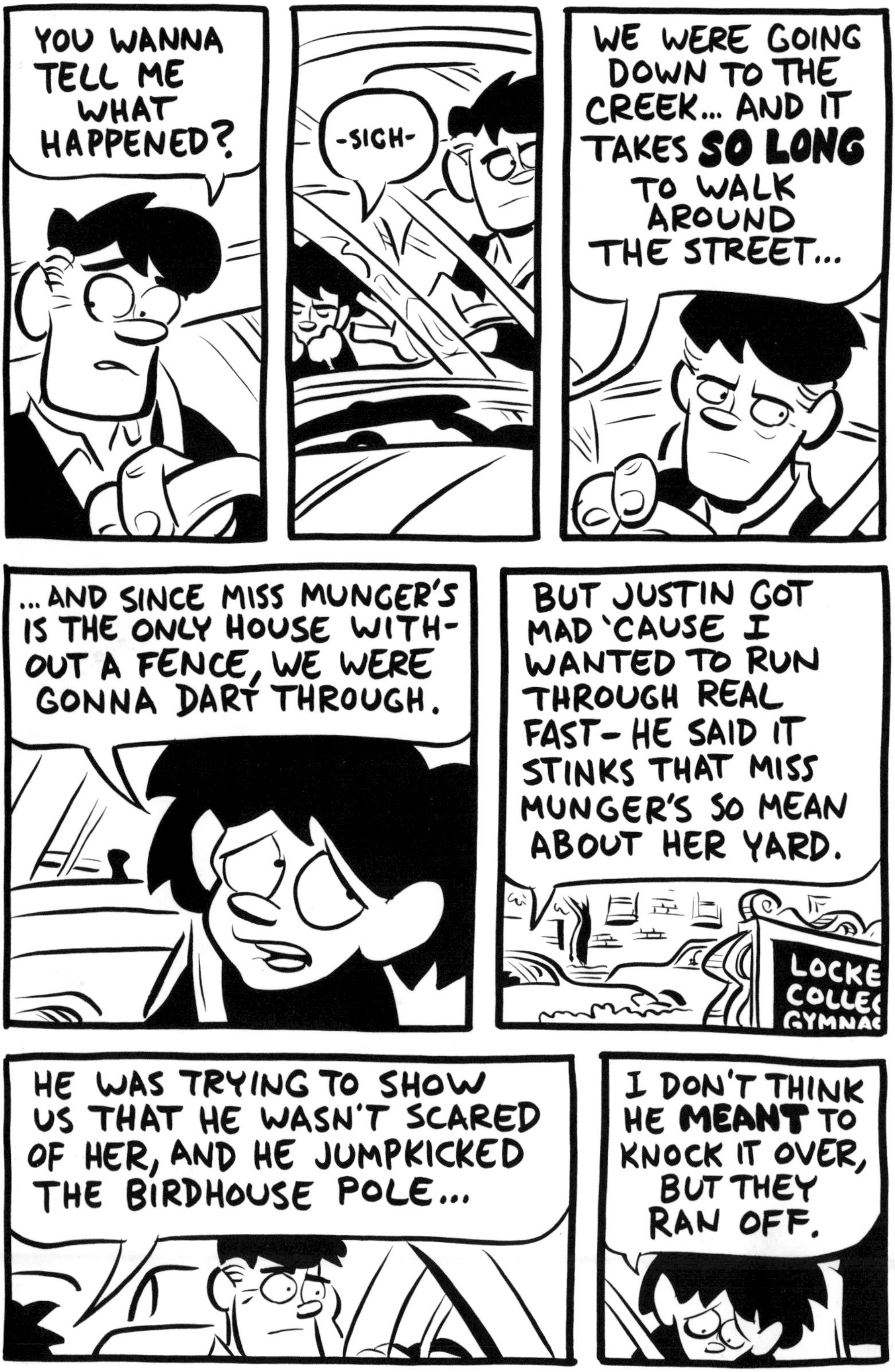
YOU WANNA TELL ME WHAT HAPPENED?
-SIGH-
WE WERE GOING DOWN TO THE CREEK... AND IT TAKES SO LONG TO WALK AROUND THE STREET...
...AND SINCE MISS MUNGER'S IS THE ONLY HOUSE WITH-OUT A FENCE, WE WERE GONNA DART THROUGH.
BUT JUSTIN GOT MAD 'CAUSE I WANTED TO RUN THROUGH REAL FAST- HE SAID IT STINKS THAT MISS MUNGER'S SO MEAN ABOUT HER YARD.
LOCKE
COLLEG
GYMNA
HE WAS TRYING TO SHOW US THAT HE WASN'T SCARED OF HER, AND HE JUMPKICKED THE BIRDHOUSE POLE...
I DON'T THINK HE MEANT TO KNOCK IT OVER, BUT THEY RAN OFF.

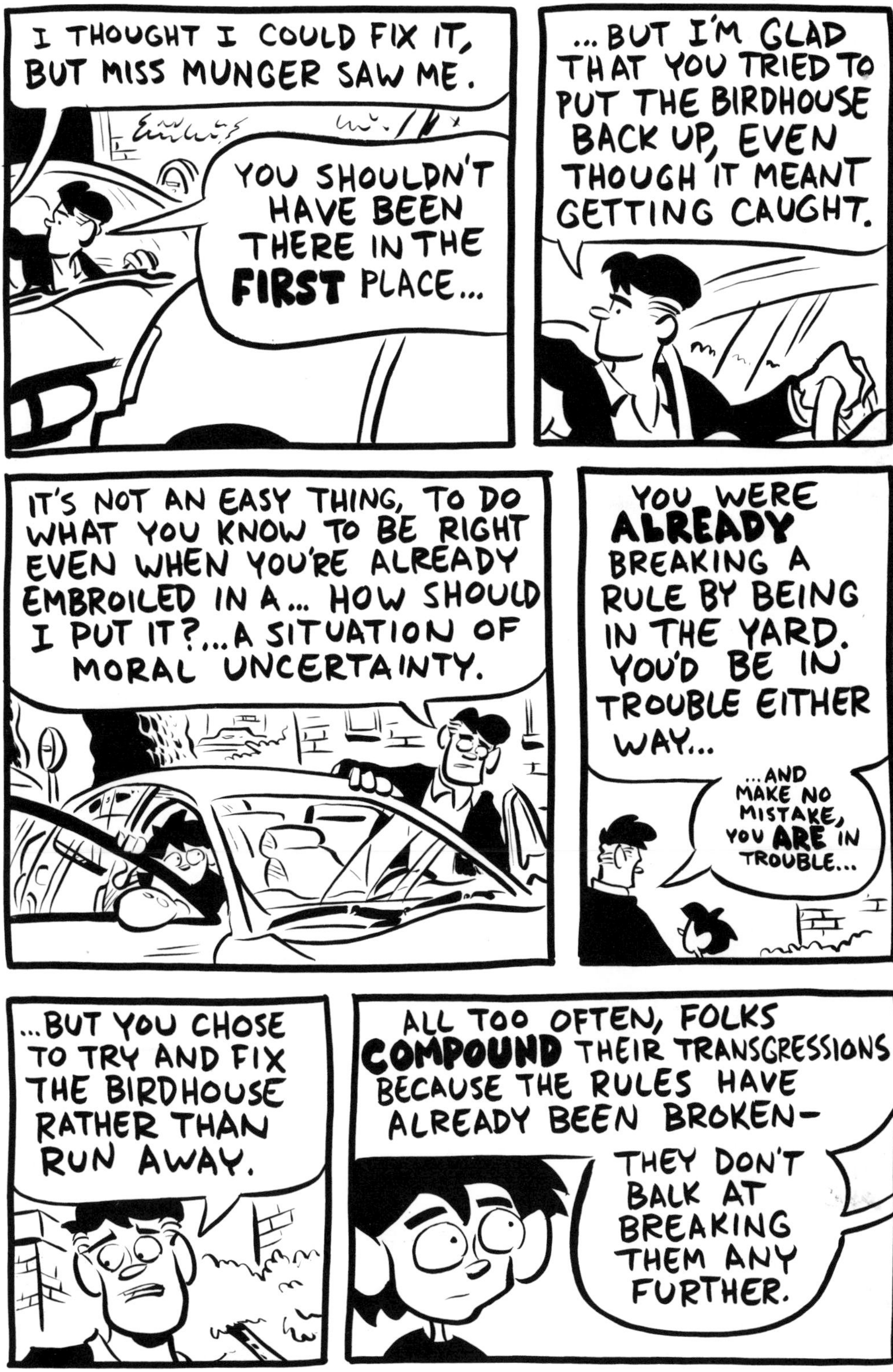
I THOUGHT I COULD FIX IT, BUT MISS MUNGER SAW ME.
YOU SHOULDN'T HAVE BEEN THERE IN THE **FIRST** PLACE...
...BUT I'M GLAD THAT YOU TRIED TO PUT THE BIRDHOUSE BACK UP, EVEN THOUGH IT MEANT GETTING CAUGHT.
IT'S NOT AN EASY THING, TO DO WHAT YOU KNOW TO BE RIGHT EVEN WHEN YOU'RE ALREADY EMBROILED IN A... HOW SHOULD I PUT IT?...A SITUATION OF MORAL UNCERTAINTY.
YOU WERE **ALREADY** BREAKING A RULE BY BEING IN THE YARD. YOU'D BE IN TROUBLE EITHER WAY...
...AND MAKE NO MISTAKE, YOU **ARE** IN TROUBLE...
...BUT YOU CHOSE TO TRY AND FIX THE BIRDHOUSE RATHER THAN RUN AWAY.
ALL TOO OFTEN, FOLKS **COMPOUND** THEIR TRANSGRESSIONS BECAUSE THE RULES HAVE ALREADY BEEN BROKEN-
THEY DON'T BALK AT BREAKING THEM ANY FURTHER.

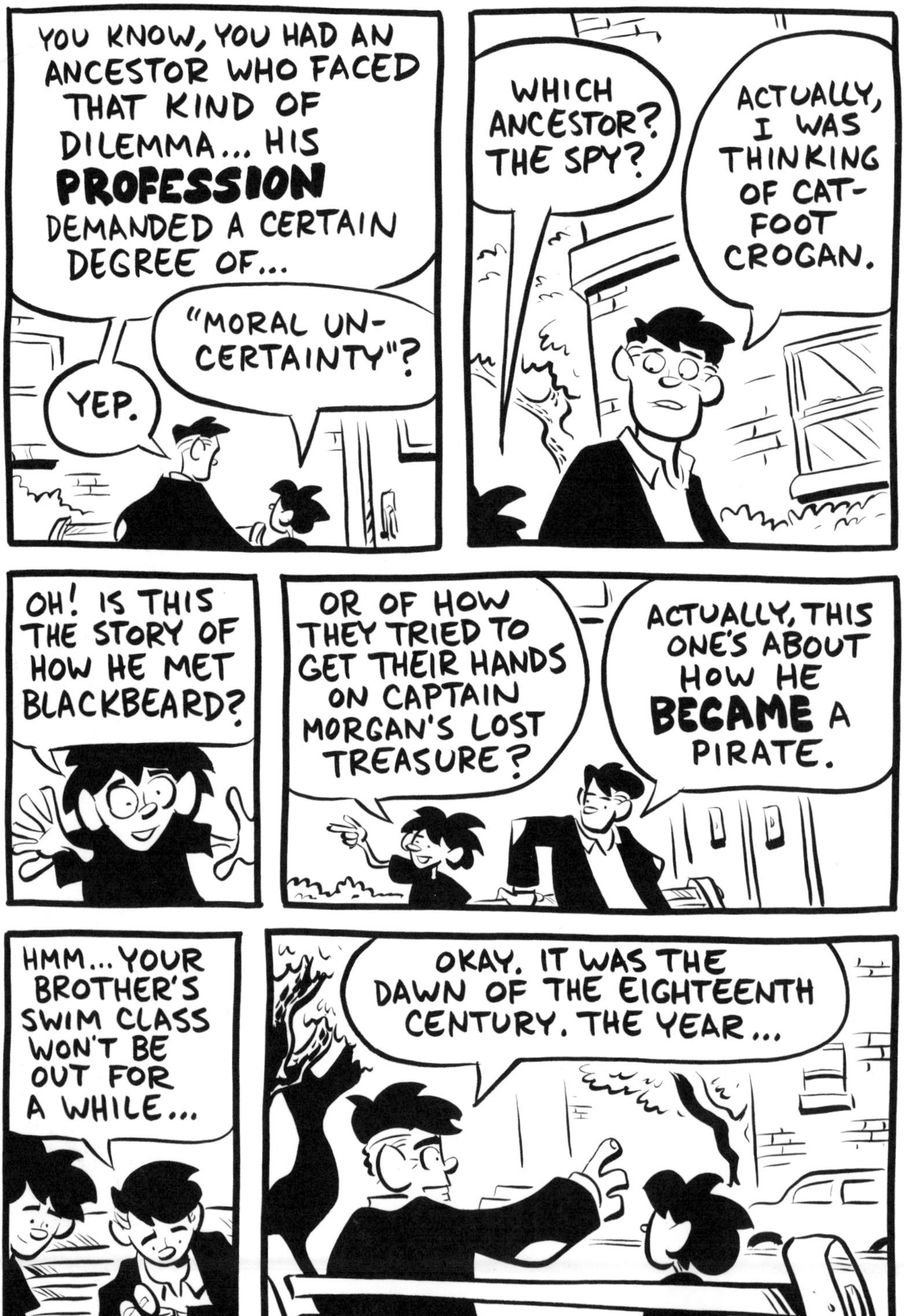
YOU KNOW, YOU HAD AN ANCESTOR WHO FACED THAT KIND OF DILEMMA... HIS PROFESSION DEMANDED A CERTAIN DEGREE OF...
"MORAL UN-CERTAINTY"?
YEP.
WHICH ANCESTOR? THE SPY?
ACTUALLY, I WAS THINKING OF CAT-FOOT CROGAN.
OH! IS THIS THE STORY OF HOW HE MET BLACKBEARD?
OR OF HOW THEY TRIED TO GET THEIR HANDS ON CAPTAIN MORGAN'S LOST TREASURE?
ACTUALLY, THIS ONE'S ABOUT HOW HE BECAME A PIRATE.
HMM... YOUR BROTHER'S SWIM CLASS WON'T BE OUT FOR A WHILE...
OKAY. IT WAS THE DAWN OF THE EIGHTEENTH CENTURY. THE YEAR...

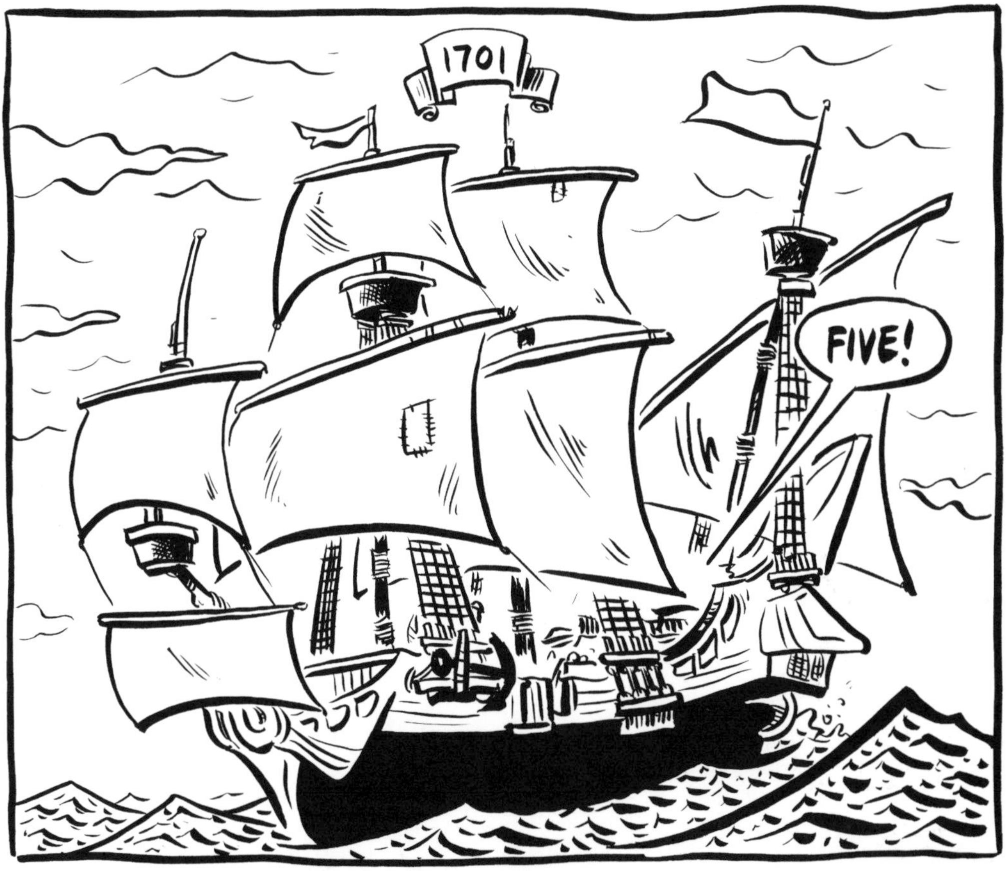
1701
FIVE!

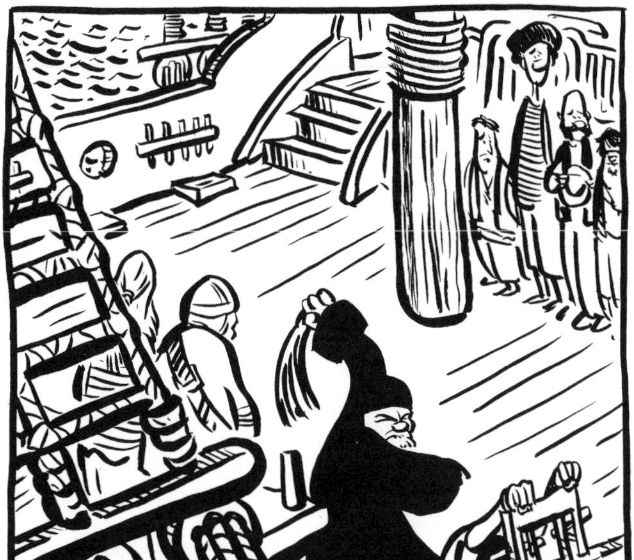

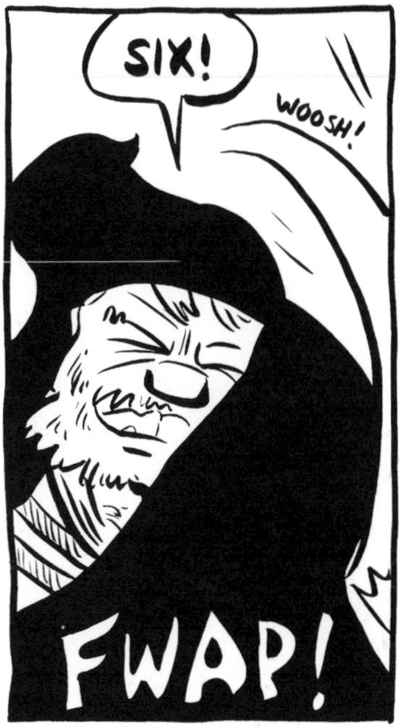
SIX!
WOOSH!
FWAP!

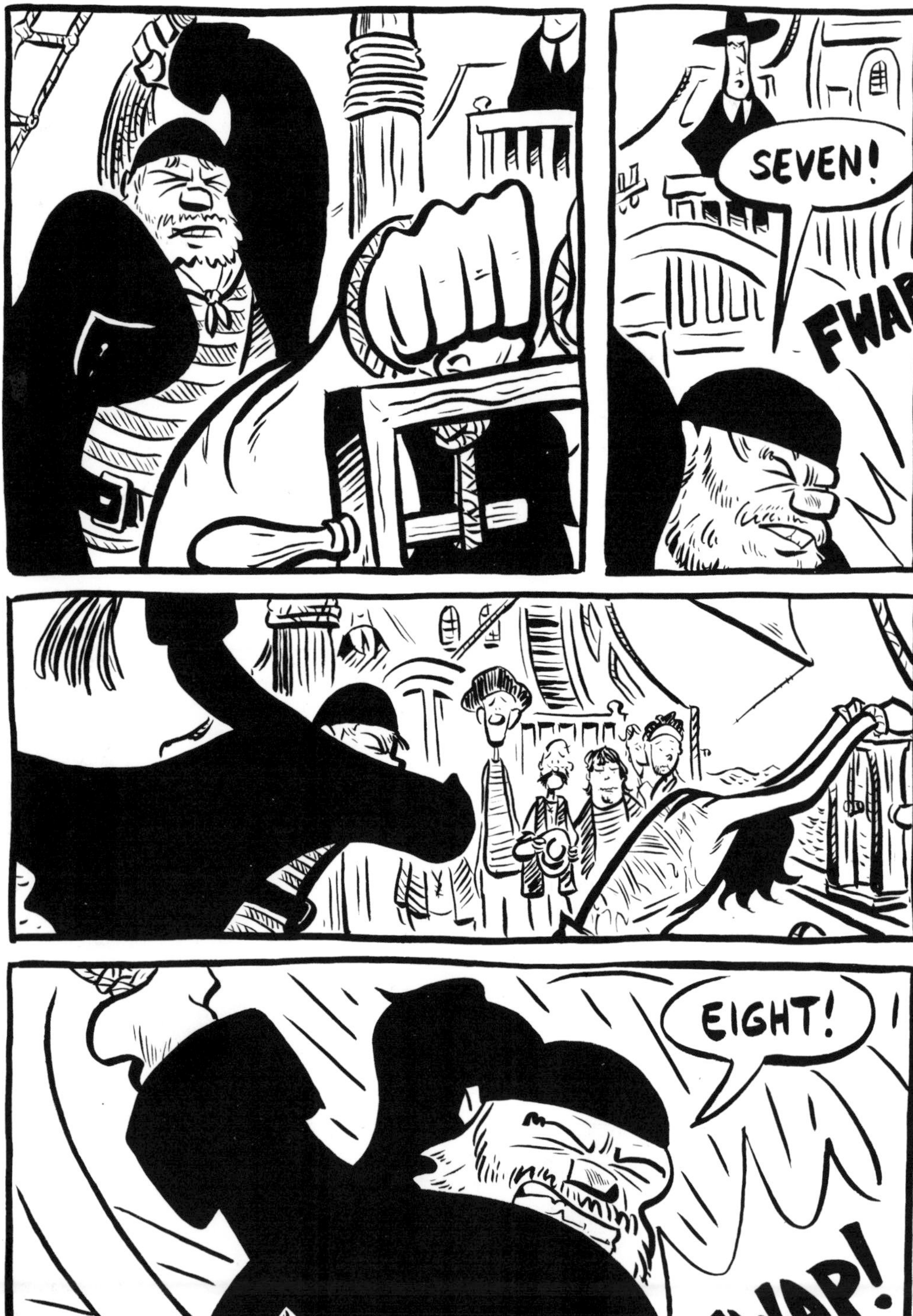
SEVEN!
FWAP!
EIGHT!
FWAP!

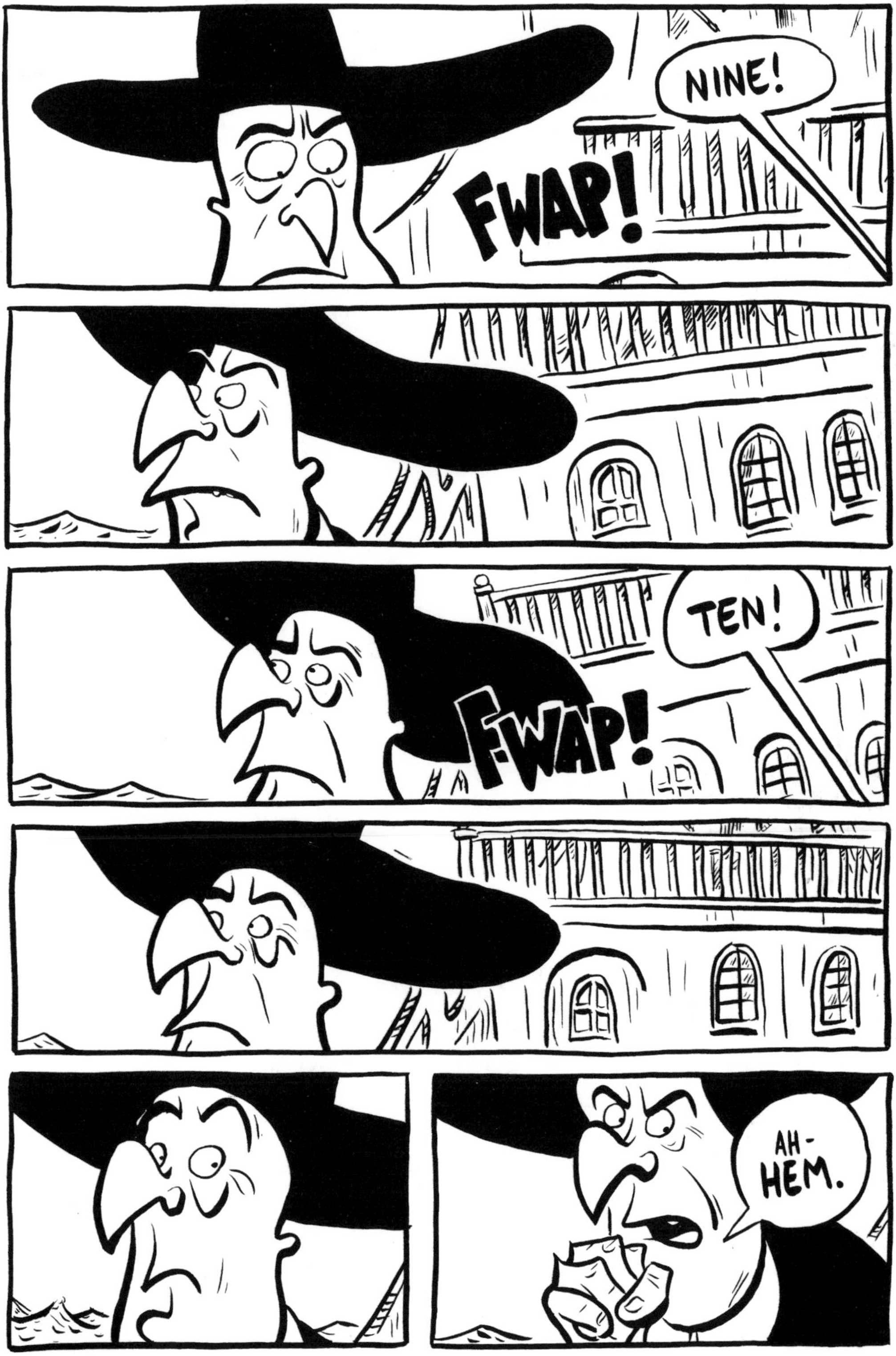
FWAP!
NINE!
F-WAP!
TEN!
AH-HEM.

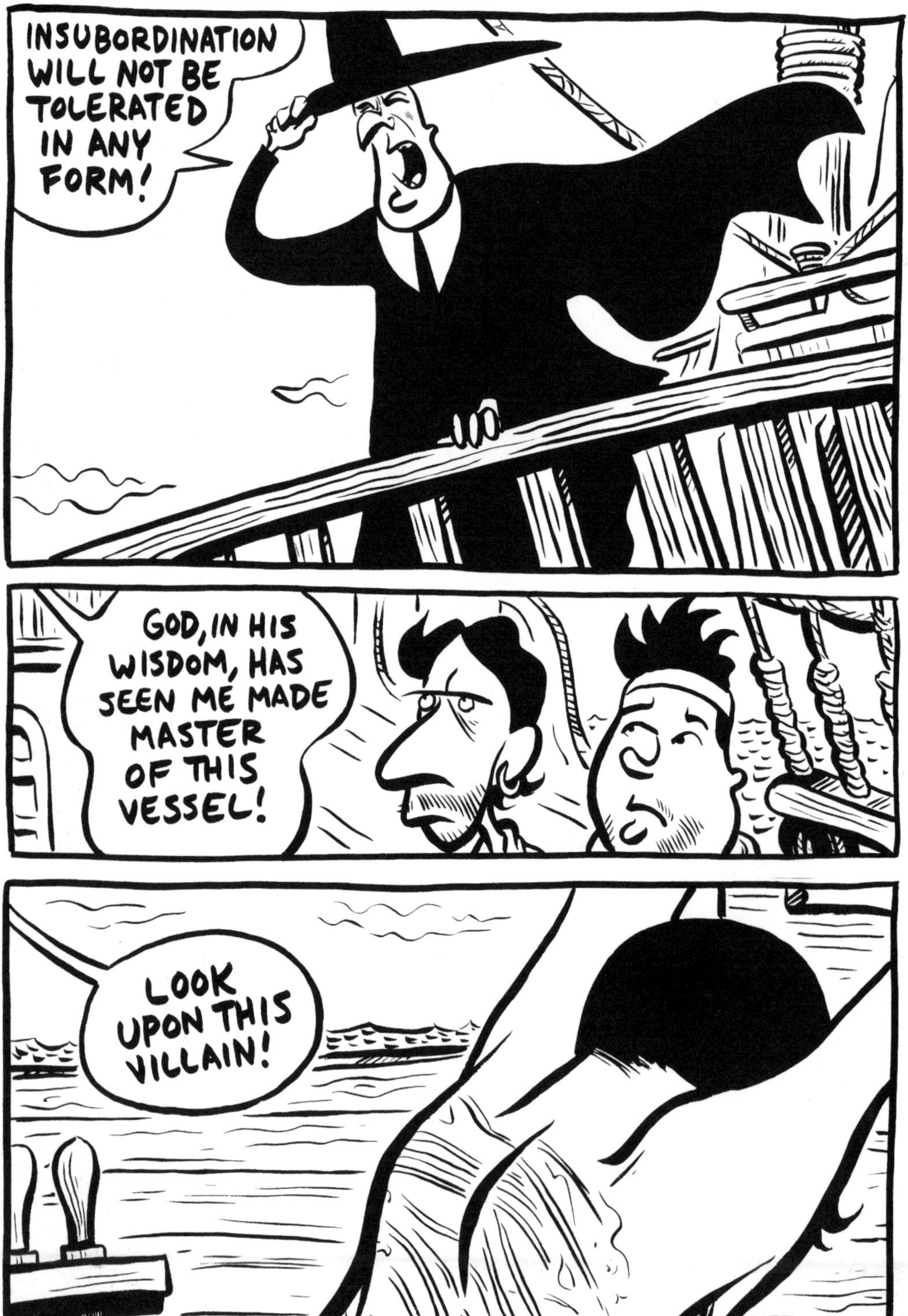
INSUBORDINATION WILL NOT BE TOLERATED IN ANY FORM!
GOD, IN HIS WISDOM, HAS SEEN ME MADE MASTER OF THIS VESSEL!
LOOK UPON THIS VILLAIN!

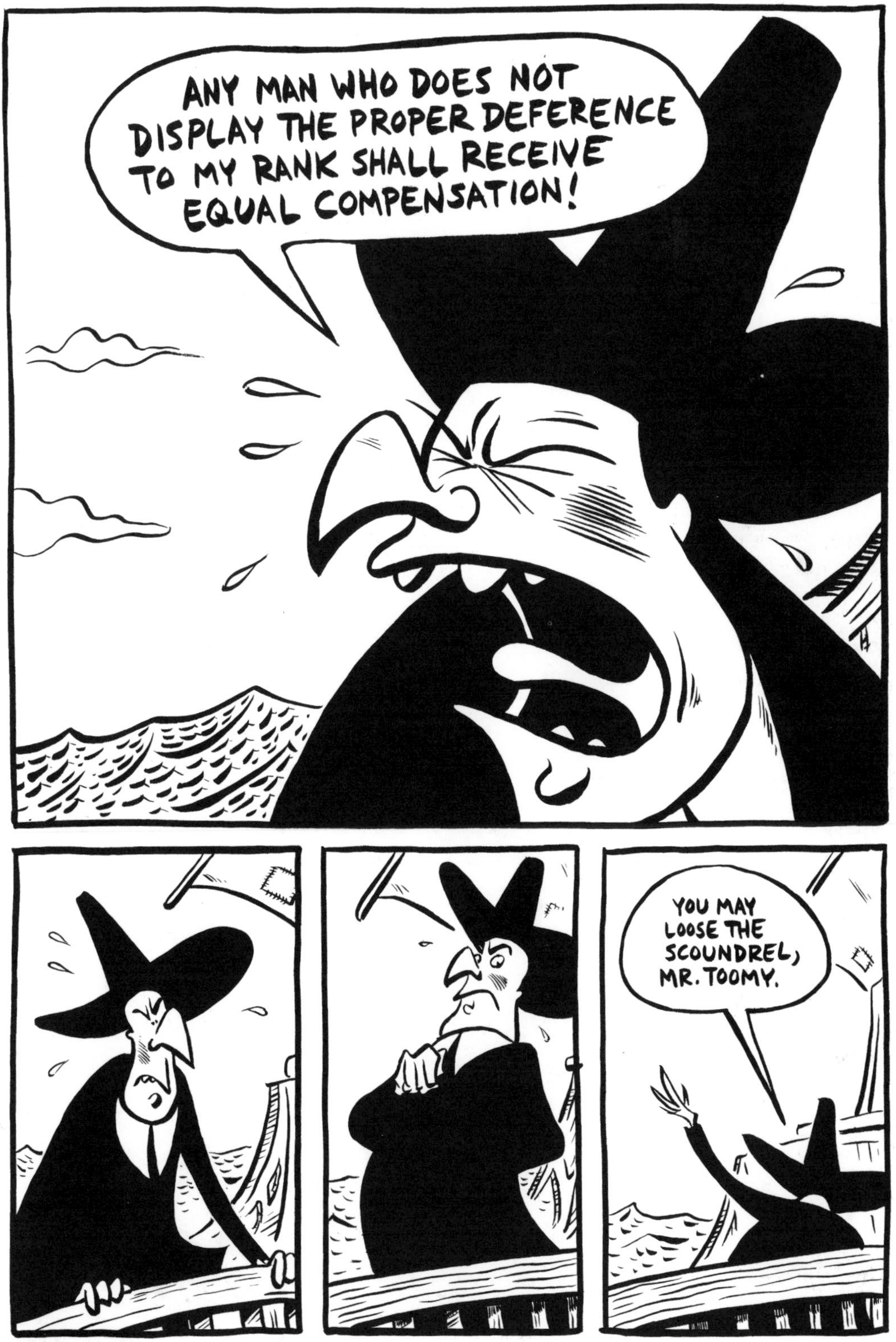
ANY MAN WHO DOES NOT DISPLAY THE PROPER DEFERENCE TO MY RANK SHALL RECEIVE EQUAL COMPENSATION!
YOU MAY LOOSE THE SCOUNDREL, MR. TOOMY.

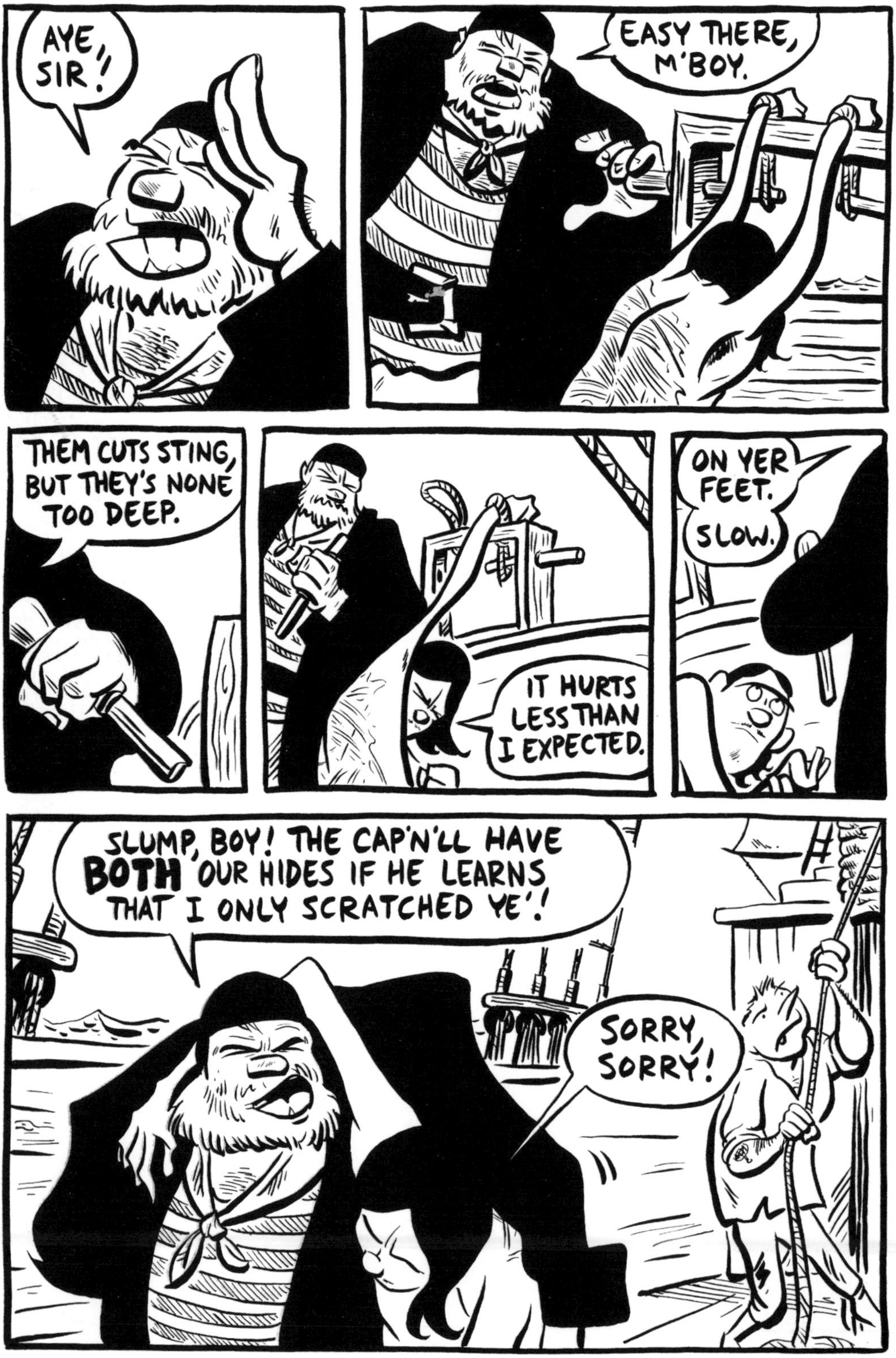
AYE, SIR!
EASY THERE, M'BOY.
THEM CUTS STING, BUT THEY'S NONE TOO DEEP.
IT HURTS LESS THAN I EXPECTED.
ON YER FEET.
SLOW.
SLUMP, BOY! THE CAP'N'LL HAVE BOTH OUR HIDES IF HE LEARNS THAT I ONLY SCRATCHED YE'!
SORRY, SORRY!

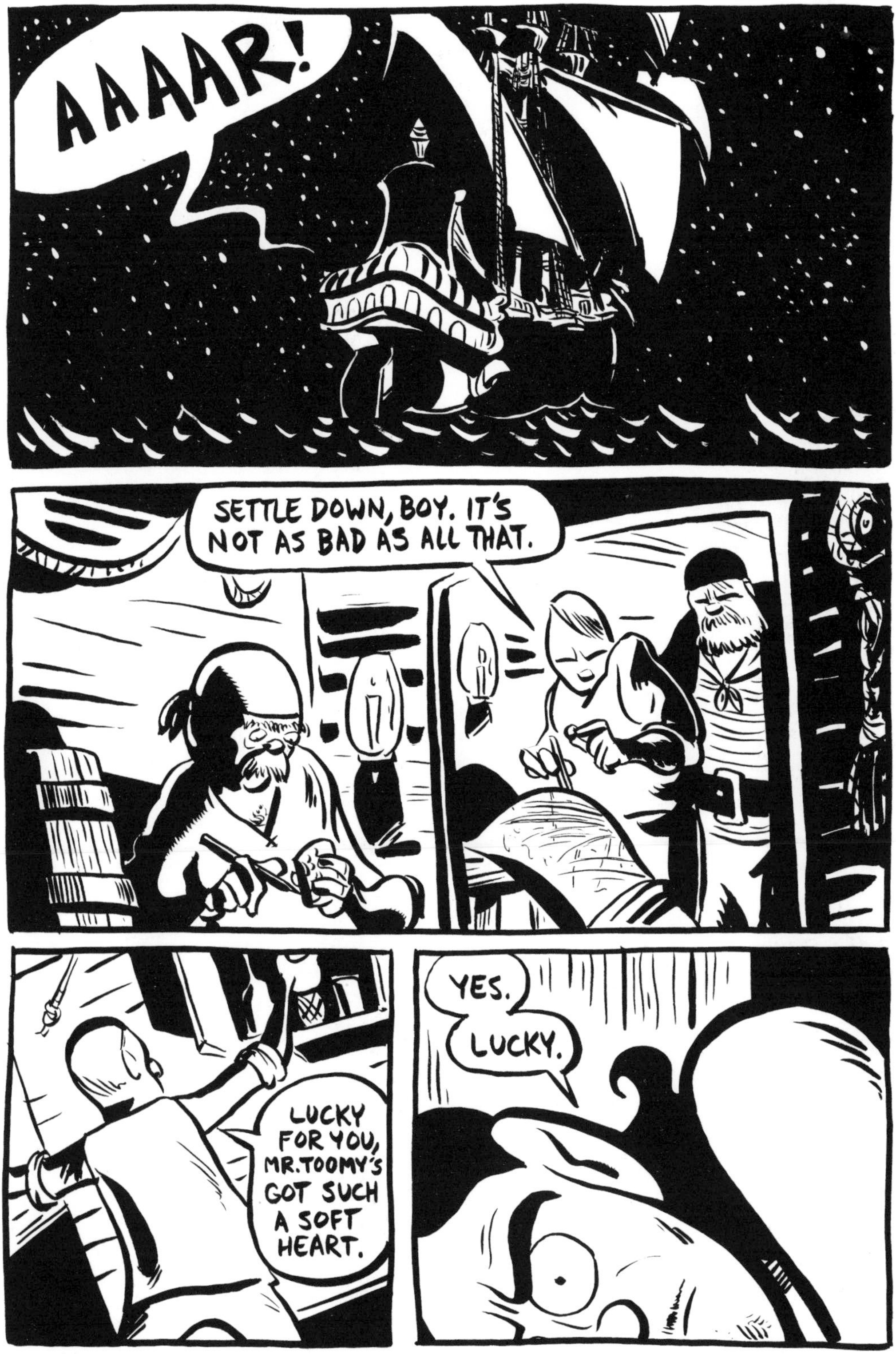
AAAAR!
SETTLE DOWN, BOY. IT'S NOT AS BAD AS ALL THAT.
LUCKY FOR YOU, MR. TOOMY'S GOT SUCH A SOFT HEART.
YES.
LUCKY.

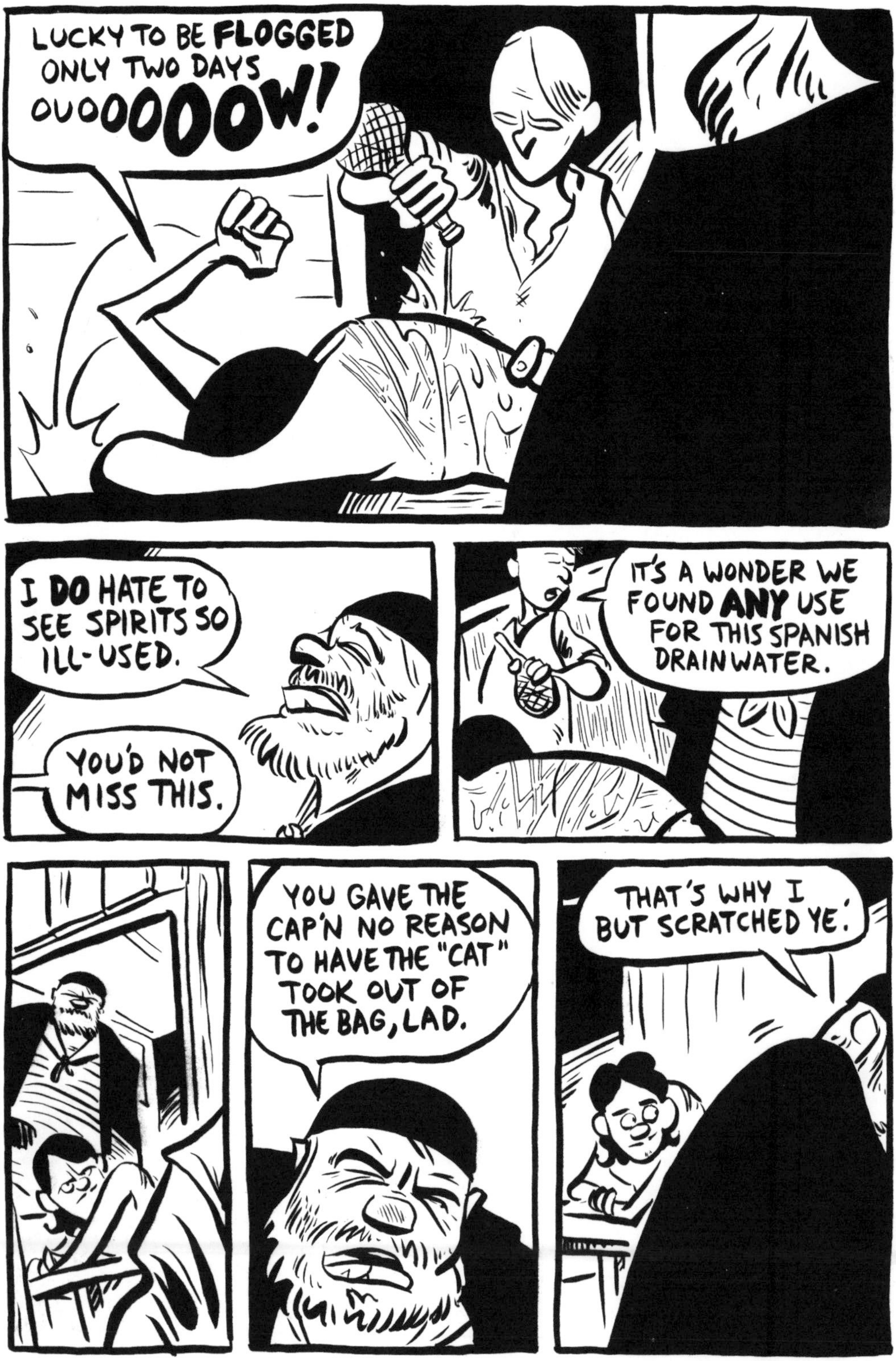
LUCKY TO BE FLOGGED ONLY TWO DAYS OUOOOOOOW!
I DO HATE TO SEE SPIRITS SO ILL-USED.
YOU'D NOT MISS THIS.
IT'S A WONDER WE FOUND ANY USE FOR THIS SPANISH DRAINWATER.
YOU GAVE THE CAP'N NO REASON TO HAVE THE "CAT" TOOK OUT OF THE BAG, LAD.
THAT'S WHY I BUT SCRATCHED YE.

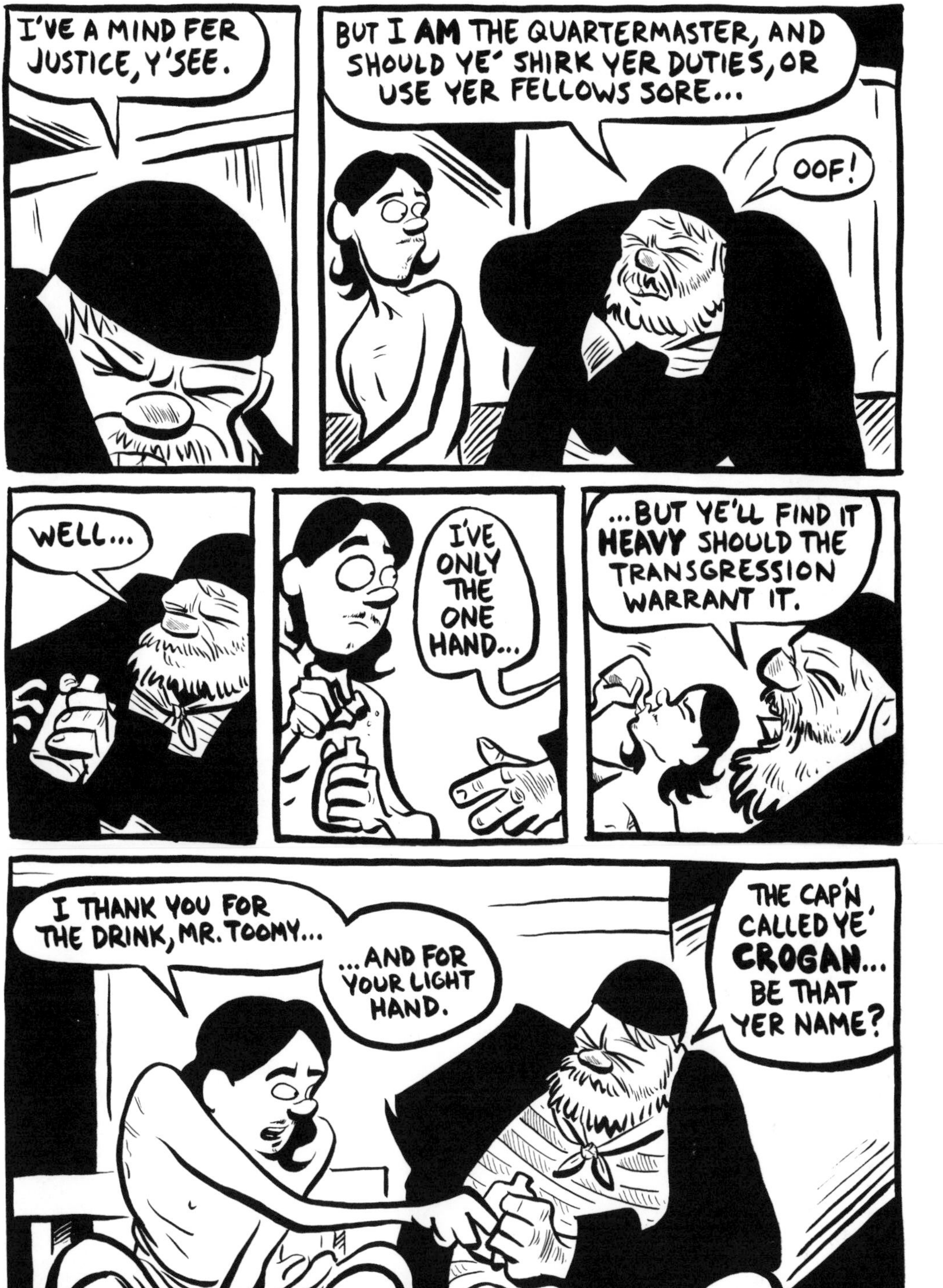
I'VE A MIND FER JUSTICE, Y'SEE.
BUT I AM THE QUARTERMASTER, AND SHOULD YE' SHIRK YER DUTIES, OR USE YER FELLOWS SORE...
OOF!
WELL...
I'VE ONLY THE ONE HAND...
...BUT YE'LL FIND IT HEAVY SHOULD THE TRANSGRESSION WARRANT IT.
I THANK YOU FOR THE DRINK, MR. TOOMY...
...AND FOR YOUR LIGHT HAND.
THE CAP'N CALLED YE' CROGAN... BE THAT YER NAME?

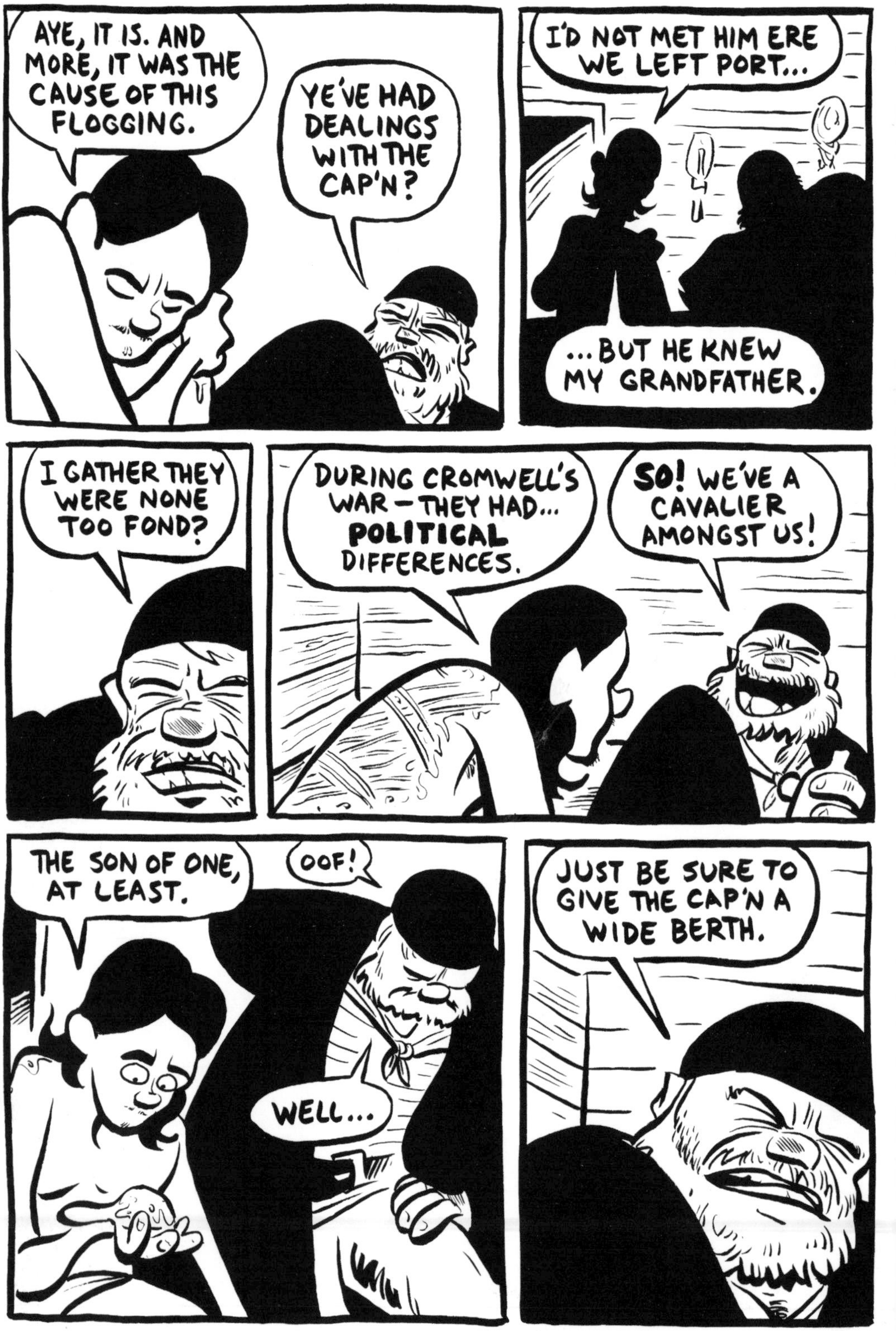
AYE, IT IS. AND MORE, IT WAS THE CAUSE OF THIS FLOGGING.
YE'VE HAD DEALINGS WITH THE CAP'N?
I'D NOT MET HIM ERE WE LEFT PORT...
...BUT HE KNEW MY GRANDFATHER.
I GATHER THEY WERE NONE TOO FOND?
DURING CROMWELL'S WAR — THEY HAD... **POLITICAL** DIFFERENCES.
SO! WE'VE A CAVALIER AMONGST US!
THE SON OF ONE, AT LEAST.
OOF!
WELL...
JUST BE SURE TO GIVE THE CAP'N A WIDE BERTH.

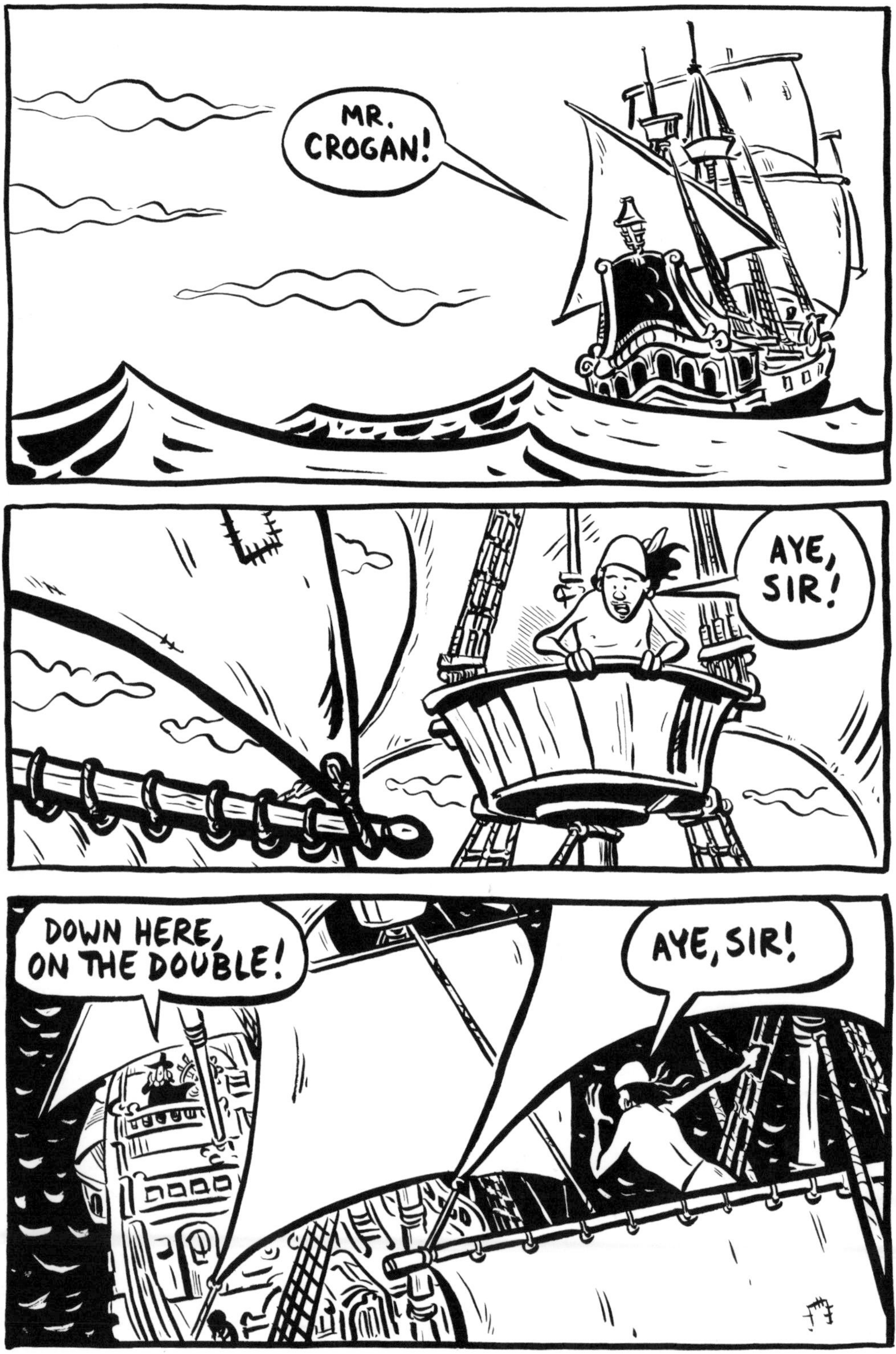
MR. CROGAN!
AYE, SIR!
DOWN HERE, ON THE DOUBLE!
AYE, SIR!

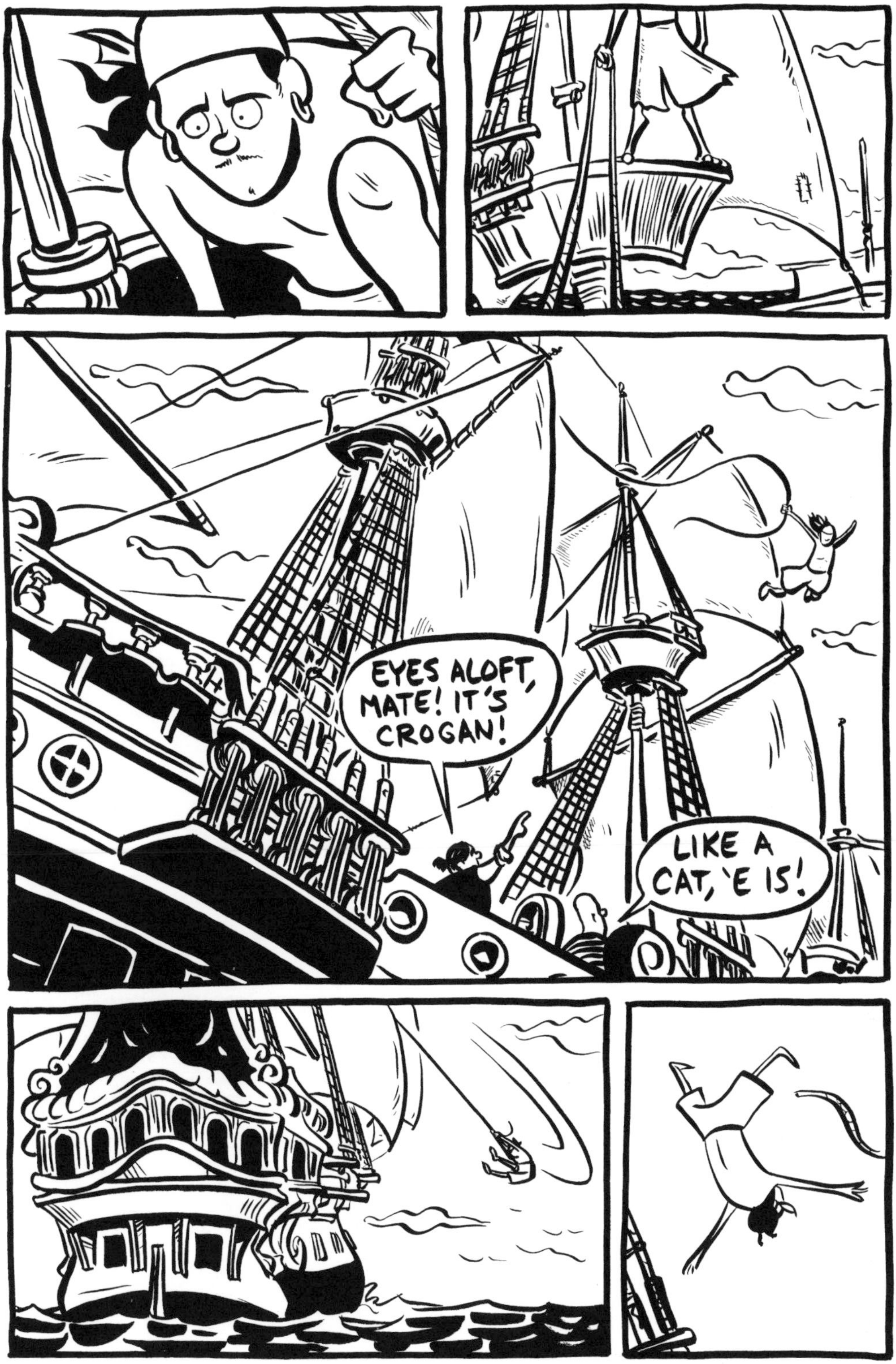
EYES ALOFT, MATE! IT'S CROGAN!
LIKE A CAT, 'E IS!

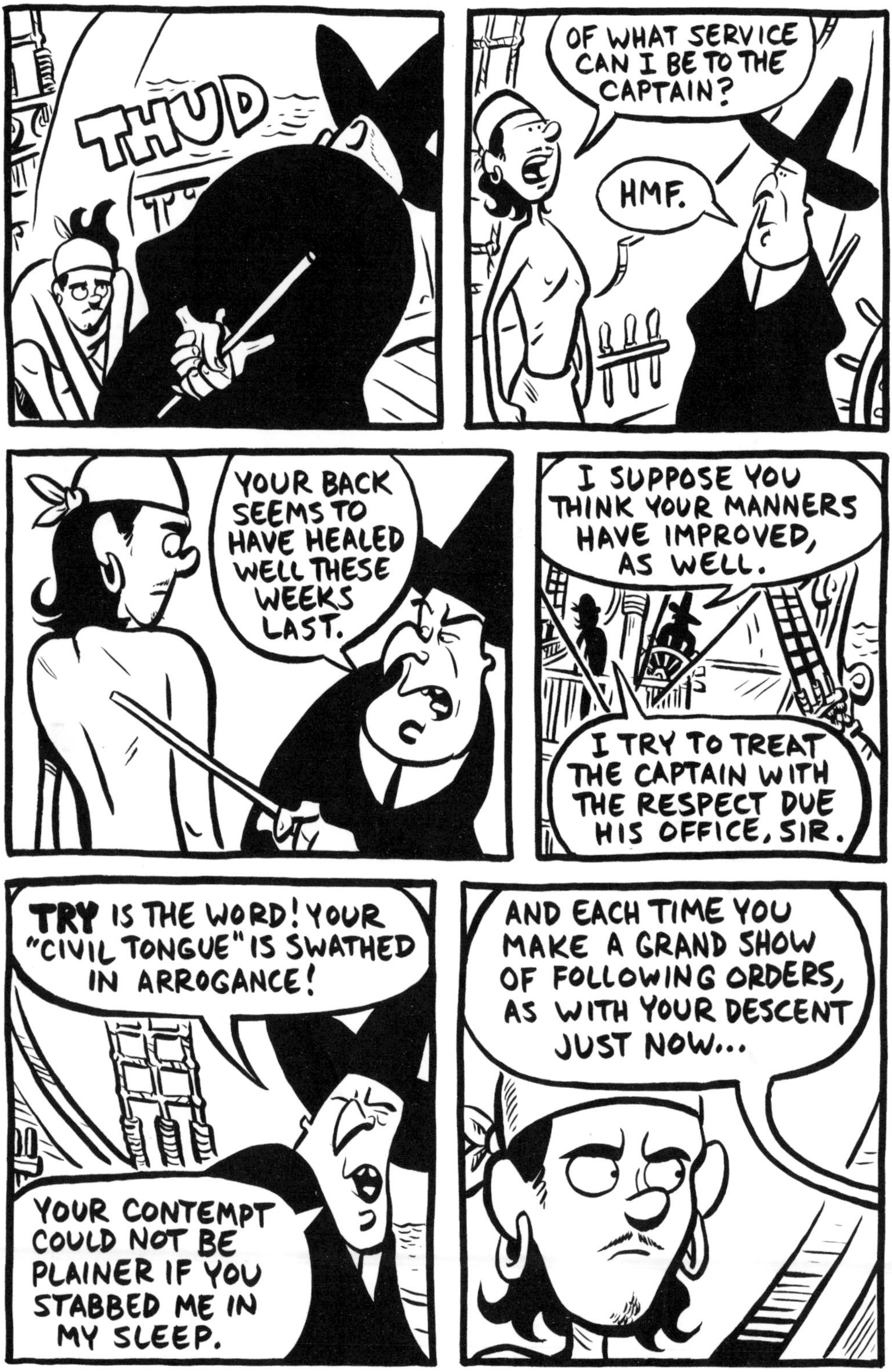
THUD
OF WHAT SERVICE CAN I BE TO THE CAPTAIN?
HMF.
YOUR BACK SEEMS TO HAVE HEALED WELL THESE WEEKS LAST.
I SUPPOSE YOU THINK YOUR MANNERS HAVE IMPROVED, AS WELL.
I TRY TO TREAT THE CAPTAIN WITH THE RESPECT DUE HIS OFFICE, SIR.
TRY IS THE WORD! YOUR "CIVIL TONGUE" IS SWATHED IN ARROGANCE!
YOUR CONTEMPT COULD NOT BE PLAINER IF YOU STABBED ME IN MY SLEEP.
AND EACH TIME YOU MAKE A GRAND SHOW OF FOLLOWING ORDERS, AS WITH YOUR DESCENT JUST NOW...

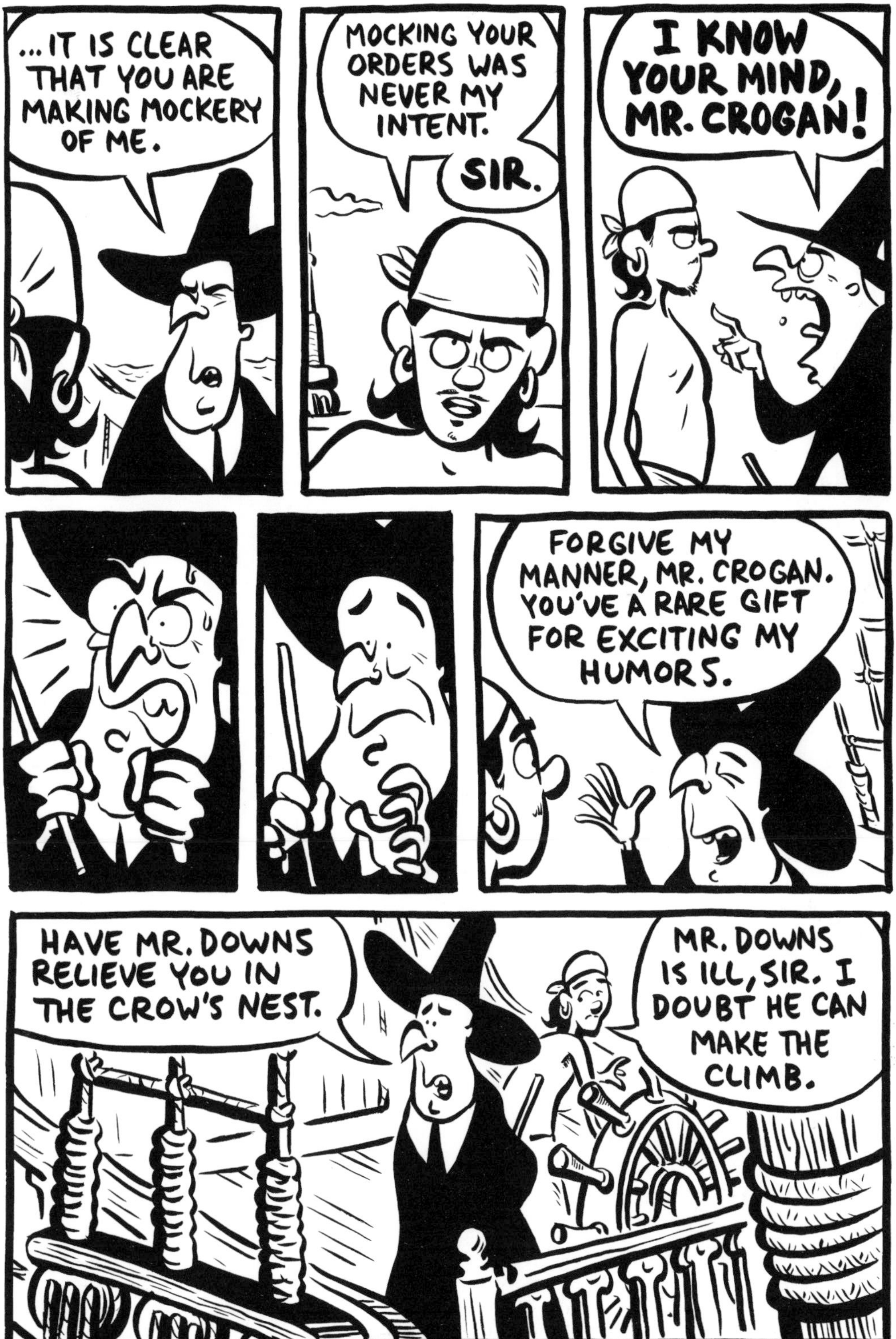
...IT IS CLEAR THAT YOU ARE MAKING MOCKERY OF ME.
MOCKING YOUR ORDERS WAS NEVER MY INTENT.
SIR.
I KNOW YOUR MIND, MR. CROGAN!
FORGIVE MY MANNER, MR. CROGAN. YOU'VE A RARE GIFT FOR EXCITING MY HUMORS.
HAVE MR. DOWNS RELIEVE YOU IN THE CROW'S NEST.
MR. DOWNS IS ILL, SIR. I DOUBT HE CAN MAKE THE CLIMB.

THE CAPTAIN IS AWARE.

SCUTTLE ME FER A BOSUN'S PIKE! HOW'S HE 'SPOSED TO WORK IF WE AIN'T FED PROPER?

CODFISH...

EH?

THE CAPTAIN'S CALLED YOU UP.

-COFF- THEN UP I MUST.

BE YOU ABLE TO CLIMB TO THE NEST?

-COFF- ABLE OR NO, I'VE LITTLE CHOICE.

-COFF-

LOOK AT HIM STAGGER! IT AIN'T RIGHT, CALLIN' HIM UP IN HIS STATE.

THAT JACK PRESBYTER'LL BE THE DEATH OF US ALL! HALF THE RATIONS AND TWICE THE WORK!

IT SURPRISES YE'?

WHAT SAY YOU, CROGAN? BE YOU AS SORE OF THE CAPTAIN AS THE REST OF US?

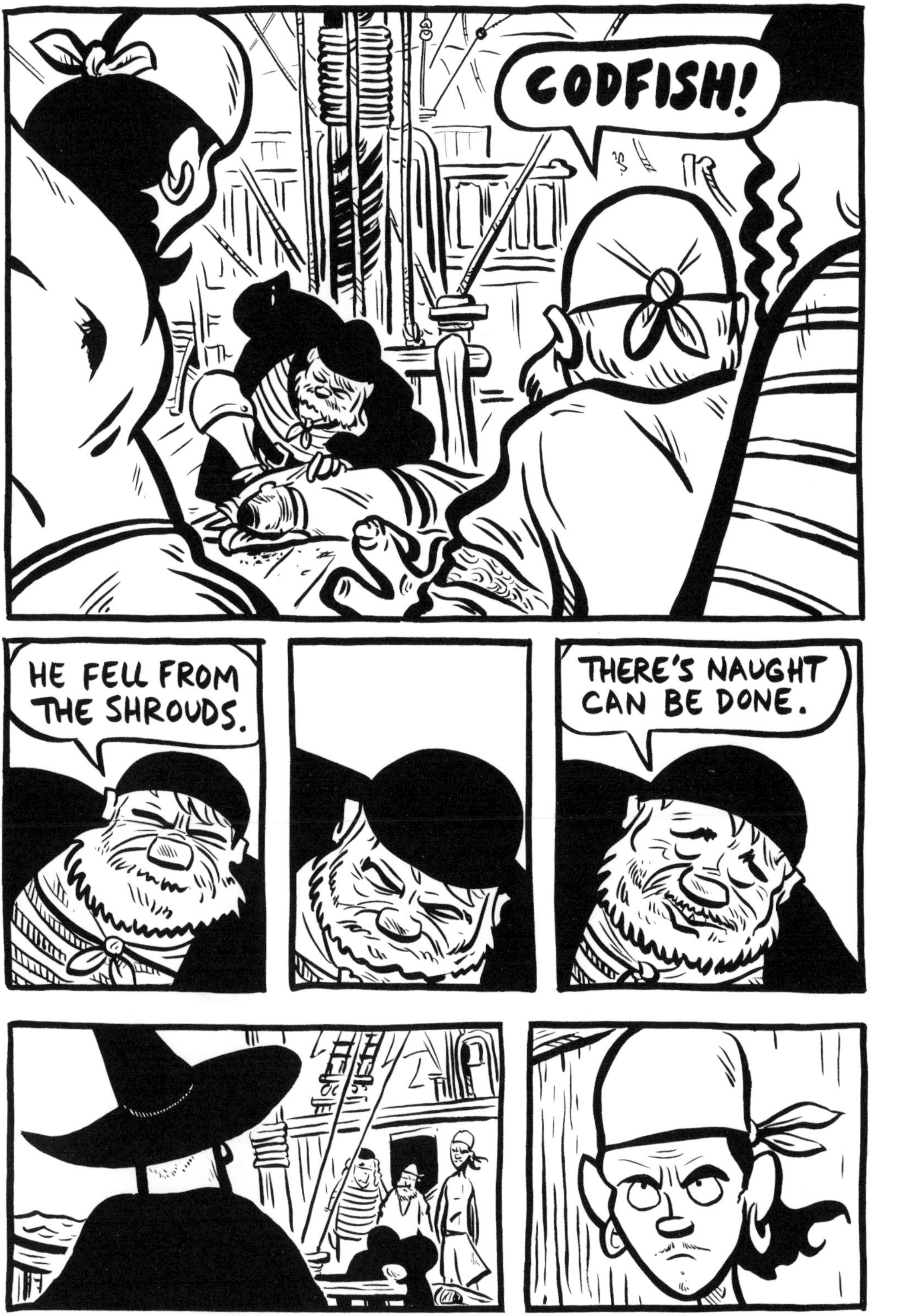
CODFISH!
HE FELL FROM THE SHROUDS.
THERE'S NAUGHT CAN BE DONE.

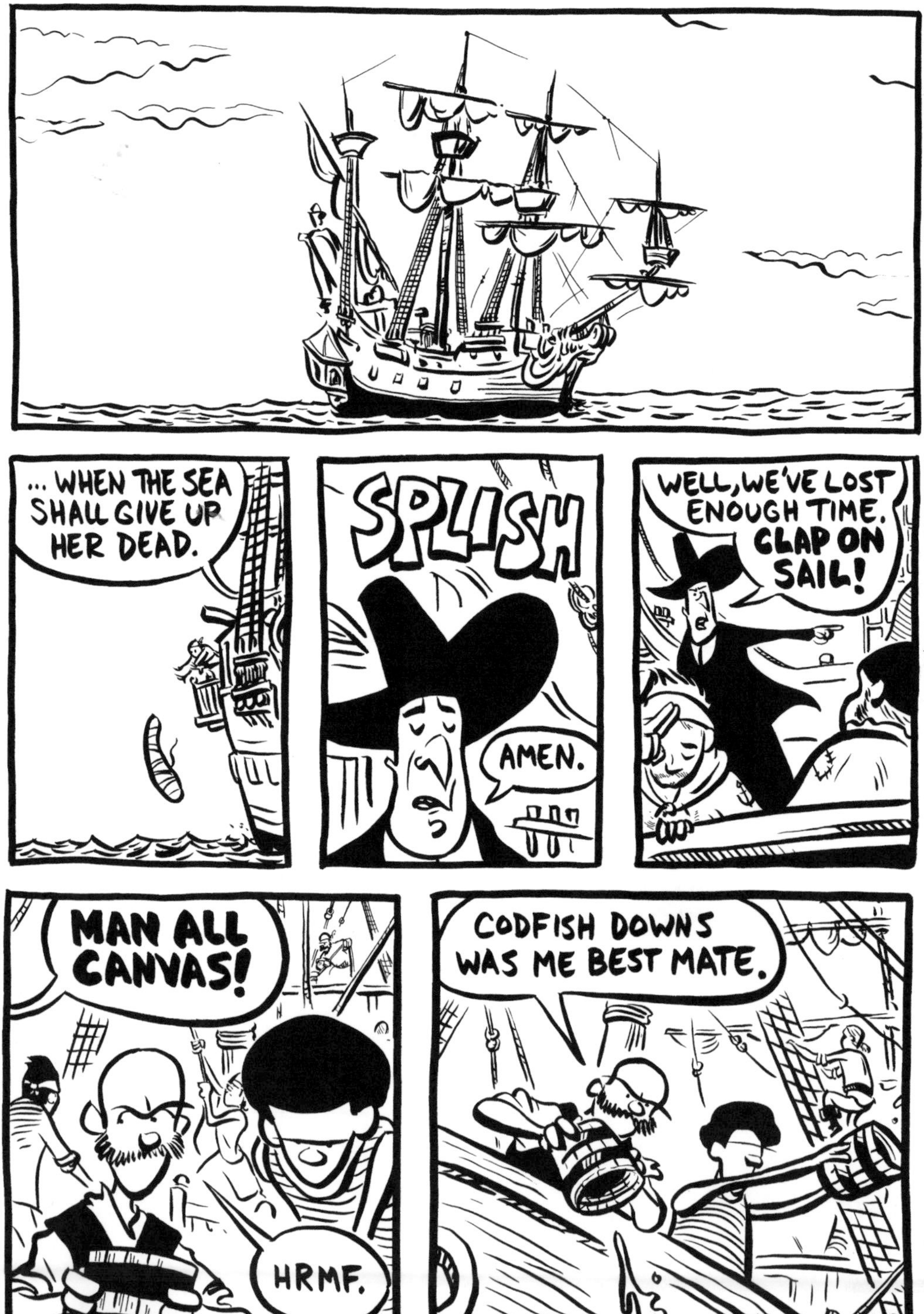
... WHEN THE SEA SHALL GIVE UP HER DEAD.
SPLISH
AMEN.
WELL, WE'VE LOST ENOUGH TIME. CLAP ON SAIL!
MAN ALL CANVAS!
HRMF.
CODFISH DOWNS WAS ME BEST MATE.

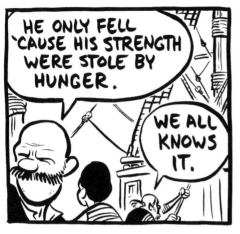

HE ONLY FELL 'CAUSE HIS STRENGTH WERE STOLE BY HUNGER.

WE ALL KNOWS IT.

DUNWELL CARES MORE FER A PROFITTING RUN THAN HE DO HIS CREW.

IT'S TRUE!

WE'VE SOME FIVE WEEKS LEFT TO PORT, AND US BUT THREE DAYS FROM HISPANIOLA!

SO WHY AIN'T WE PUTTING IN FOR FOOD? WE GOT RIGHTS!

AND WE **SHOULD** DEMAND 'EM, SINK ME FER A PARSON ELSE!

DON'T TRY IT.

EH?

THE CAPTAIN WILL CRY "MUTINY."

WE DON'T WANT TO TAKE THE SHIP! WE JUST WANT OUR RIGHTS! **STAND WITH US!**

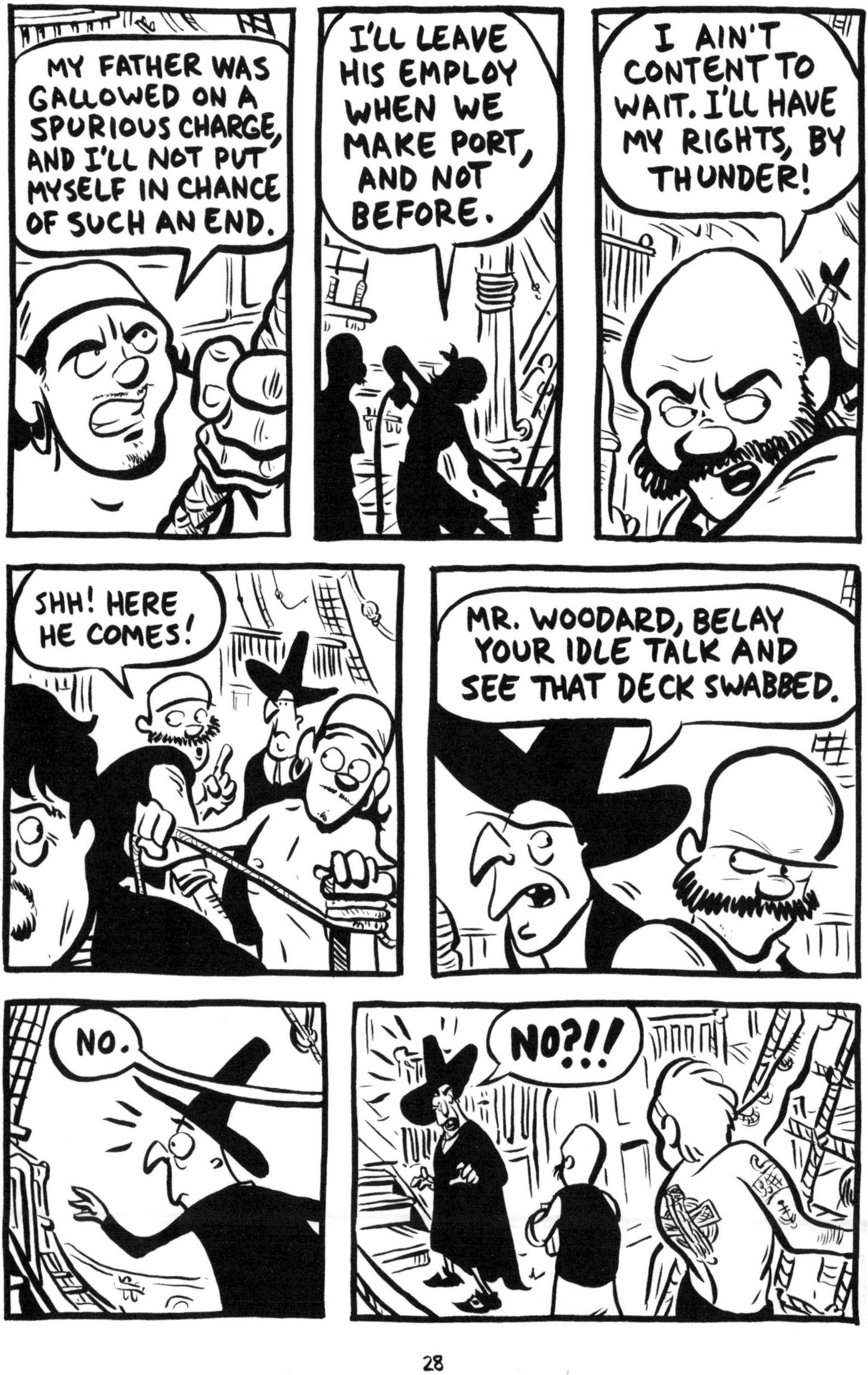
MY FATHER WAS GALLOWED ON A SPURIOUS CHARGE, AND I'LL NOT PUT MYSELF IN CHANCE OF SUCH AN END.
I'LL LEAVE HIS EMPLOY WHEN WE MAKE PORT, AND NOT BEFORE.
I AIN'T CONTENT TO WAIT. I'LL HAVE MY RIGHTS, BY THUNDER!
SHH! HERE HE COMES!
MR. WOODARD, BELAY YOUR IDLE TALK AND SEE THAT DECK SWABBED.
NO.
NO?!!

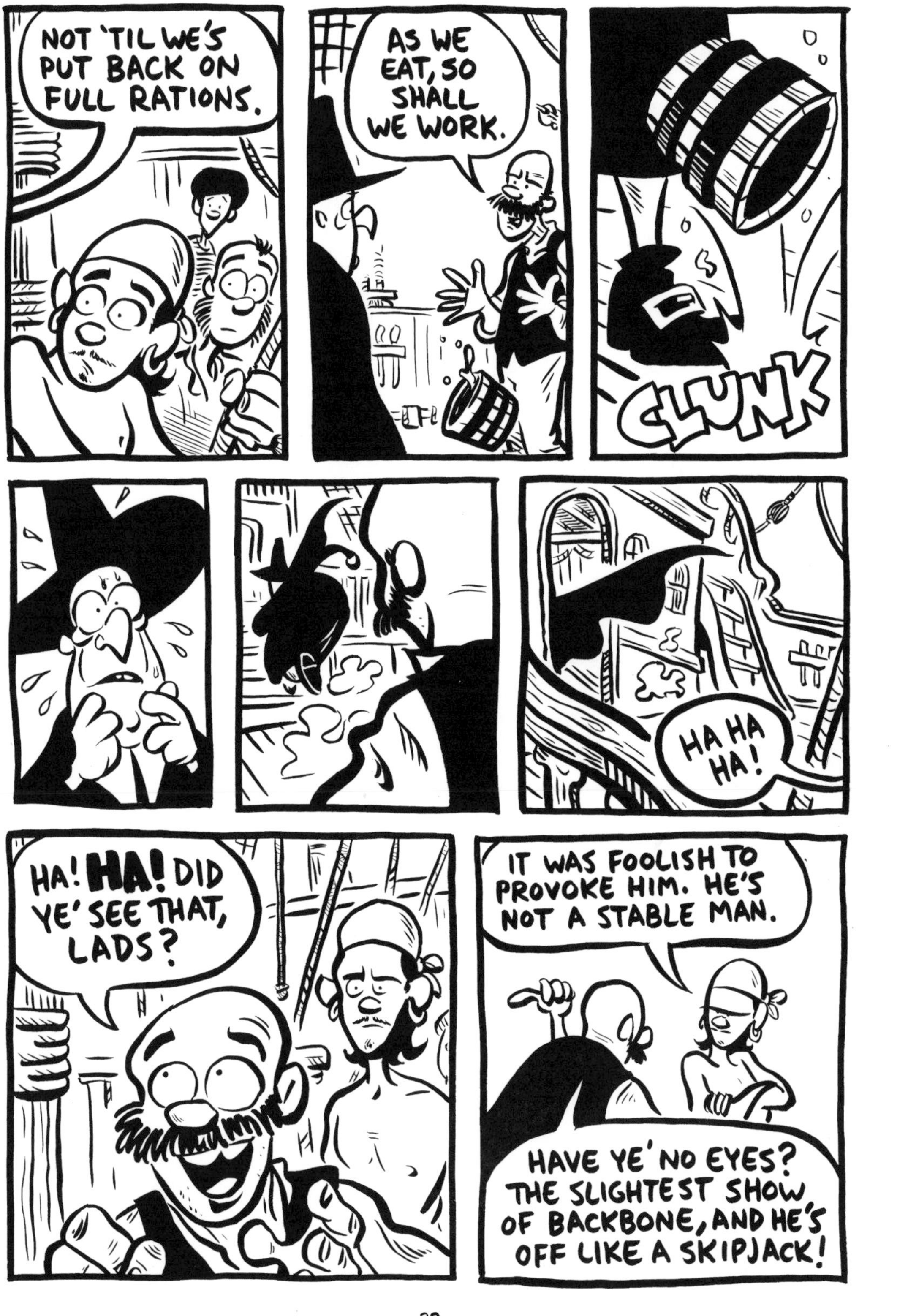
NOT 'TIL WE'S PUT BACK ON FULL RATIONS.
AS WE EAT, SO SHALL WE WORK.
CLUNK
HA HA HA!
HA! HA! DID YE' SEE THAT, LADS?
IT WAS FOOLISH TO PROVOKE HIM. HE'S NOT A STABLE MAN.
HAVE YE' NO EYES? THE SLIGHTEST SHOW OF BACKBONE, AND HE'S OFF LIKE A SKIPJACK!

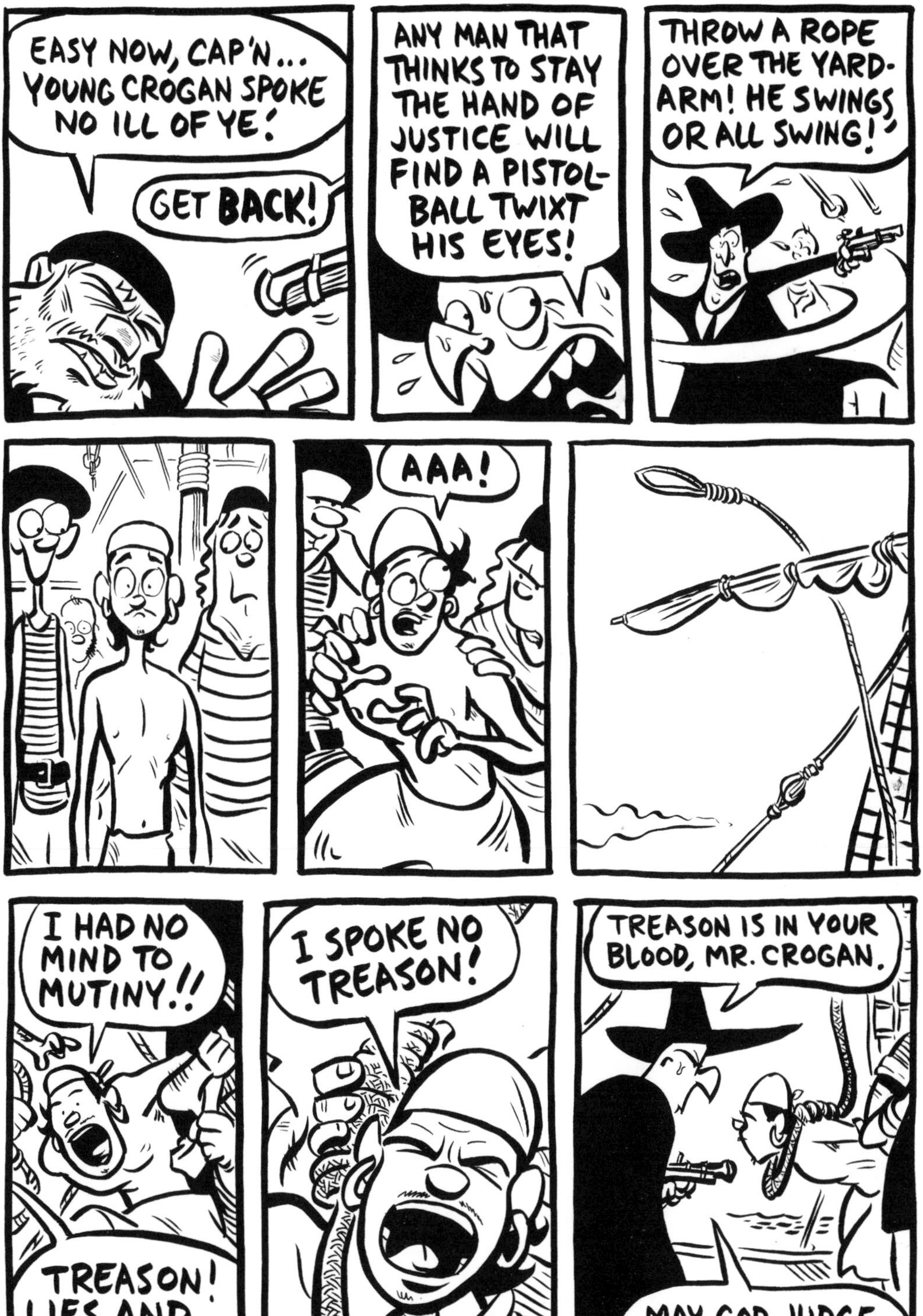
EASY NOW, CAP'N... YOUNG CROGAN SPOKE NO ILL OF YE!
GET BACK!
ANY MAN THAT THINKS TO STAY THE HAND OF JUSTICE WILL FIND A PISTOL-BALL TWIXT HIS EYES!
THROW A ROPE OVER THE YARD-ARM! HE SWINGS OR ALL SWING!
AAA!
I HAD NO MIND TO MUTINY!!
TREASON! LIES AND TREASON!
I SPOKE NO TREASON!
TREASON IS IN YOUR BLOOD, MR. CROGAN.
MAY GOD JUDGE YOU AS I HAVE.

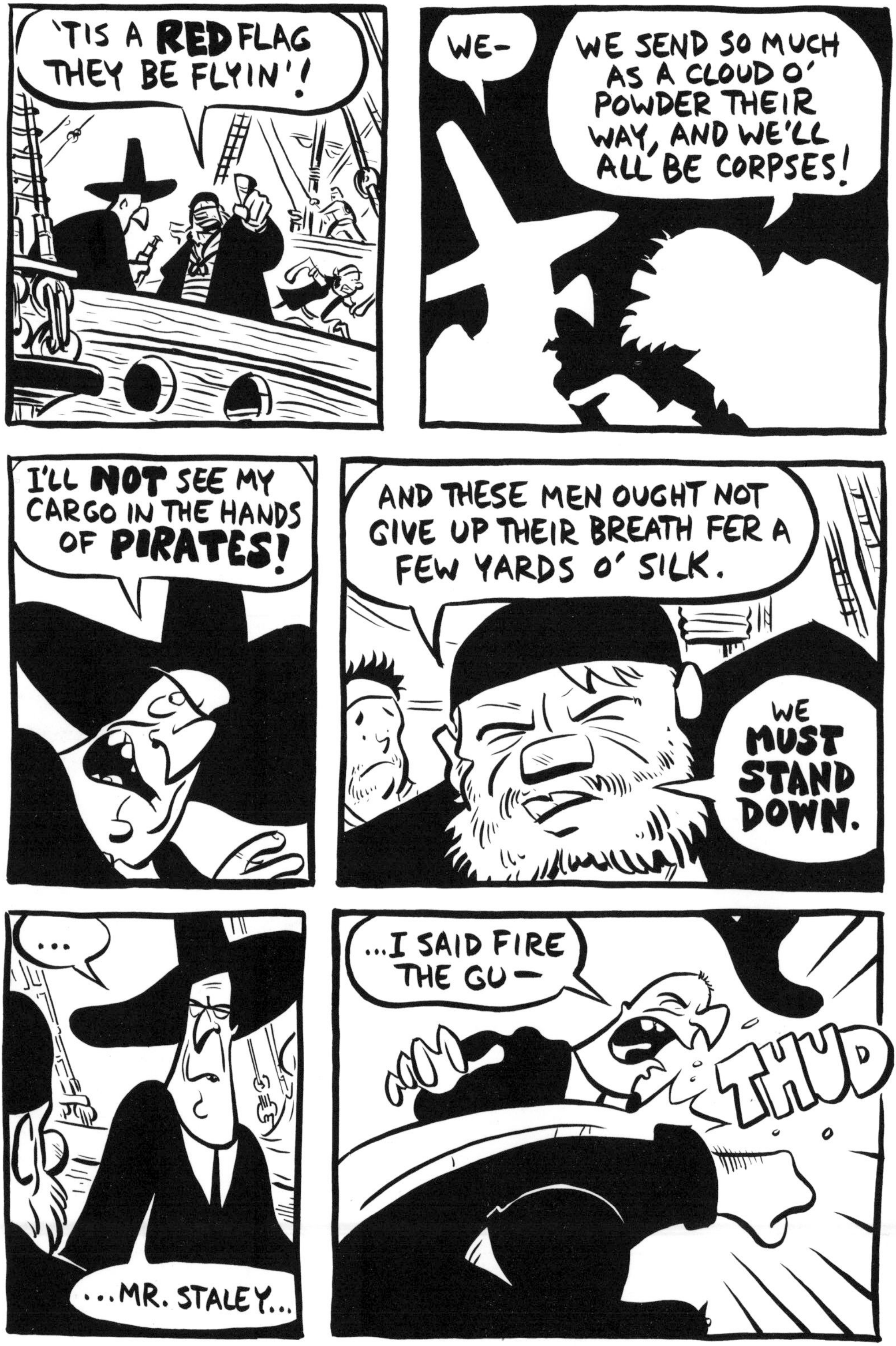
'TIS A RED FLAG THEY BE FLYIN'!
WE-
WE SEND SO MUCH AS A CLOUD O' POWDER THEIR WAY, AND WE'LL ALL BE CORPSES!
I'LL NOT SEE MY CARGO IN THE HANDS OF PIRATES!
AND THESE MEN OUGHT NOT GIVE UP THEIR BREATH FER A FEW YARDS O' SILK.
WE MUST STAND DOWN.
...
...MR. STALEY...
...I SAID FIRE THE GU-
THUD

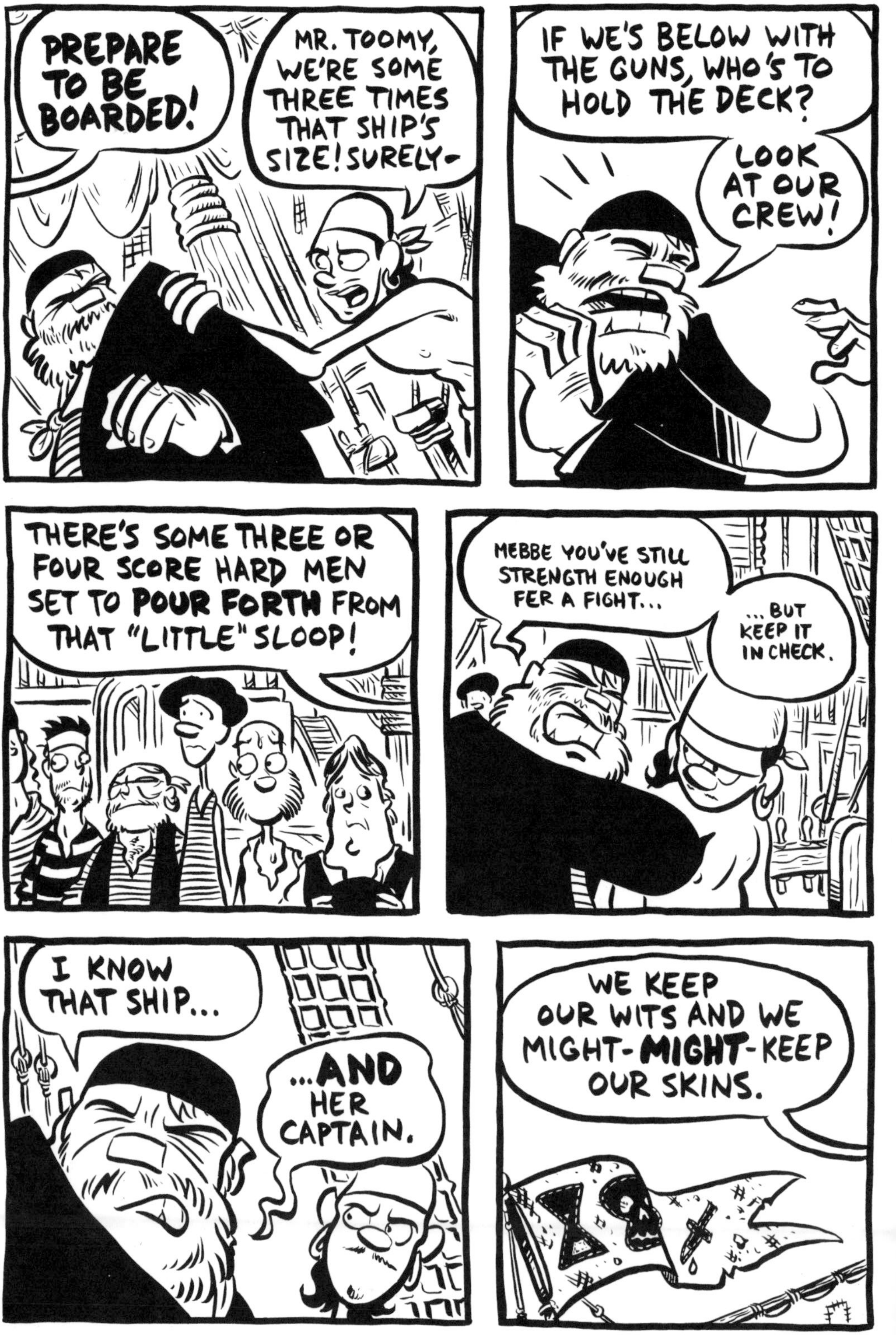
PREPARE TO BE BOARDED!
MR. TOOMY, WE'RE SOME THREE TIMES THAT SHIP'S SIZE! SURELY-
IF WE'S BELOW WITH THE GUNS, WHO'S TO HOLD THE DECK?
LOOK AT OUR CREW!
THERE'S SOME THREE OR FOUR SCORE HARD MEN SET TO POUR FORTH FROM THAT "LITTLE" SLOOP!
MEBBE YOU'VE STILL STRENGTH ENOUGH FER A FIGHT...
...BUT KEEP IT IN CHECK.
I KNOW THAT SHIP...
...AND HER CAPTAIN.
WE KEEP OUR WITS AND WE MIGHT-MIGHT-KEEP OUR SKINS.

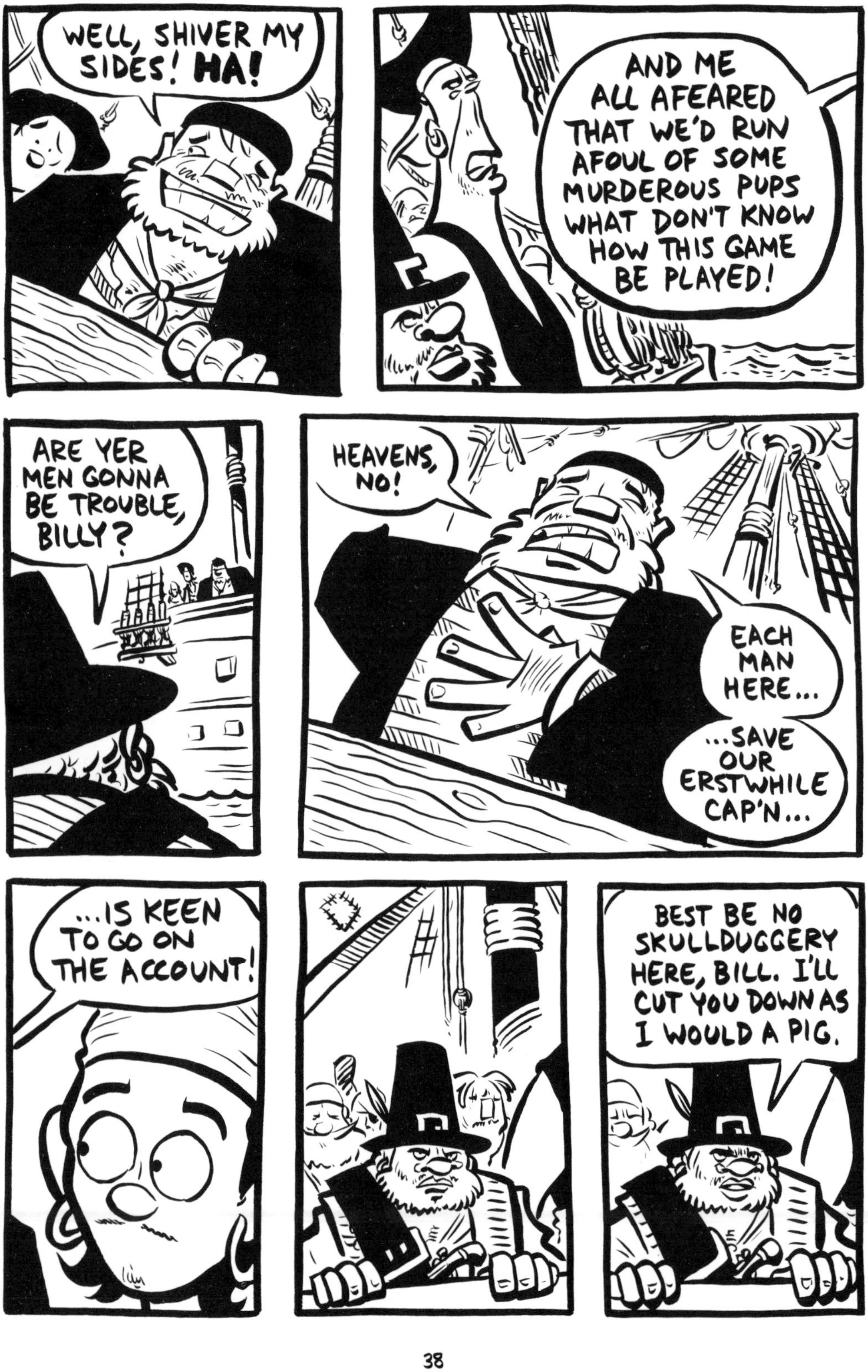
WELL, SHIVER MY SIDES! HA!
AND ME ALL AFEARED THAT WE'D RUN AFOUL OF SOME MURDEROUS PUPS WHAT DON'T KNOW HOW THIS GAME BE PLAYED!
ARE YER MEN GONNA BE TROUBLE, BILLY?
HEAVENS, NO!
EACH MAN HERE...
...SAVE OUR ERSTWHILE CAP'N...
...IS KEEN TO GO ON THE ACCOUNT!
BEST BE NO SKULLDUGGERY HERE, BILL. I'LL CUT YOU DOWN AS I WOULD A PIG.

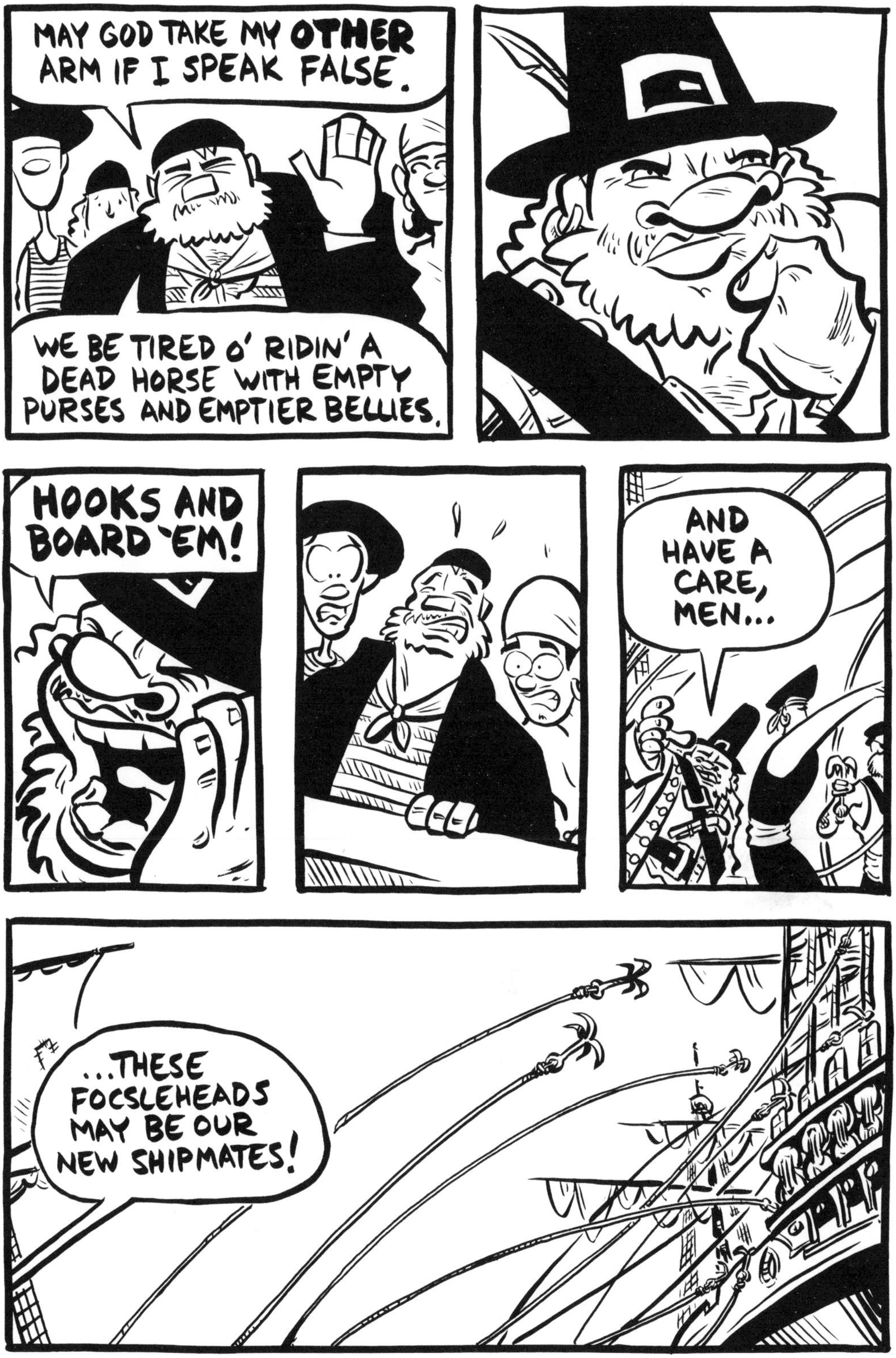
MAY GOD TAKE MY OTHER ARM IF I SPEAK FALSE.
WE BE TIRED O' RIDIN' A DEAD HORSE WITH EMPTY PURSES AND EMPTIER BELLIES.
HOOKS AND BOARD 'EM!
AND HAVE A CARE, MEN...
...THESE FOCSLEHEADS MAY BE OUR NEW SHIPMATES!

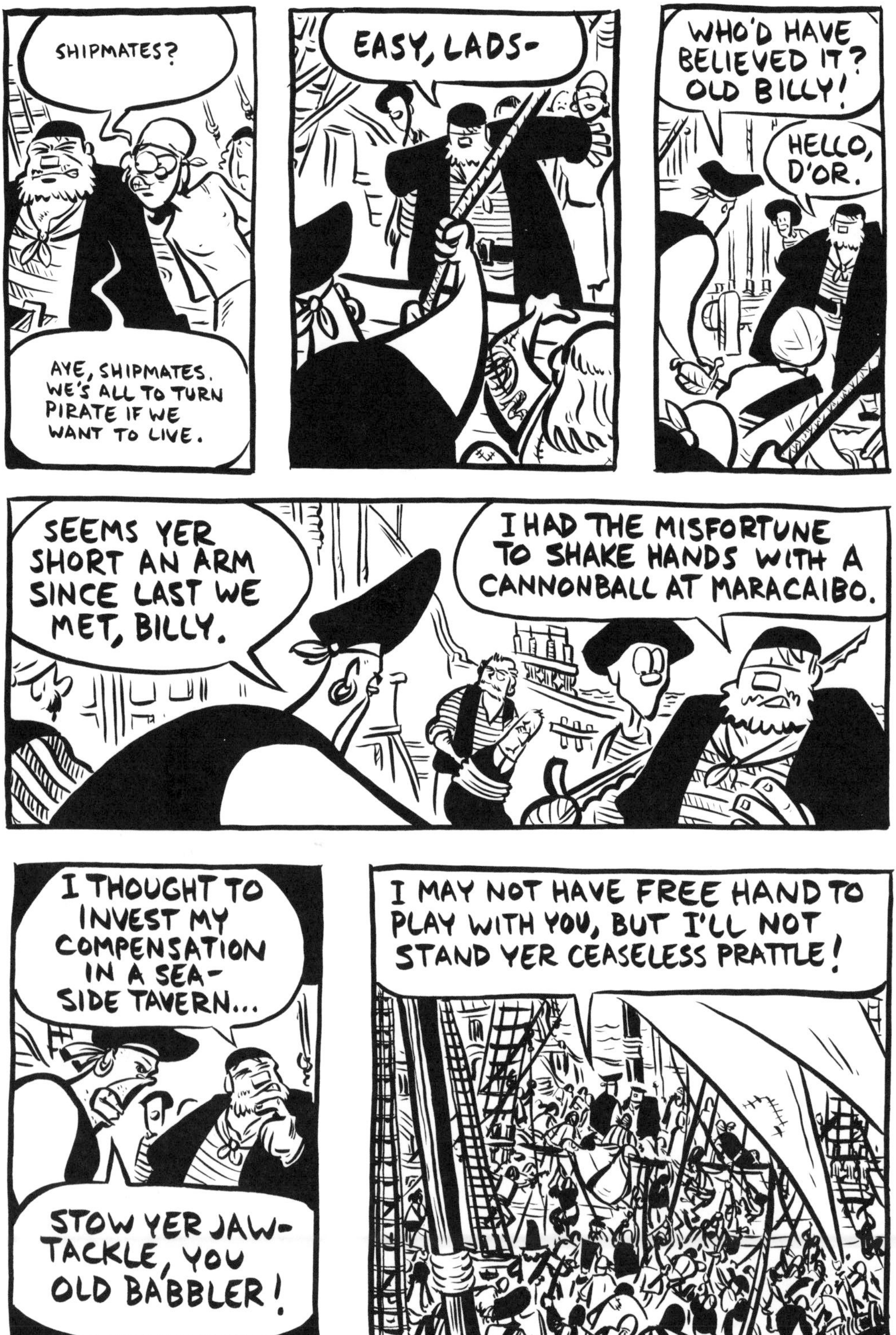
SHIPMATES?
AYE, SHIPMATES. WE'S ALL TO TURN PIRATE IF WE WANT TO LIVE.
EASY, LADS-
WHO'D HAVE BELIEVED IT? OLD BILLY!
HELLO, D'OR.
SEEMS YER SHORT AN ARM SINCE LAST WE MET, BILLY.
I HAD THE MISFORTUNE TO SHAKE HANDS WITH A CANNONBALL AT MARACAIBO.
I THOUGHT TO INVEST MY COMPENSATION IN A SEA-SIDE TAVERN...
STOW YER JAW-TACKLE, YOU OLD BABBLER!
I MAY NOT HAVE FREE HAND TO PLAY WITH YOU, BUT I'LL NOT STAND YER CEASELESS PRATTLE!

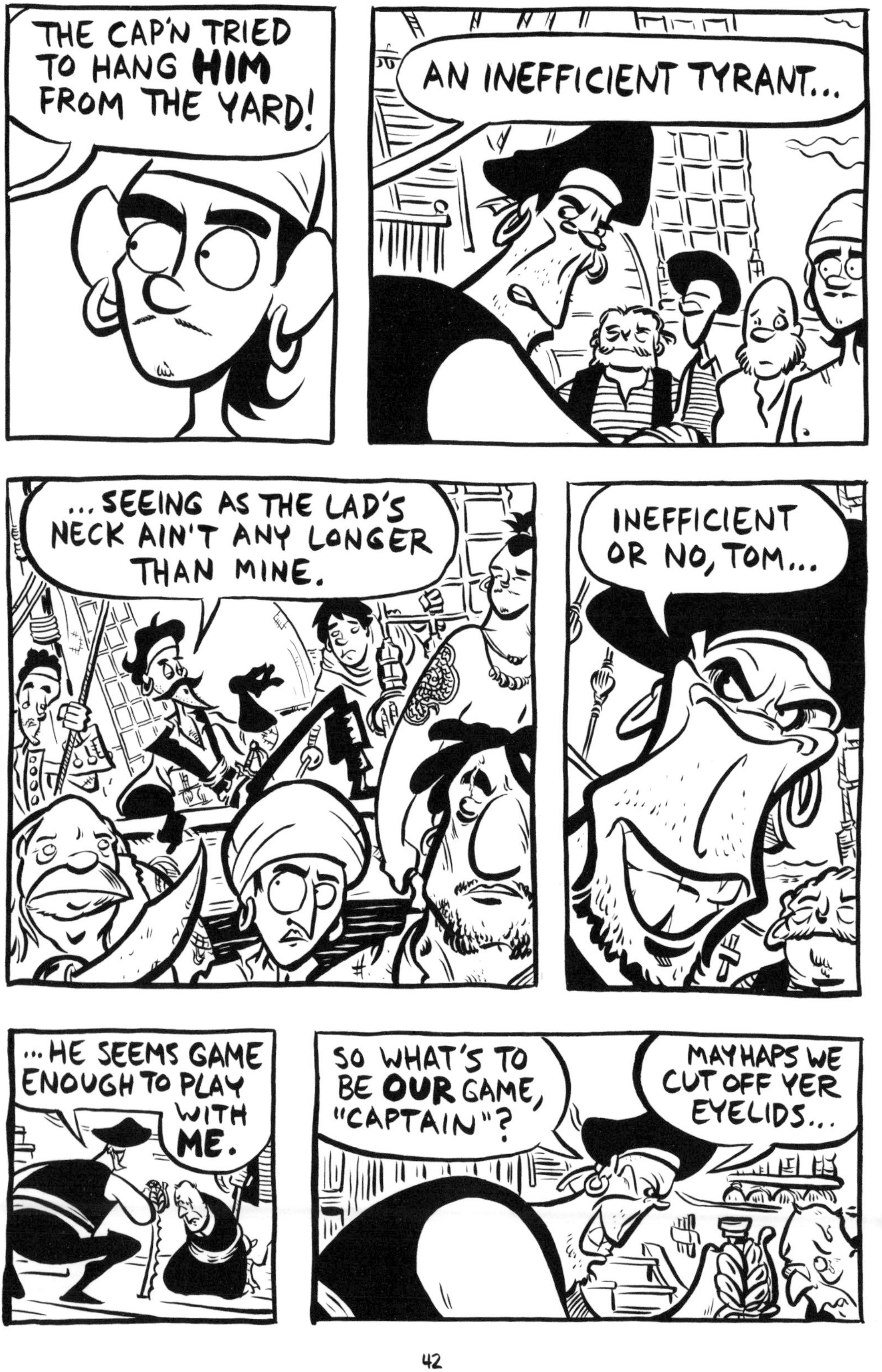
THE CAP'N TRIED TO HANG **HIM** FROM THE YARD!
AN INEFFICIENT TYRANT...
...SEEING AS THE LAD'S NECK AIN'T ANY LONGER THAN MINE.
INEFFICIENT OR NO, TOM...
...HE SEEMS GAME ENOUGH TO PLAY WITH **ME**.
SO WHAT'S TO BE **OUR** GAME, "CAPTAIN"?
MAYHAPS WE CUT OFF YER EYELIDS...

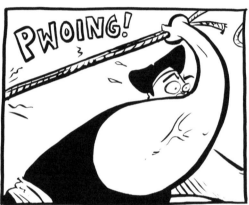

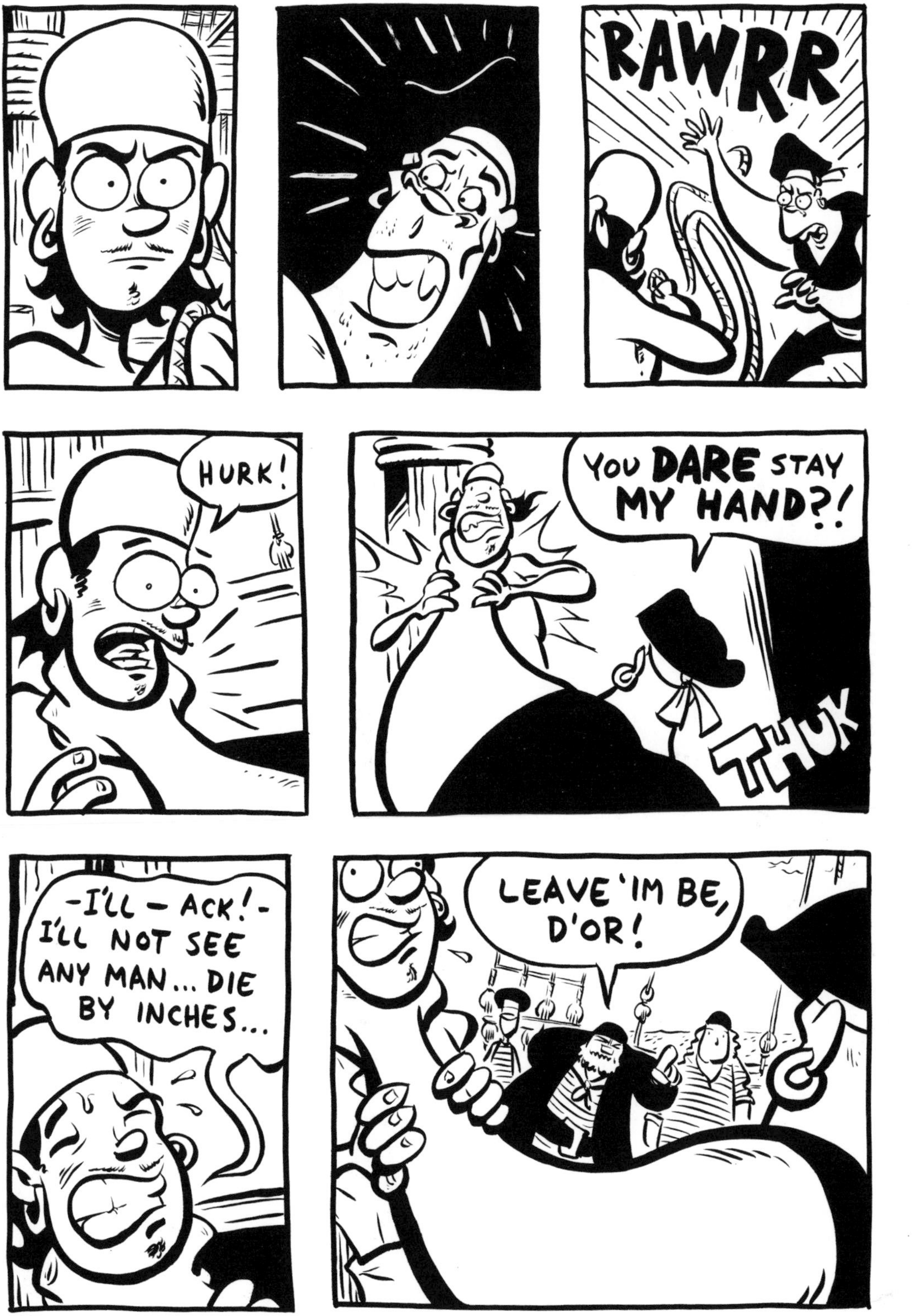
RAWRR
HURK!
YOU DARE STAY MY HAND?!
THUK
-I'LL - ACK! - I'LL NOT SEE ANY MAN... DIE BY INCHES...
LEAVE 'IM BE, D'OR!

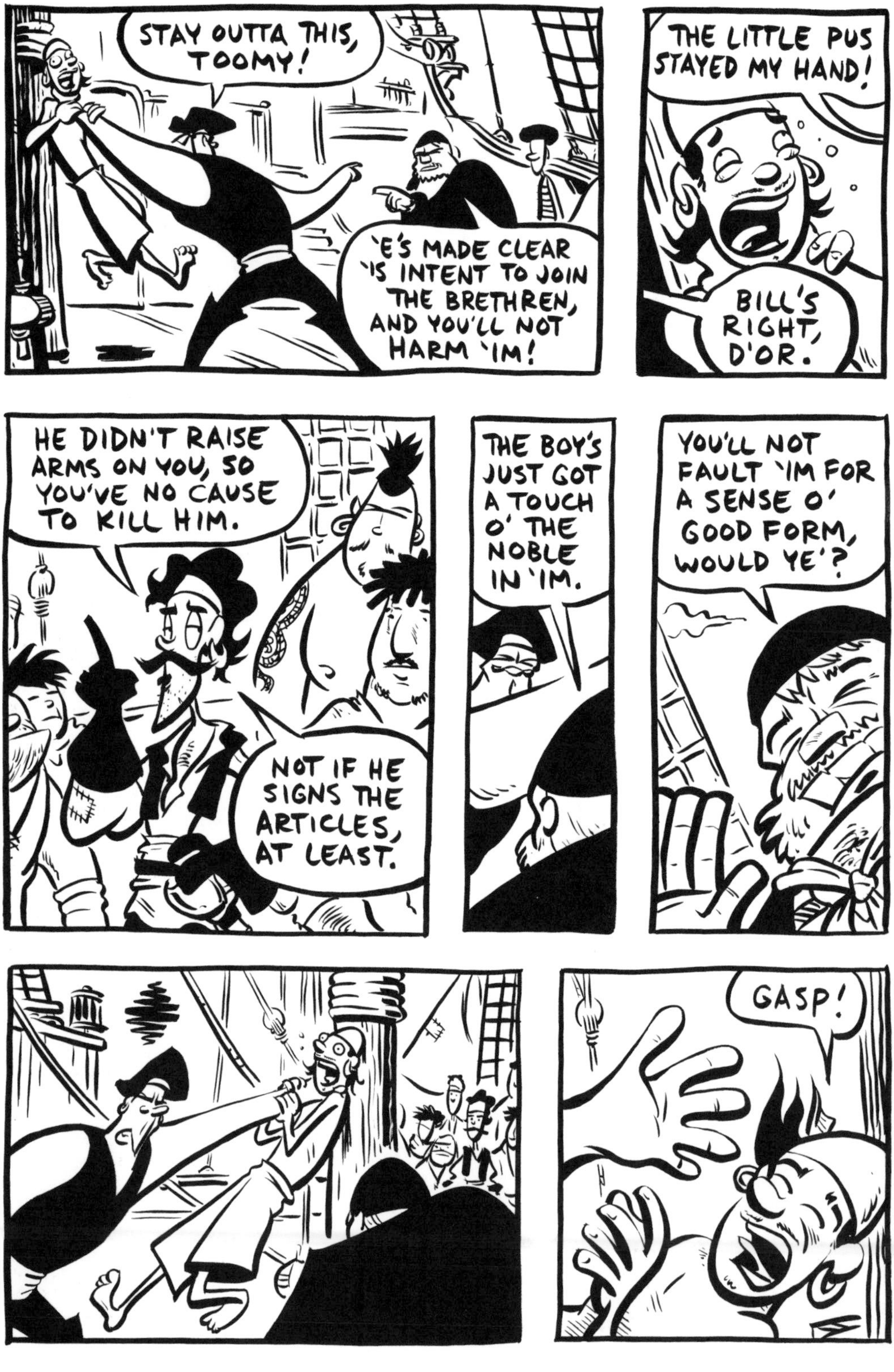
STAY OUTTA THIS, TOOMY!
`E'S MADE CLEAR `IS INTENT TO JOIN THE BRETHREN, AND YOU'LL NOT HARM `IM!
THE LITTLE PUS STAYED MY HAND!
BILL'S RIGHT, D'OR.
HE DIDN'T RAISE ARMS ON YOU, SO YOU'VE NO CAUSE TO KILL HIM.
NOT IF HE SIGNS THE ARTICLES, AT LEAST.
THE BOY'S JUST GOT A TOUCH O' THE NOBLE IN `IM.
YOU'LL NOT FAULT `IM FOR A SENSE O' GOOD FORM, WOULD YE'?
GASP!

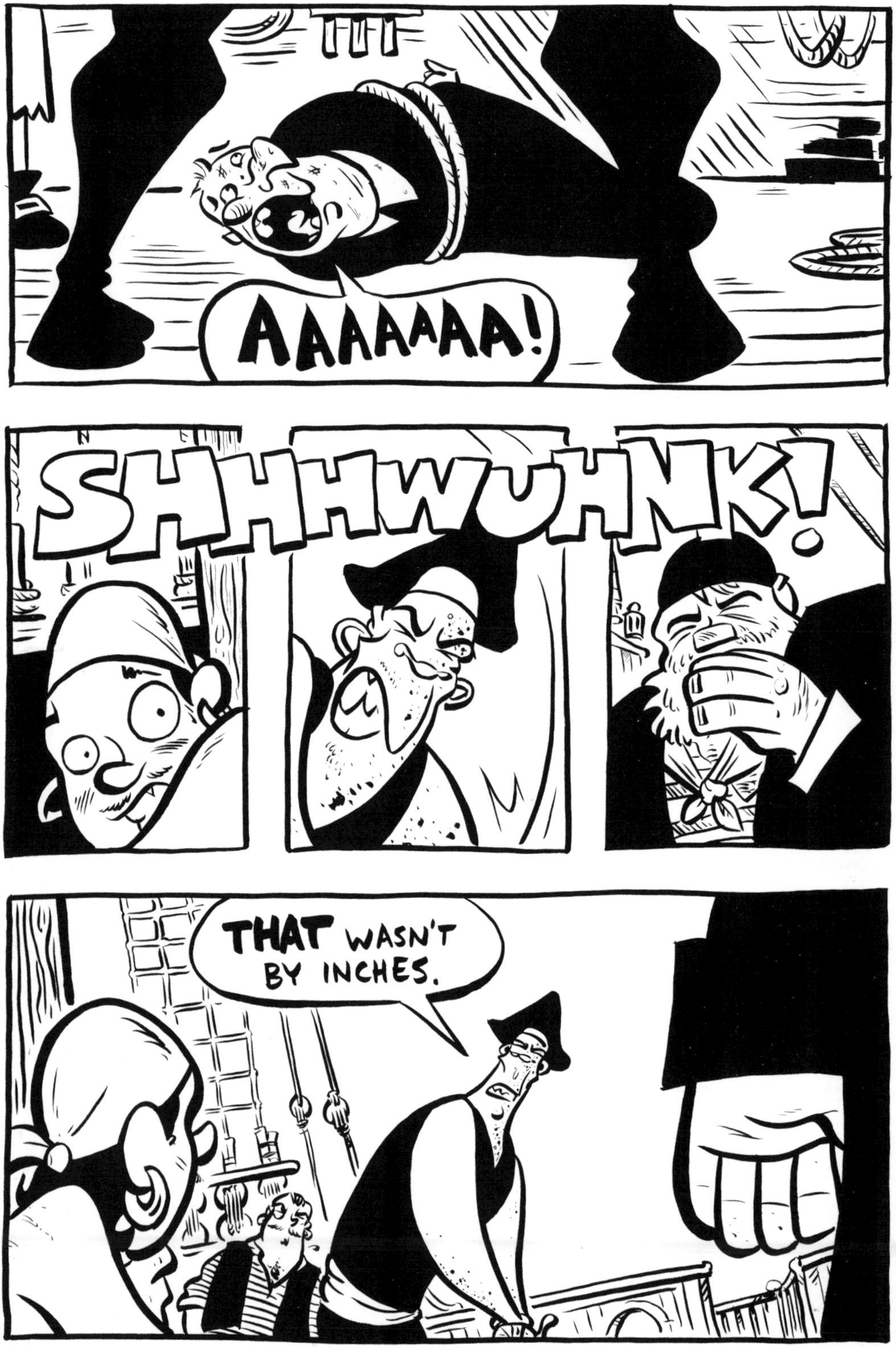
AAAAAAA!
SHHHWUHNK!
THAT WASN'T BY INCHES.

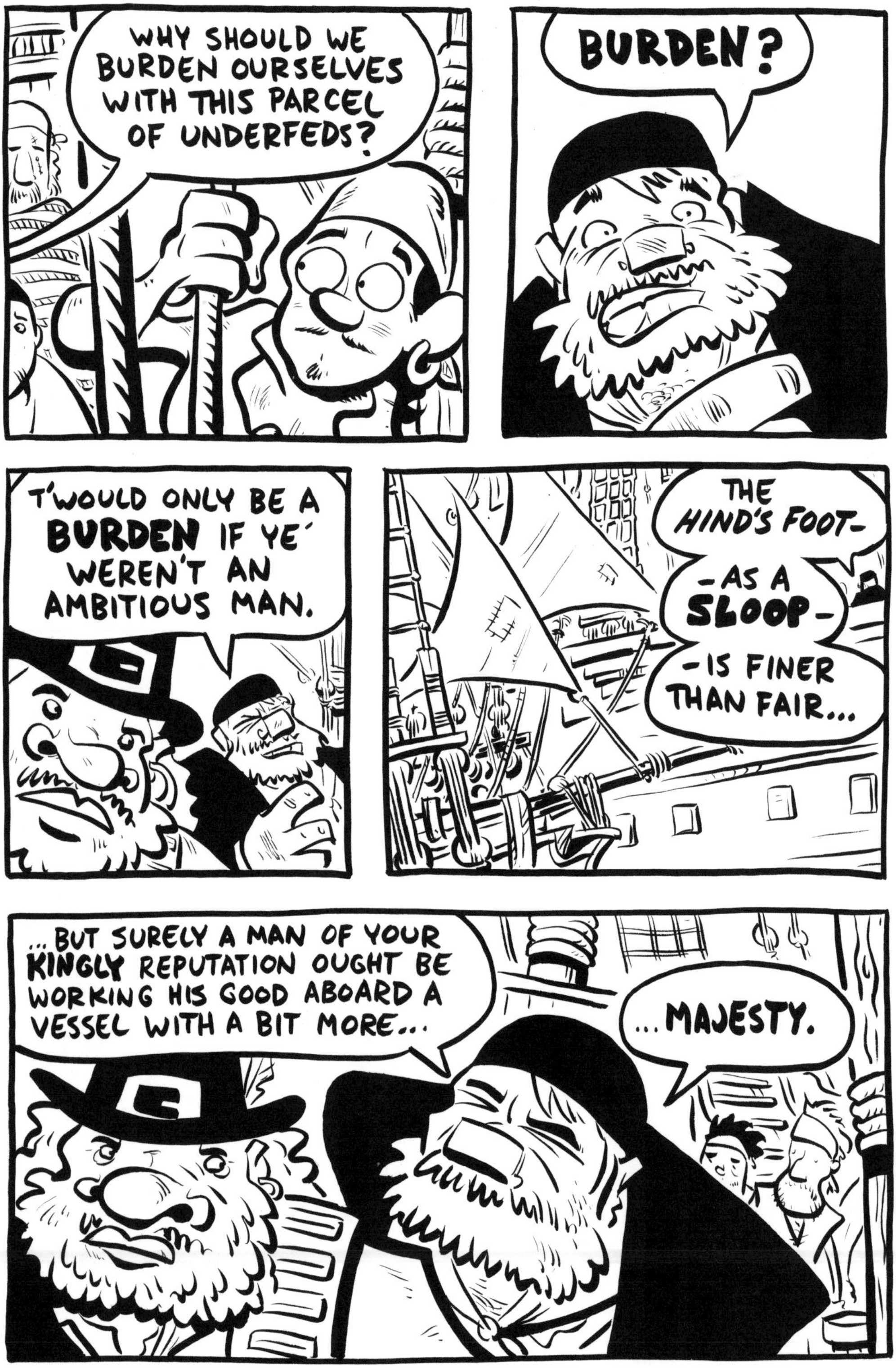
WHY SHOULD WE BURDEN OURSELVES WITH THIS PARCEL OF UNDERFEDS?
BURDEN?
T'WOULD ONLY BE A BURDEN IF YE WEREN'T AN AMBITIOUS MAN.
THE HIND'S FOOT-
-AS A SLOOP-
-IS FINER THAN FAIR...
...BUT SURELY A MAN OF YOUR KINGLY REPUTATION OUGHT BE WORKING HIS GOOD ABOARD A VESSEL WITH A BIT MORE...
...MAJESTY.

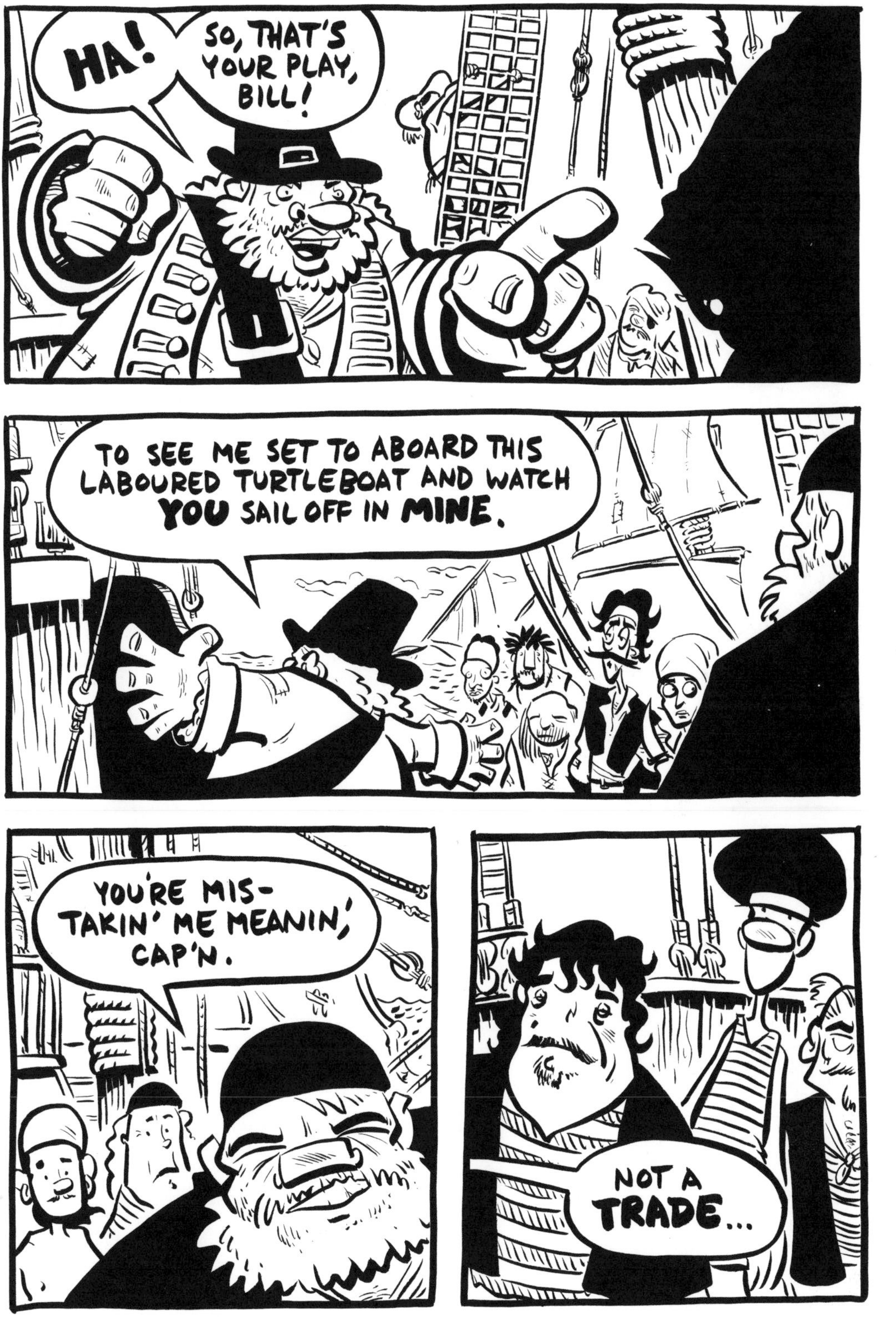
HA!
SO, THAT'S YOUR PLAY, BILL!
TO SEE ME SET TO ABOARD THIS LABOURED TURTLEBOAT AND WATCH **YOU** SAIL OFF IN **MINE**.
YOU'RE MIS-TAKIN' ME MEANIN', CAP'N.
NOT A **TRADE**...

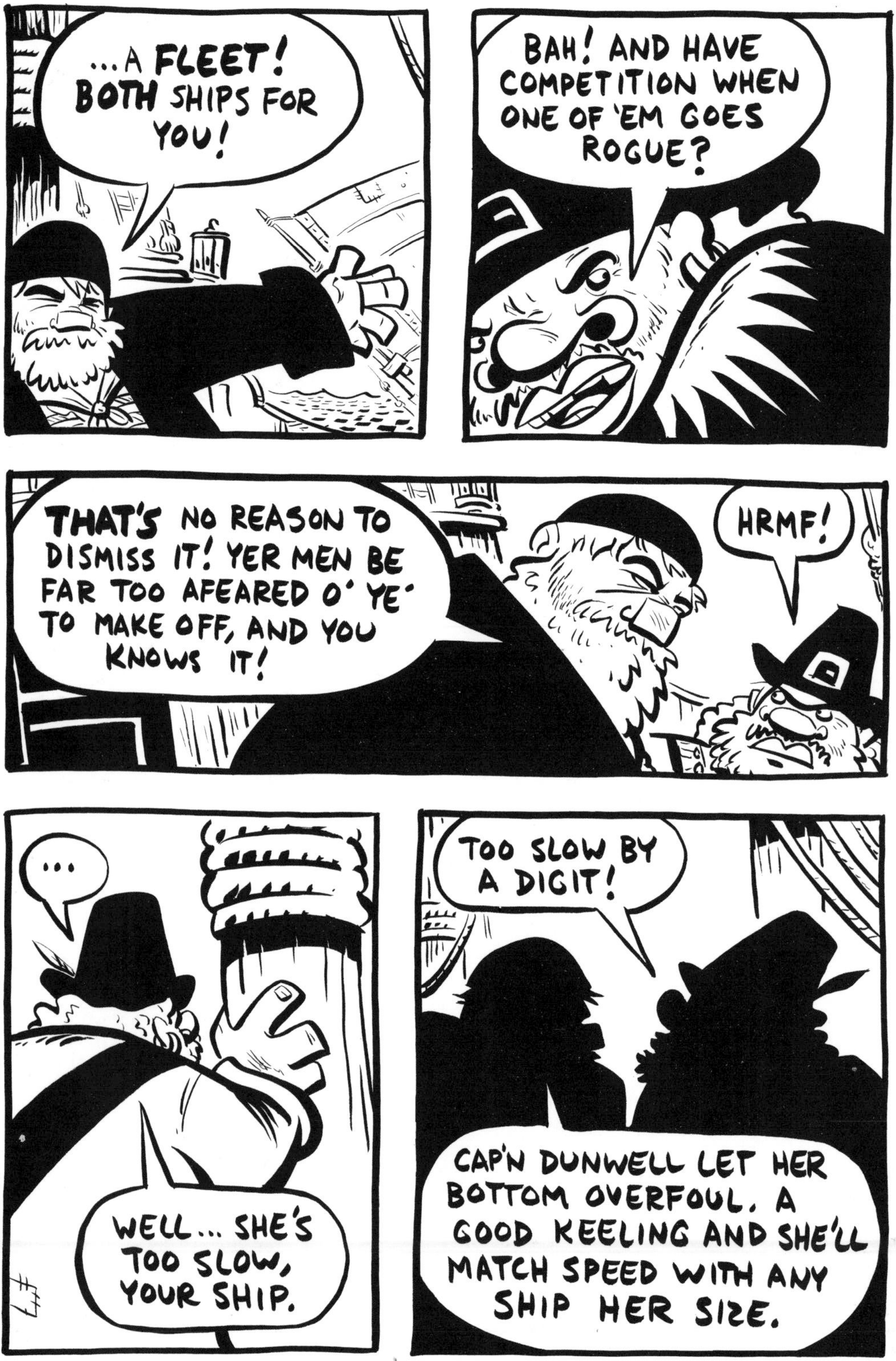
...A FLEET! BOTH SHIPS FOR YOU!
BAH! AND HAVE COMPETITION WHEN ONE OF 'EM GOES ROGUE?
THAT'S NO REASON TO DISMISS IT! YER MEN BE FAR TOO AFEARED O' YE TO MAKE OFF, AND YOU KNOWS IT!
HRMF!
...
WELL... SHE'S TOO SLOW, YOUR SHIP.
TOO SLOW BY A DIGIT!
CAP'N DUNWELL LET HER BOTTOM OVERFOUL. A GOOD KEELING AND SHE'LL MATCH SPEED WITH ANY SHIP HER SIZE.

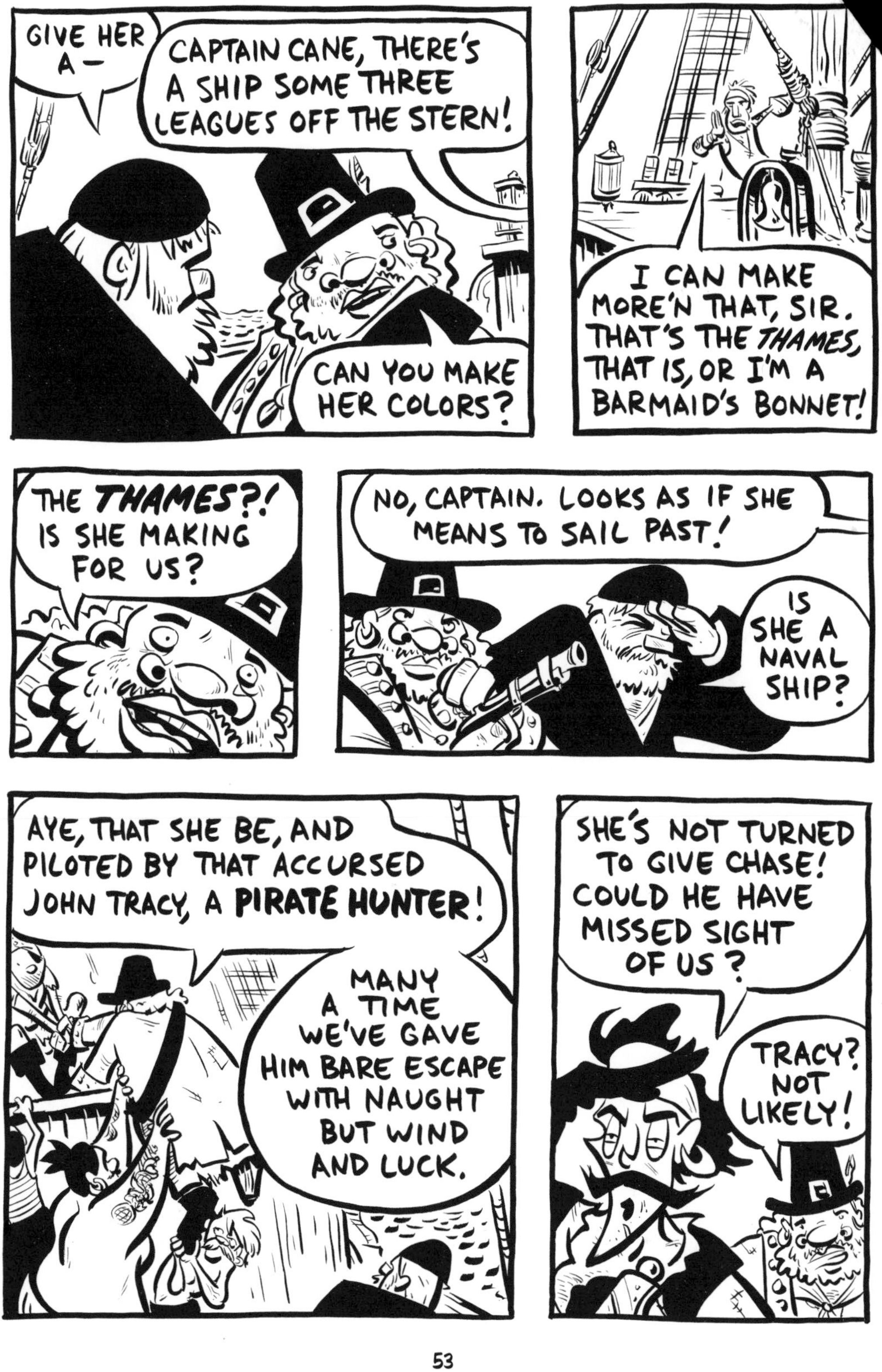
GIVE HER A—
CAPTAIN CANE, THERE'S A SHIP SOME THREE LEAGUES OFF THE STERN!
CAN YOU MAKE HER COLORS?
I CAN MAKE MORE'N THAT, SIR. THAT'S THE *THAMES*, THAT IS, OR I'M A BARMAID'S BONNET!
THE ***THAMES***?! IS SHE MAKING FOR US?
NO, CAPTAIN. LOOKS AS IF SHE MEANS TO SAIL PAST!
IS SHE A NAVAL SHIP?
AYE, THAT SHE BE, AND PILOTED BY THAT ACCURSED JOHN TRACY, A **PIRATE HUNTER**!
MANY A TIME WE'VE GAVE HIM BARE ESCAPE WITH NAUGHT BUT WIND AND LUCK.
SHE'S NOT TURNED TO GIVE CHASE! COULD HE HAVE MISSED SIGHT OF US?
TRACY? NOT LIKELY!

HEARD FROM ...ARLY THE GREEK THAT THE *THAMES* IS TAKING THE JAMAICA TAXES TO ENGLAND.

HER HOLD BE **STUFFED** WITH PLATE AND COIN, IF OL' CHARLY TELLS TRUE.

SO **THAT'S** WHY SHE AIN'T VEERED TO!

BY THUNDER! A TREASURE SHIP!

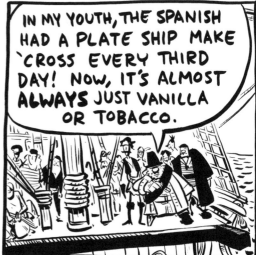

IN MY YOUTH, THE SPANISH HAD A PLATE SHIP MAKE `CROSS EVERY THIRD DAY! NOW, IT'S ALMOST **ALWAYS** JUST VANILLA OR TOBACCO.

NEVER THOUGHT I'D SEE ANOTHER TREASURE SHIP.

CAN WE CATCH `ER?

THE *HIND'S FOOT* COULD CATCH HER, BUT TO WHAT PURPOSE? THE *THAMES* HAS **TWENTY GUNS,** AND TRACY IS NO BABE AT THE HELM.

SHE'D SINK US `ERE WE FIRED A SECOND VOLLEY.

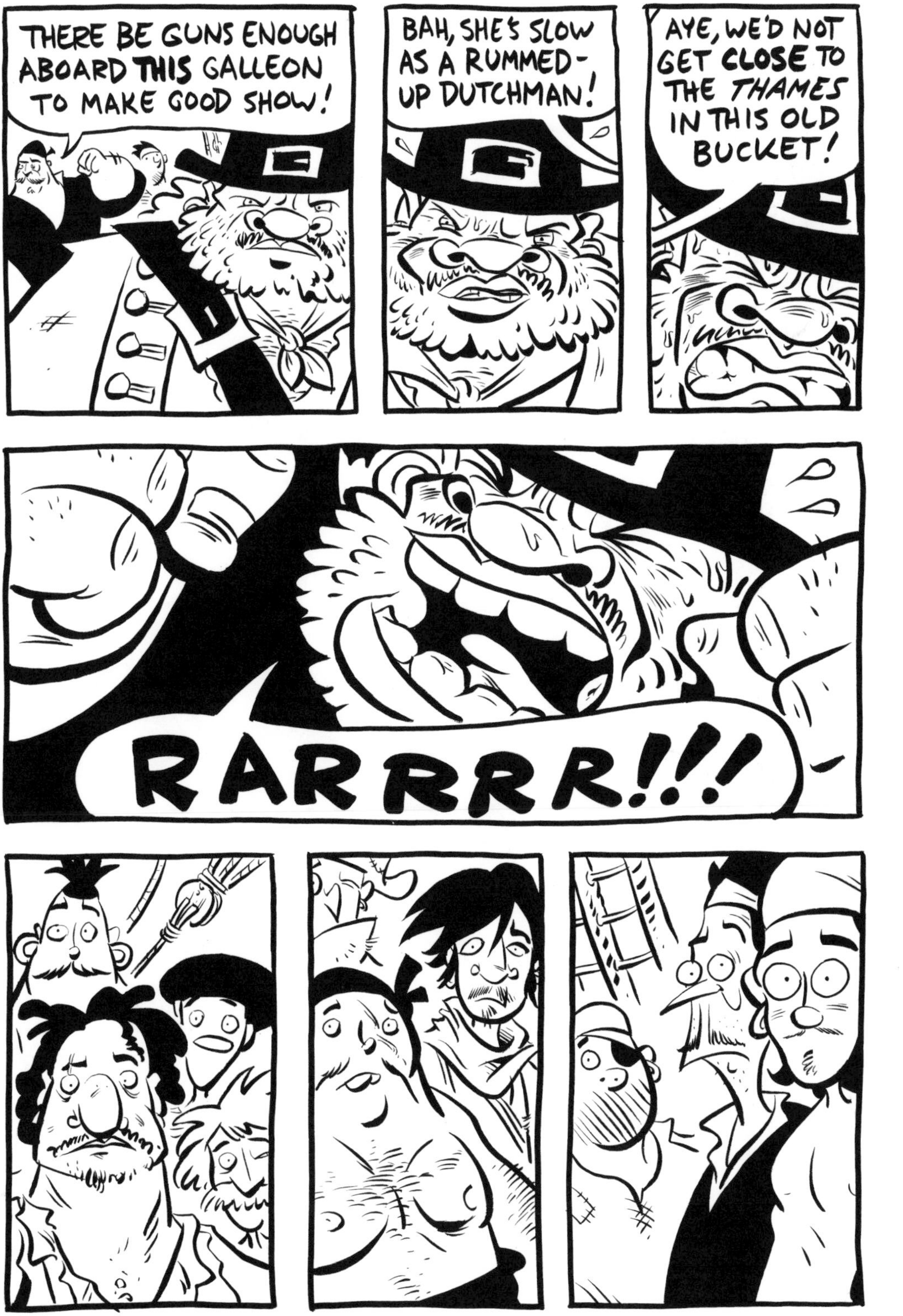
THERE BE GUNS ENOUGH ABOARD **THIS** GALLEON TO MAKE GOOD SHOW!
BAH, SHE'S SLOW AS A RUMMED-UP DUTCHMAN!
AYE, WE'D NOT GET **CLOSE** TO THE *THAMES* IN THIS OLD BUCKET!
RARRRR!!!

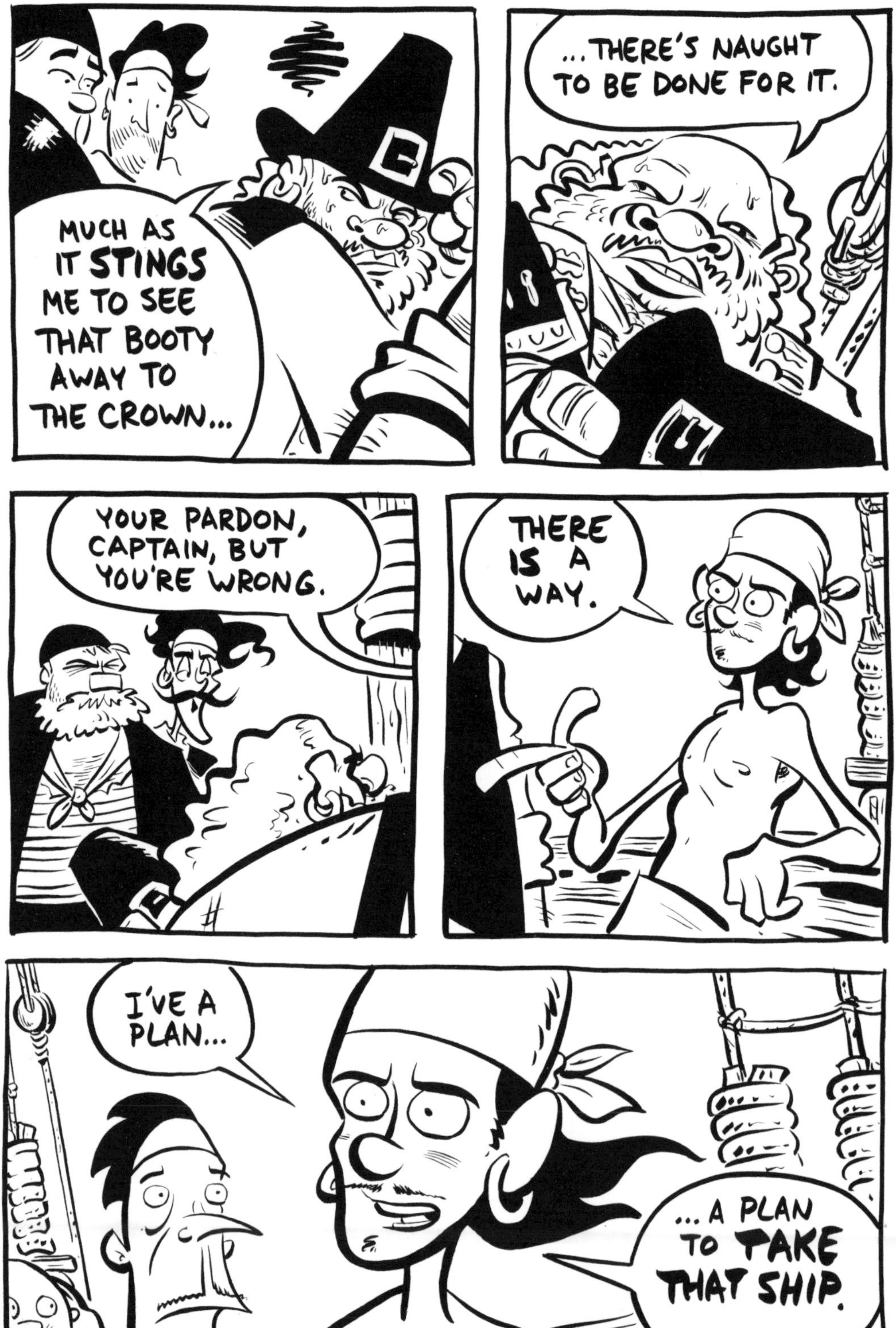
MUCH AS IT STINGS ME TO SEE THAT BOOTY AWAY TO THE CROWN...
...THERE'S NAUGHT TO BE DONE FOR IT.
YOUR PARDON, CAPTAIN, BUT YOU'RE WRONG.
THERE IS A WAY.
I'VE A PLAN...
...A PLAN TO TAKE THAT SHIP.

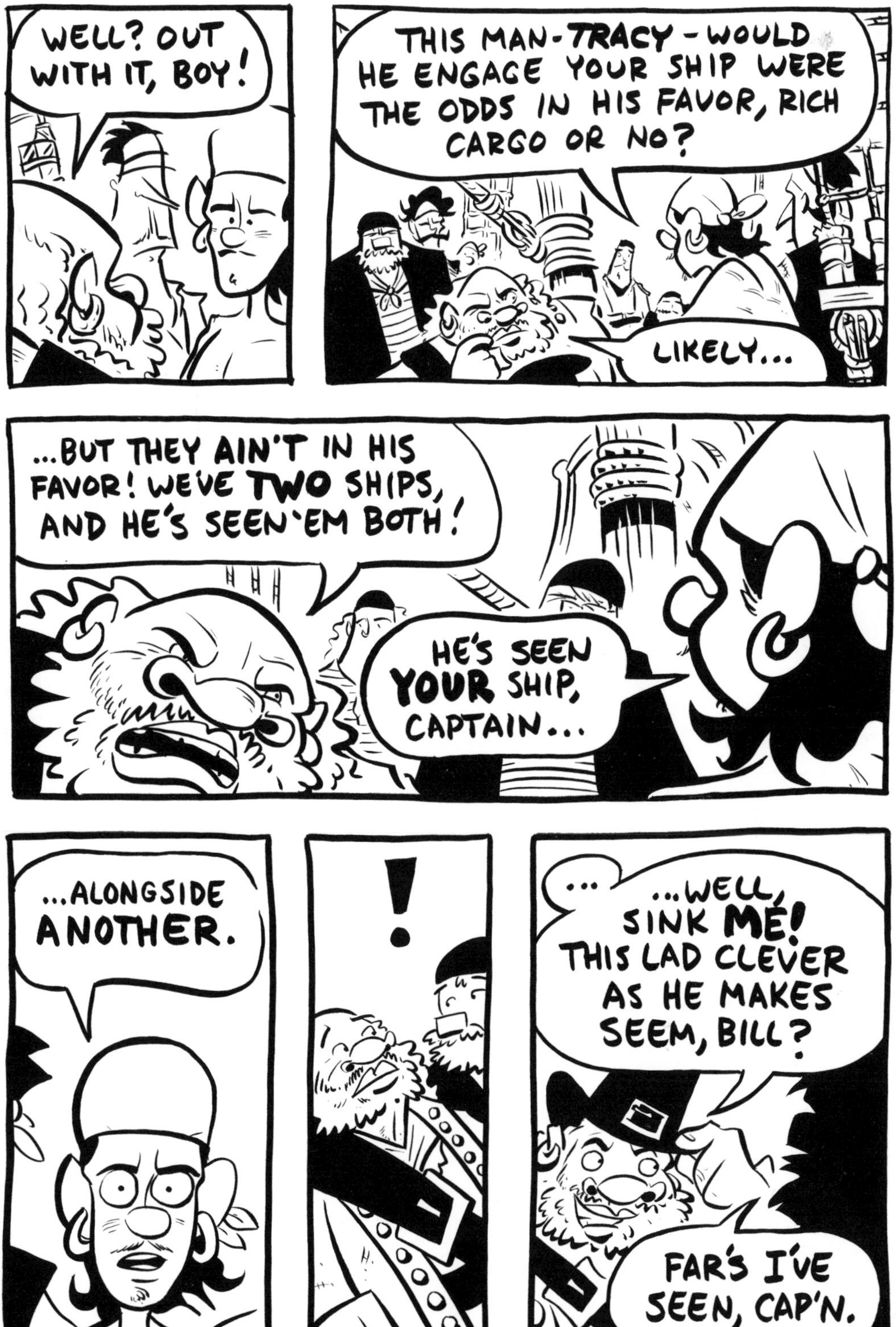
WELL? OUT WITH IT, BOY!
THIS MAN-TRACY-WOULD HE ENGAGE YOUR SHIP WERE THE ODDS IN HIS FAVOR, RICH CARGO OR NO?
LIKELY...
...BUT THEY AIN'T IN HIS FAVOR! WE'VE TWO SHIPS, AND HE'S SEEN 'EM BOTH!
HE'S SEEN YOUR SHIP, CAPTAIN...
...ALONGSIDE ANOTHER.
!
...
...WELL, SINK ME! THIS LAD CLEVER AS HE MAKES SEEM, BILL?
FAR'S I'VE SEEN, CAP'N.

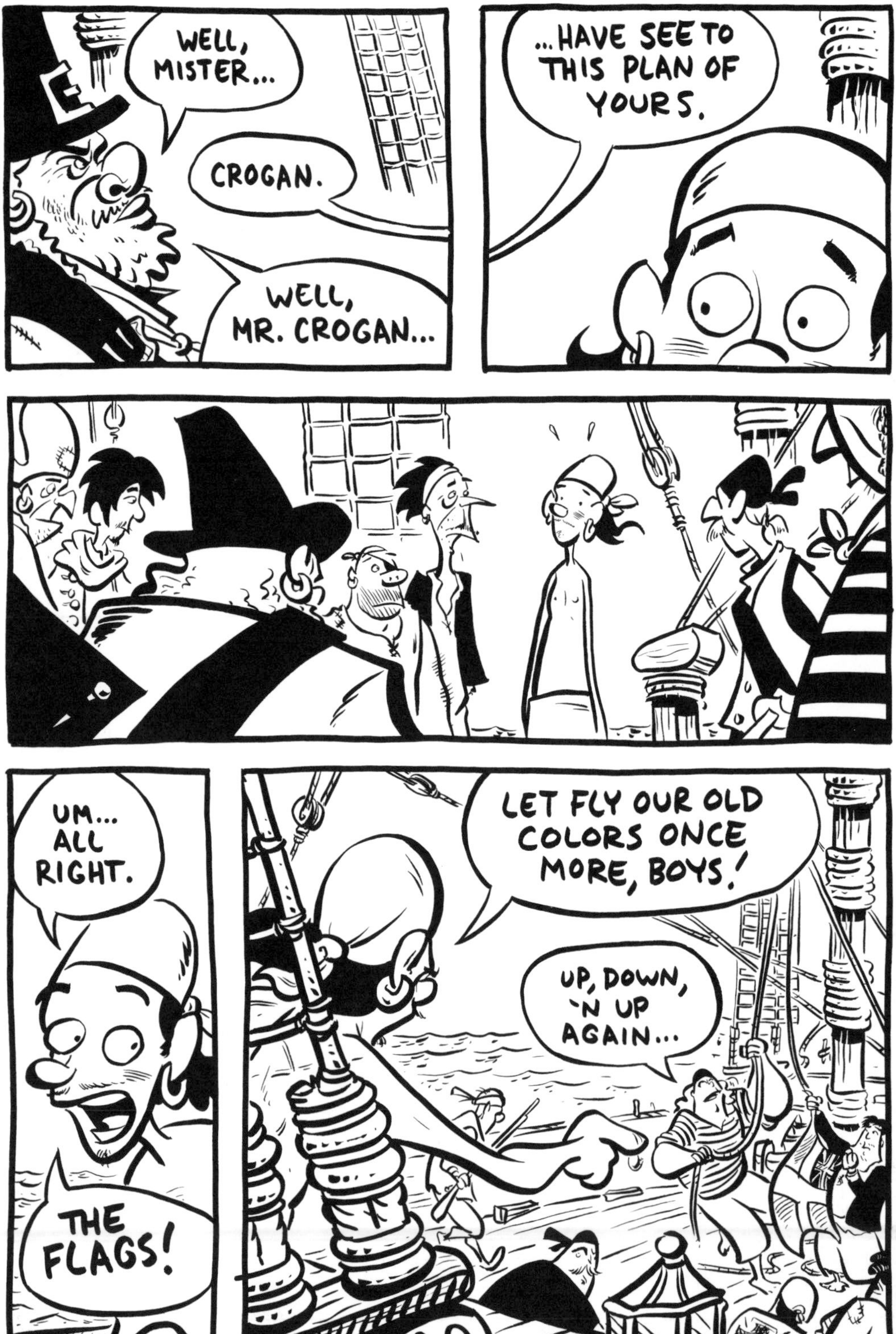
WELL, MISTER...
CROGAN.
WELL, MR. CROGAN...
...HAVE SEE TO THIS PLAN OF YOURS.
UM... ALL RIGHT.
THE FLAGS!
LET FLY OUR OLD COLORS ONCE MORE, BOYS!
UP, DOWN, 'N UP AGAIN...

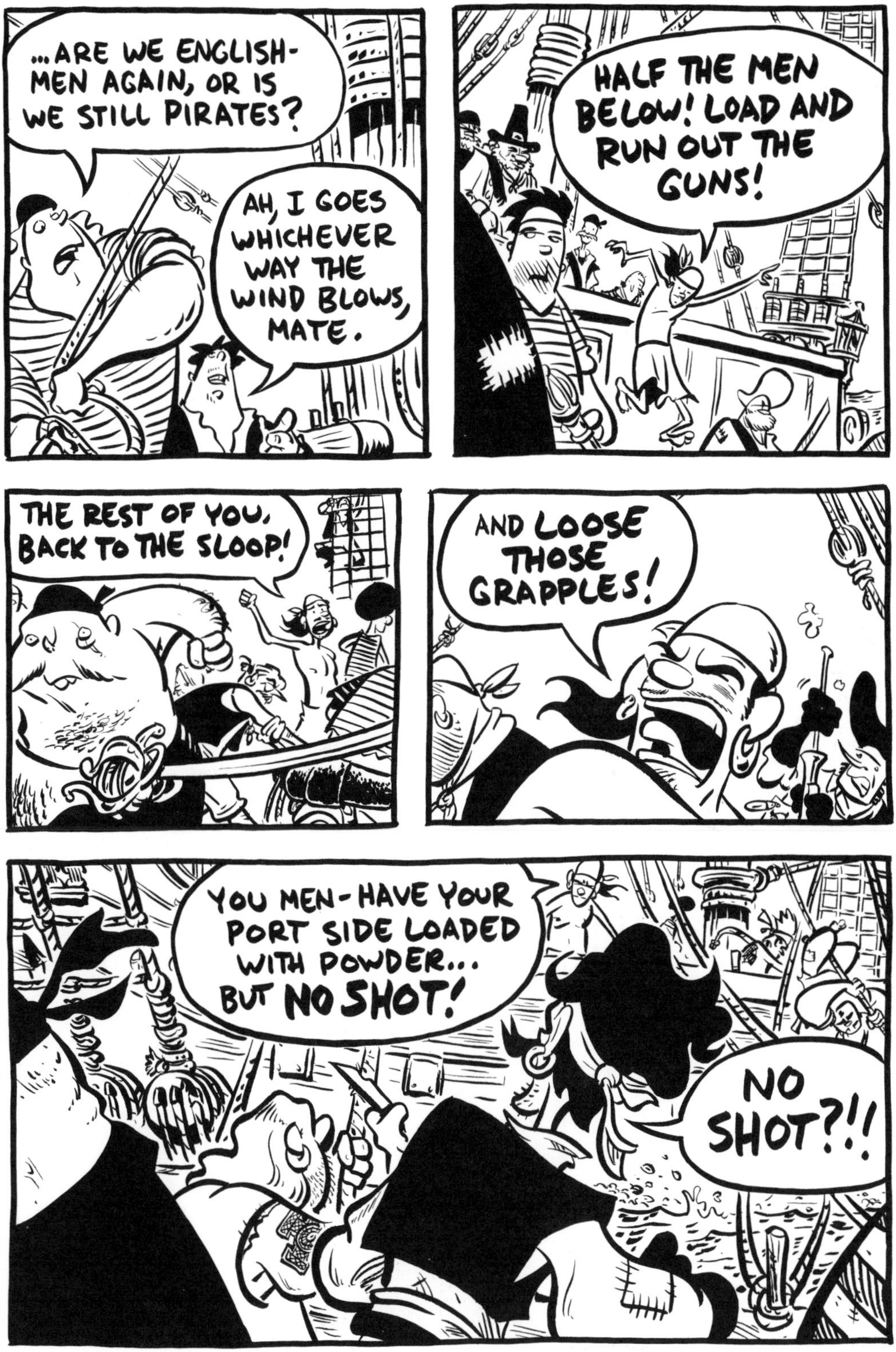
...ARE WE ENGLISH-MEN AGAIN, OR IS WE STILL PIRATES?
AH, I GOES WHICHEVER WAY THE WIND BLOWS, MATE.
HALF THE MEN BELOW! LOAD AND RUN OUT THE GUNS!
THE REST OF YOU, BACK TO THE SLOOP!
AND LOOSE THOSE GRAPPLES!
YOU MEN-HAVE YOUR PORT SIDE LOADED WITH POWDER... BUT NO SHOT!
NO SHOT?!!

NO SHOT. AND ON MY SIGNAL, FIRE INTO OUR SIDES!

TRACY WILL THINK THE GALLEON IS UNDER ATTACK!

AND HE'LL SWING ROUND TO THEIR AID, SURE ENOUGH!

WELL THOUGHT, LAD!

IT'S NOT WORKED YET, CAPTAIN.

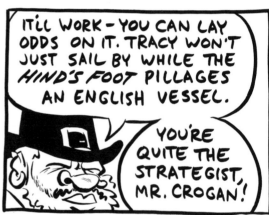

IT'LL WORK — YOU CAN LAY ODDS ON IT. TRACY WON'T JUST SAIL BY WHILE THE *HIND'S FOOT* PILLAGES AN ENGLISH VESSEL.

YOU'RE QUITE THE STRATEGIST, MR. CROGAN!

WE'LL SOON SEE. LOOSE THE SAILS!

YOU MEN IN THE SLOOP - BE SURE THERE'S NOT BUT WADDING IN YOUR GUNS—

FIRE!!!

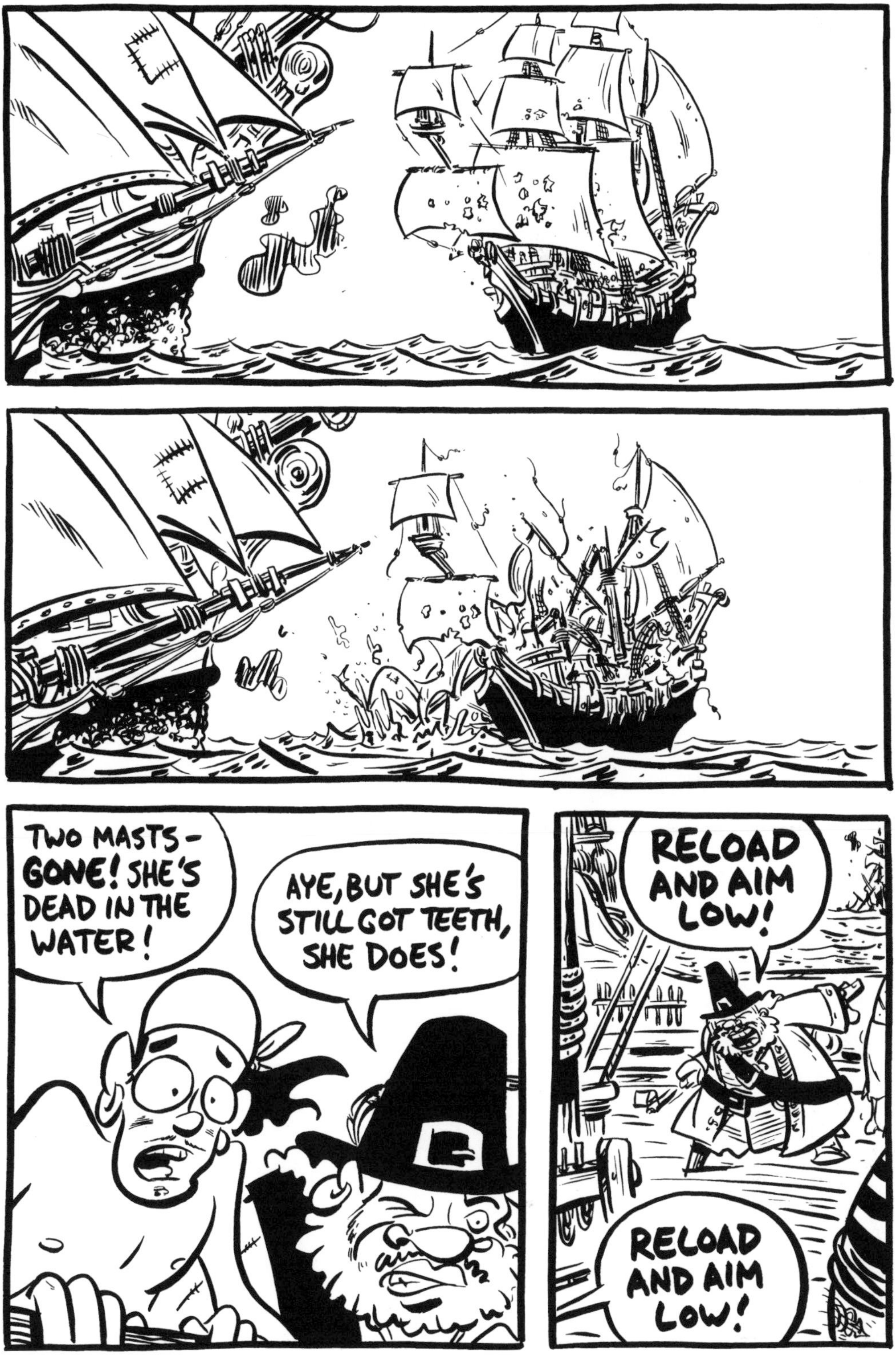
TWO MASTS - GONE! SHE'S DEAD IN THE WATER!
AYE, BUT SHE'S STILL GOT TEETH, SHE DOES!
RELOAD AND AIM LOW!
RELOAD AND AIM LOW!

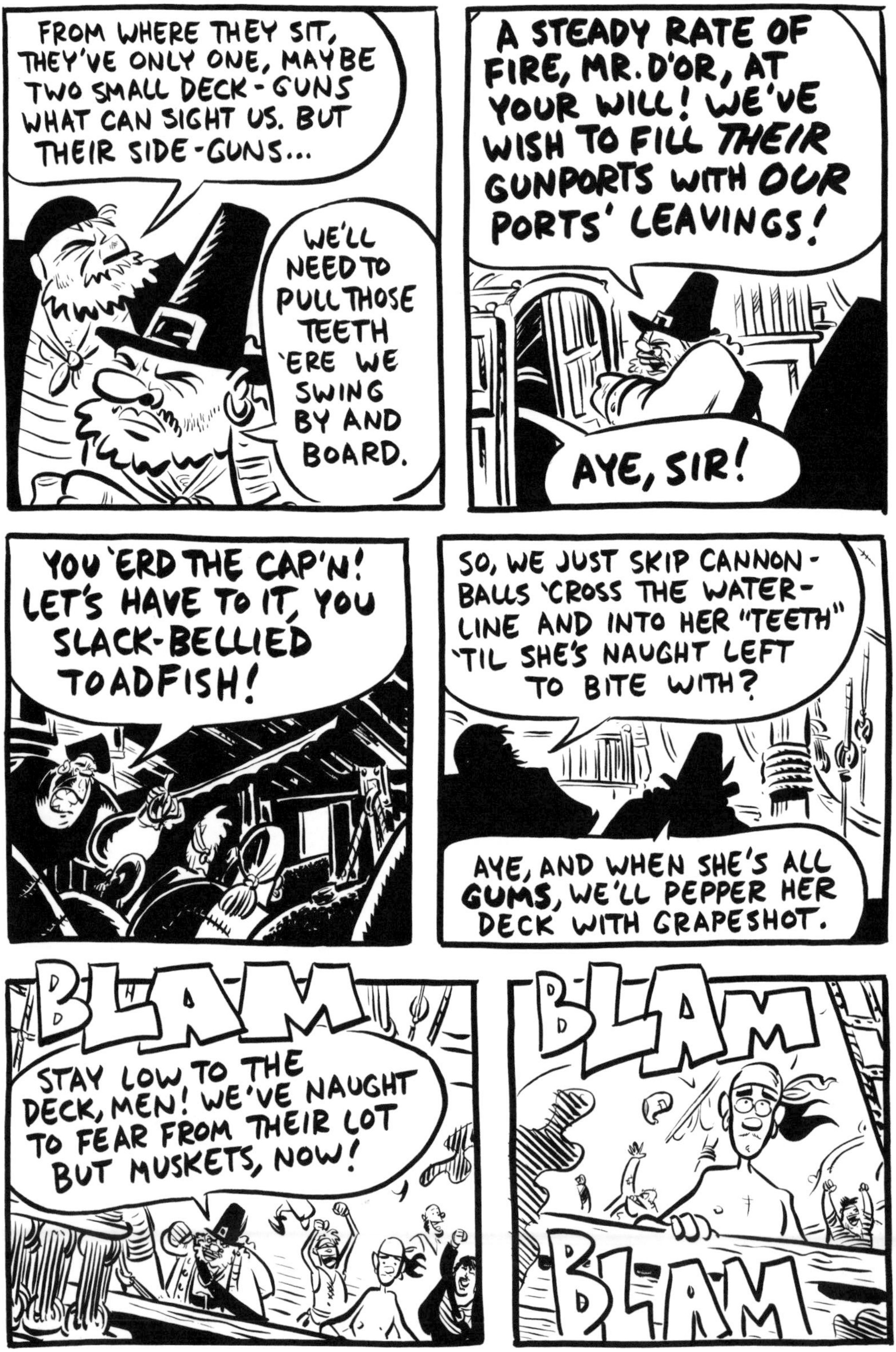
FROM WHERE THEY SIT, THEY'VE ONLY ONE, MAYBE TWO SMALL DECK-GUNS WHAT CAN SIGHT US. BUT THEIR SIDE-GUNS...
WE'LL NEED TO PULL THOSE TEETH 'ERE WE SWING BY AND BOARD.
A STEADY RATE OF FIRE, MR. D'OR, AT YOUR WILL! WE'VE WISH TO FILL THEIR GUNPORTS WITH OUR PORTS' LEAVINGS!
AYE, SIR!
YOU 'ERD THE CAP'N! LET'S HAVE TO IT, YOU SLACK-BELLIED TOADFISH!
SO, WE JUST SKIP CANNON-BALLS 'CROSS THE WATER-LINE AND INTO HER "TEETH" 'TIL SHE'S NAUGHT LEFT TO BITE WITH?
AYE, AND WHEN SHE'S ALL GUMS, WE'LL PEPPER HER DECK WITH GRAPESHOT.
BLAM
STAY LOW TO THE DECK, MEN! WE'VE NAUGHT TO FEAR FROM THEIR LOT BUT MUSKETS, NOW!
BLAM
BLAM

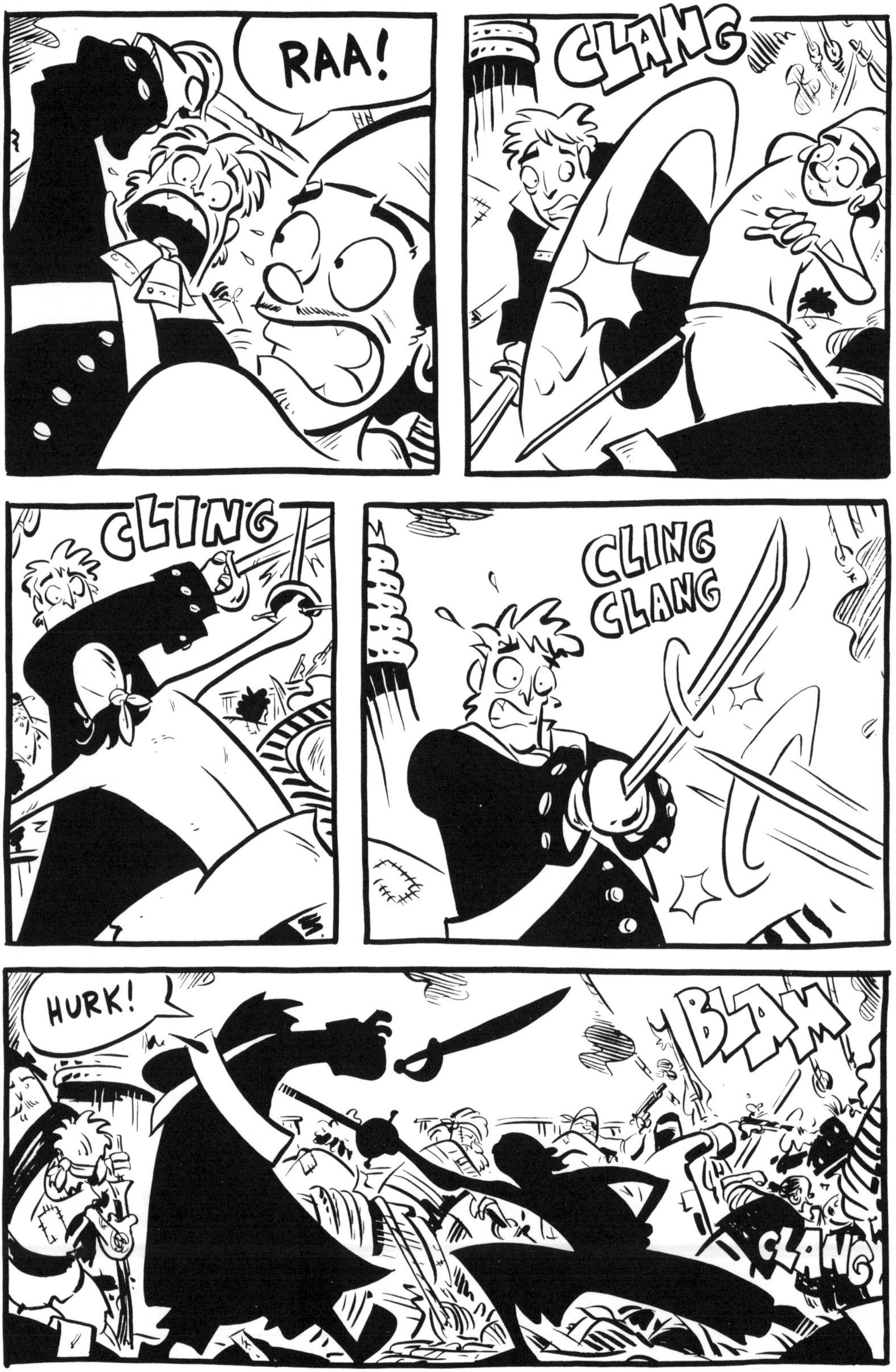
RAA!
CLANG
CLING
CLING
CLANG
HURK!
BLAM
CLANG

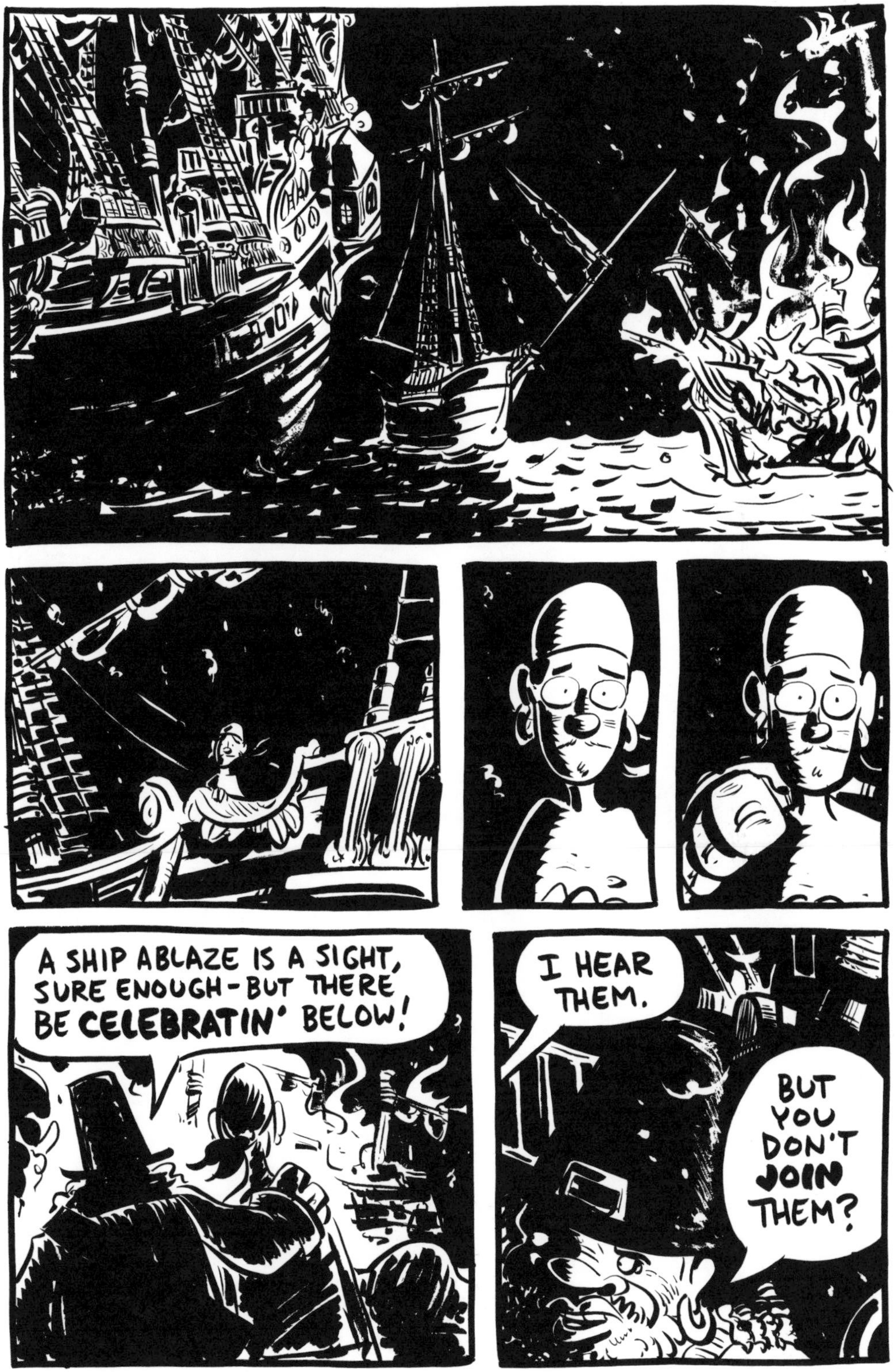
A SHIP ABLAZE IS A SIGHT, SURE ENOUGH - BUT THERE BE CELEBRATIN' BELOW!
I HEAR THEM.
BUT YOU DON'T JOIN THEM?

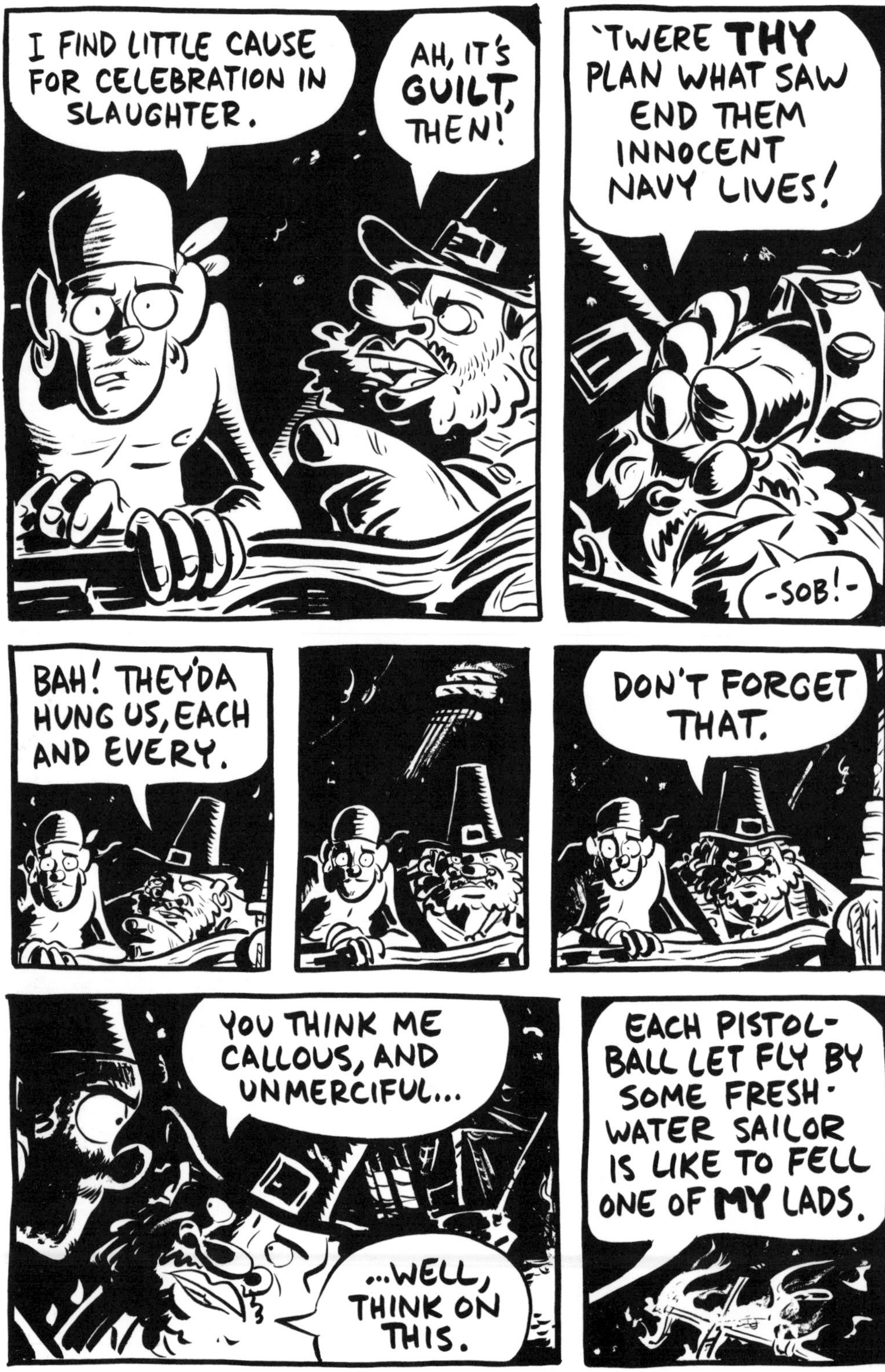
I FIND LITTLE CAUSE FOR CELEBRATION IN SLAUGHTER.
AH, IT'S GUILT, THEN!
'TWERE THY PLAN WHAT SAW END THEM INNOCENT NAVY LIVES!
-SOB!-
BAH! THEY'DA HUNG US, EACH AND EVERY.
DON'T FORGET THAT.
YOU THINK ME CALLOUS, AND UNMERCIFUL...
...WELL, THINK ON THIS.
EACH PISTOL-BALL LET FLY BY SOME FRESH-WATER SAILOR IS LIKE TO FELL ONE OF MY LADS.

SOME LUBBER WITH A CUTLASS AND A BELLYFUL OF TERROR MIGHT **LAY LOW** ONE OF THESE FINE BOYS!

IF EACH AND EVERY O'ER THE SEAS IS SURE-**SURE**-THAT TAKING ARMS TO US MEANS HIS CERTAIN DEATH...

...THEN HE'LL BE DISINCLINED TO FIGHT MY MEN.

AND THOSE WHOSE CARE IS **MY** VOCATION LIVE ANOTHER DAY.

71

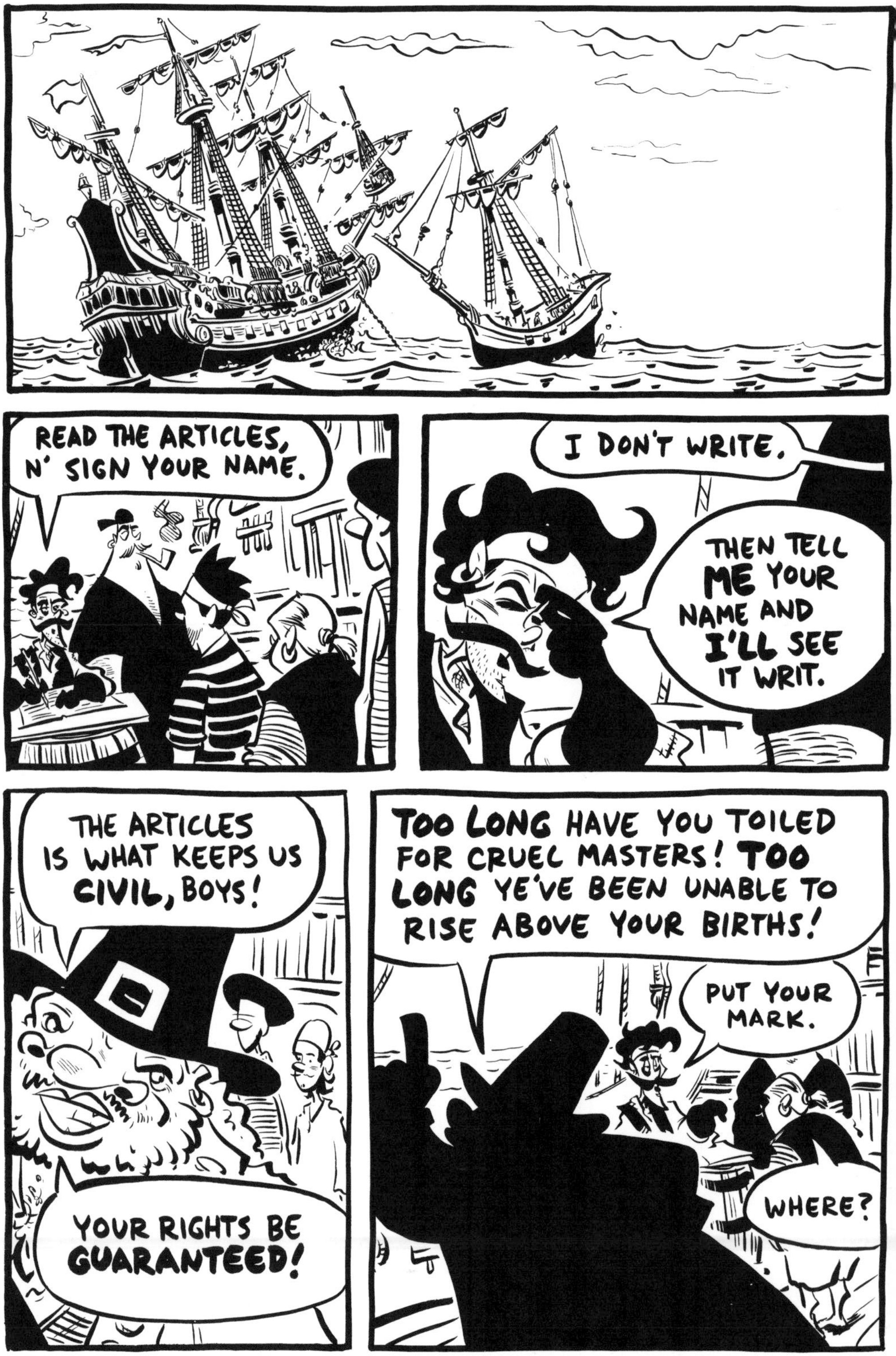
READ THE ARTICLES, N' SIGN YOUR NAME.
I DON'T WRITE.
THEN TELL ME YOUR NAME AND I'LL SEE IT WRIT.
THE ARTICLES IS WHAT KEEPS US CIVIL, BOYS!
YOUR RIGHTS BE GUARANTEED!
TOO LONG HAVE YOU TOILED FOR CRUEL MASTERS! TOO LONG YE'VE BEEN UNABLE TO RISE ABOVE YOUR BIRTHS!
PUT YOUR MARK.
WHERE?

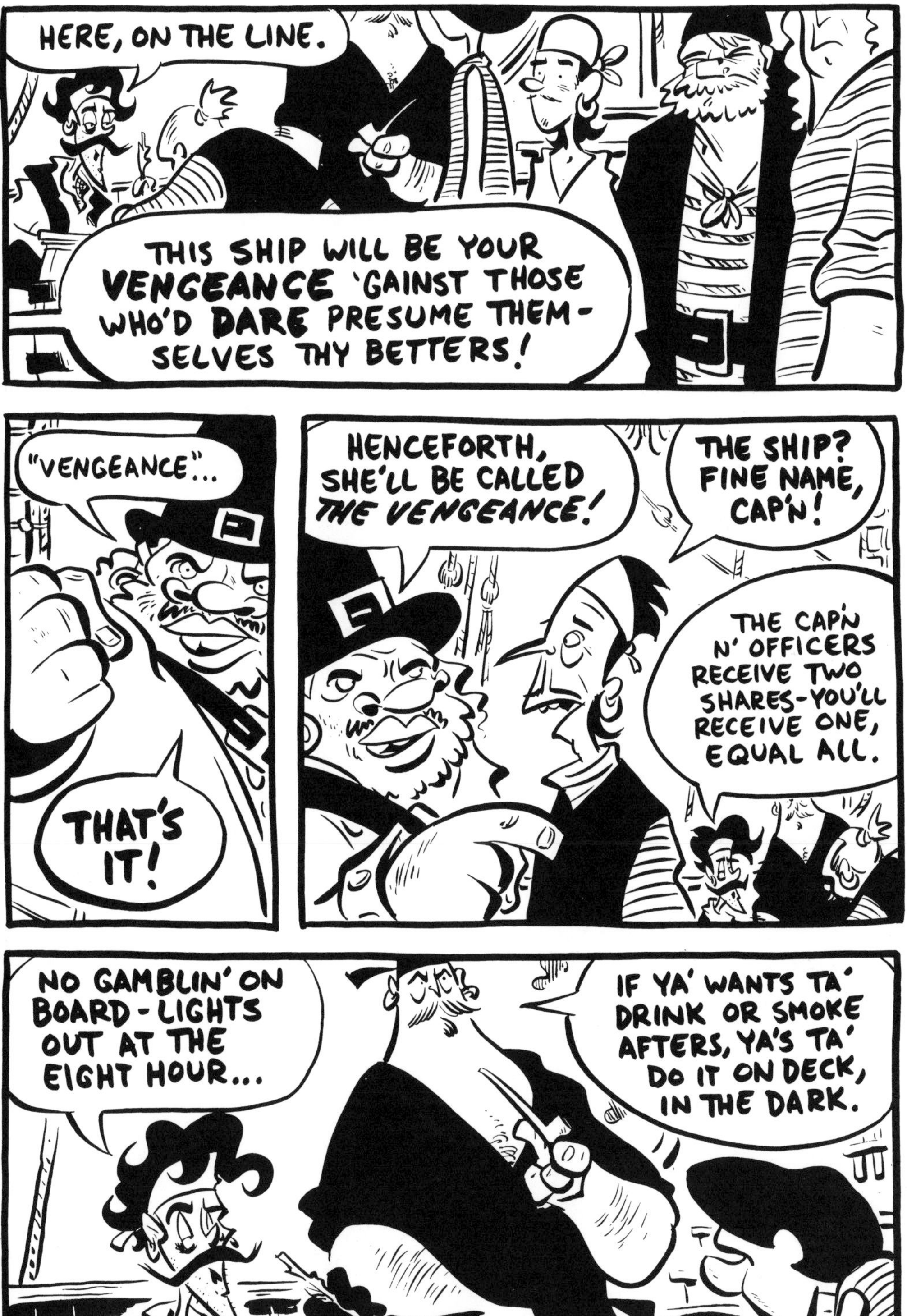
HERE, ON THE LINE.
THIS SHIP WILL BE YOUR VENGEANCE 'GAINST THOSE WHO'D DARE PRESUME THEM-SELVES THY BETTERS!
"VENGEANCE"...
THAT'S IT!
HENCEFORTH, SHE'LL BE CALLED THE VENGEANCE!
THE SHIP? FINE NAME, CAP'N!
THE CAP'N N' OFFICERS RECEIVE TWO SHARES-YOU'LL RECEIVE ONE, EQUAL ALL.
NO GAMBLIN' ON BOARD-LIGHTS OUT AT THE EIGHT HOUR...
IF YA' WANTS TA' DRINK OR SMOKE AFTERS, YA'S TA' DO IT ON DECK, IN THE DARK.

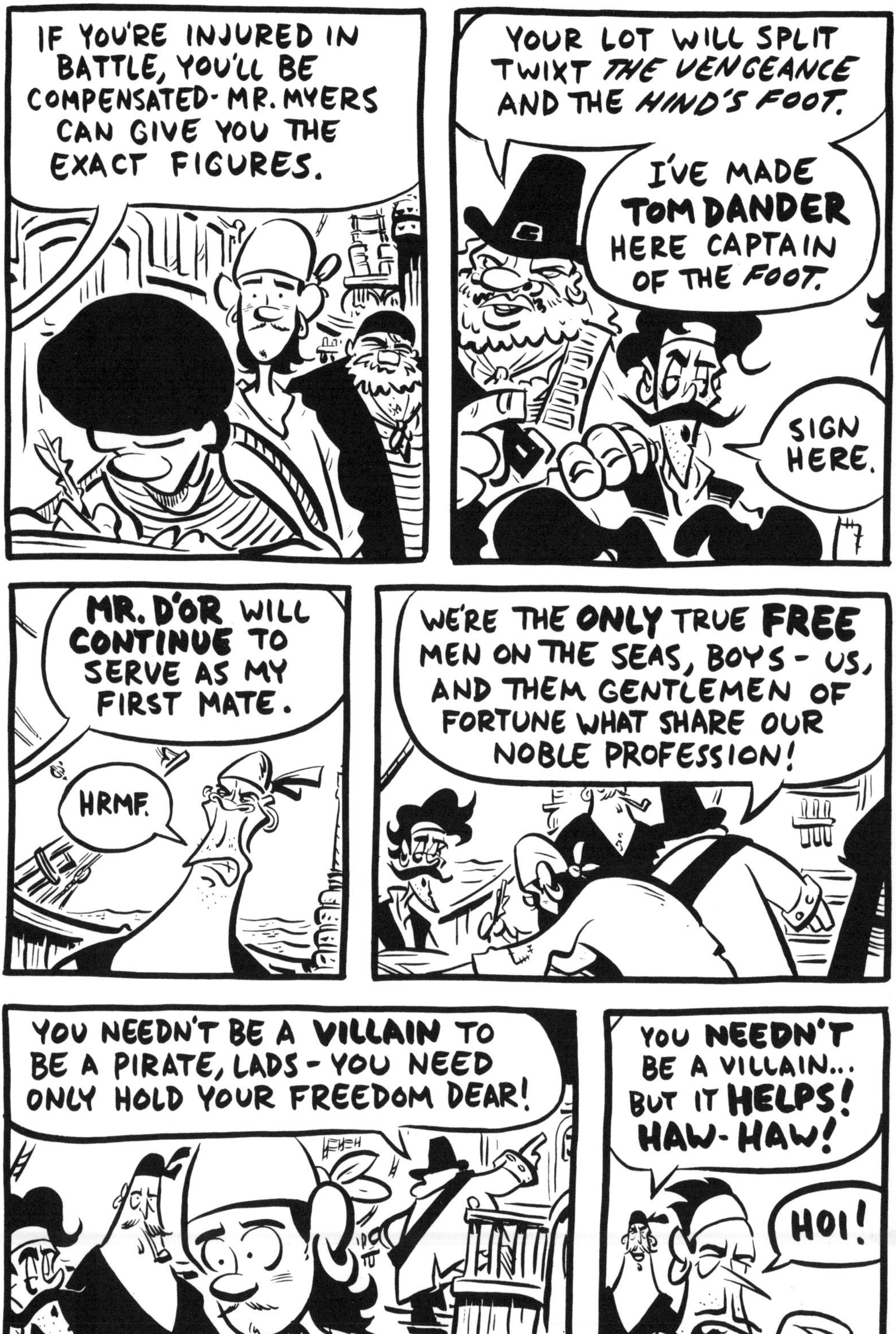
IF YOU'RE INJURED IN BATTLE, YOU'LL BE COMPENSATED- MR. MYERS CAN GIVE YOU THE EXACT FIGURES.
YOUR LOT WILL SPLIT TWIXT *THE VENGEANCE* AND THE *HIND'S FOOT.*
I'VE MADE **TOM DANDER** HERE CAPTAIN OF THE *FOOT.*
SIGN HERE.
MR. D'OR WILL **CONTINUE** TO SERVE AS MY FIRST MATE.
HRMF.
WE'RE THE **ONLY** TRUE **FREE** MEN ON THE SEAS, BOYS - US, AND THEM GENTLEMEN OF FORTUNE WHAT SHARE OUR NOBLE PROFESSION!
YOU NEEDN'T BE A **VILLAIN** TO BE A PIRATE, LADS - YOU NEED ONLY HOLD YOUR FREEDOM DEAR!
YOU **NEEDN'T** BE A VILLAIN... BUT IT **HELPS**! **HAW-HAW!**
HOI!

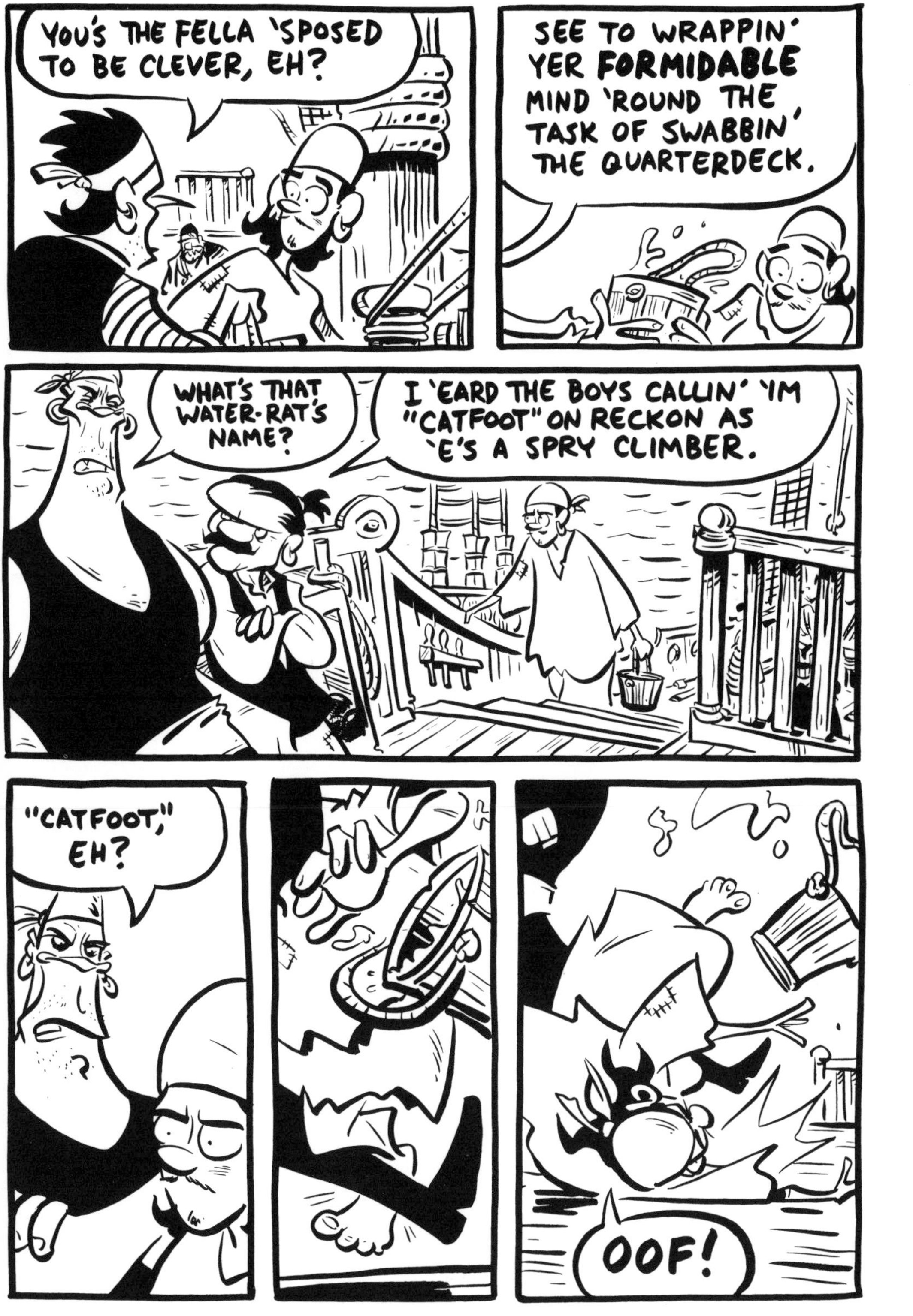
YOU'S THE FELLA 'SPOSED TO BE CLEVER, EH?
SEE TO WRAPPIN' YER FORMIDABLE MIND 'ROUND THE TASK OF SWABBIN' THE QUARTERDECK.
WHAT'S THAT WATER-RAT'S NAME?
I 'EARD THE BOYS CALLIN' 'IM "CATFOOT" ON RECKON AS 'E'S A SPRY CLIMBER.
"CATFOOT," EH?
OOF!

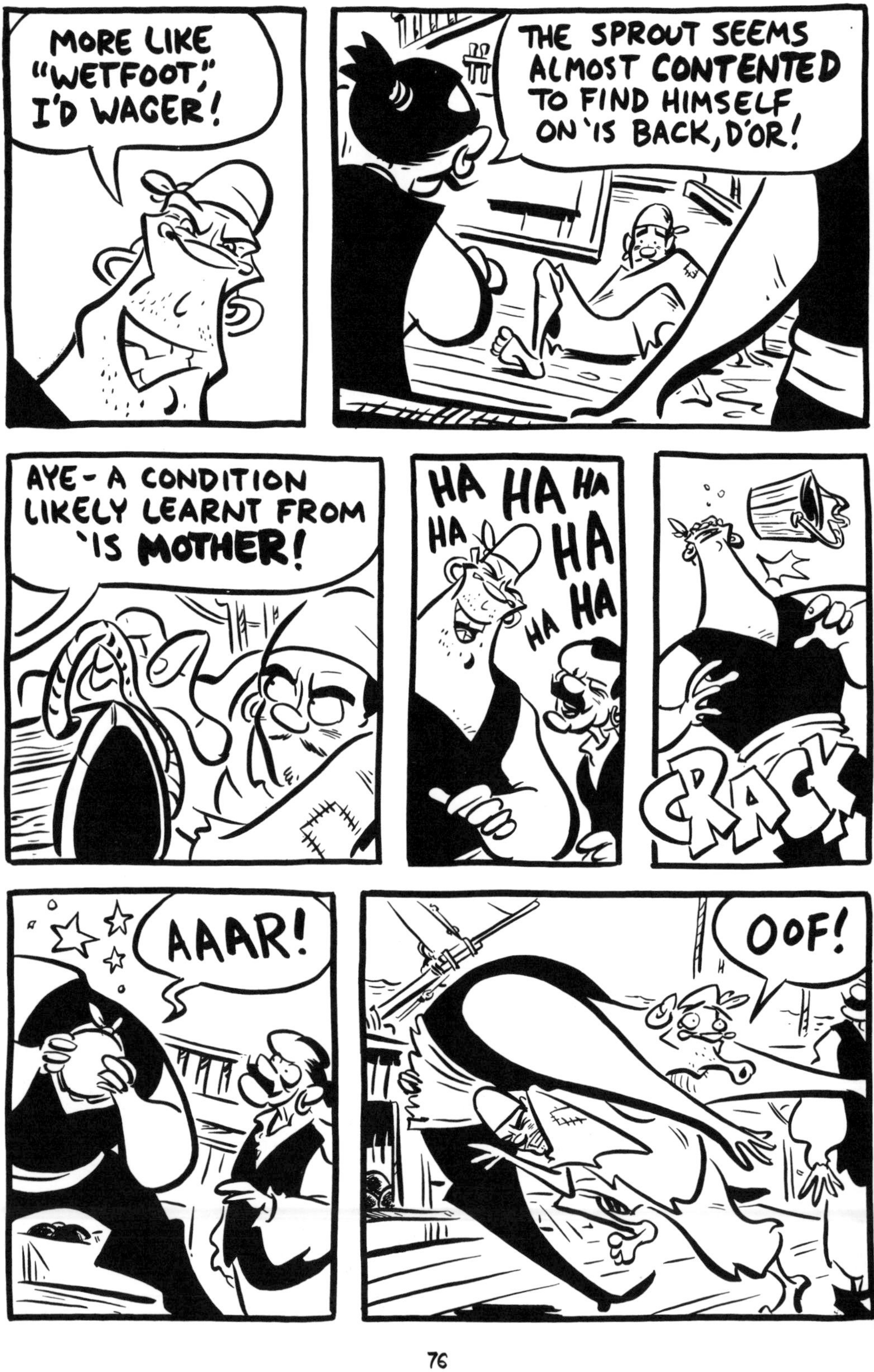
MORE LIKE "WETFOOT," I'D WAGER!
THE SPROUT SEEMS ALMOST CONTENTED TO FIND HIMSELF ON 'IS BACK, D'OR!
AYE - A CONDITION LIKELY LEARNT FROM 'IS MOTHER!
HA HA HA HA HA HA HA HA
CRACK
AAAR!
OOF!

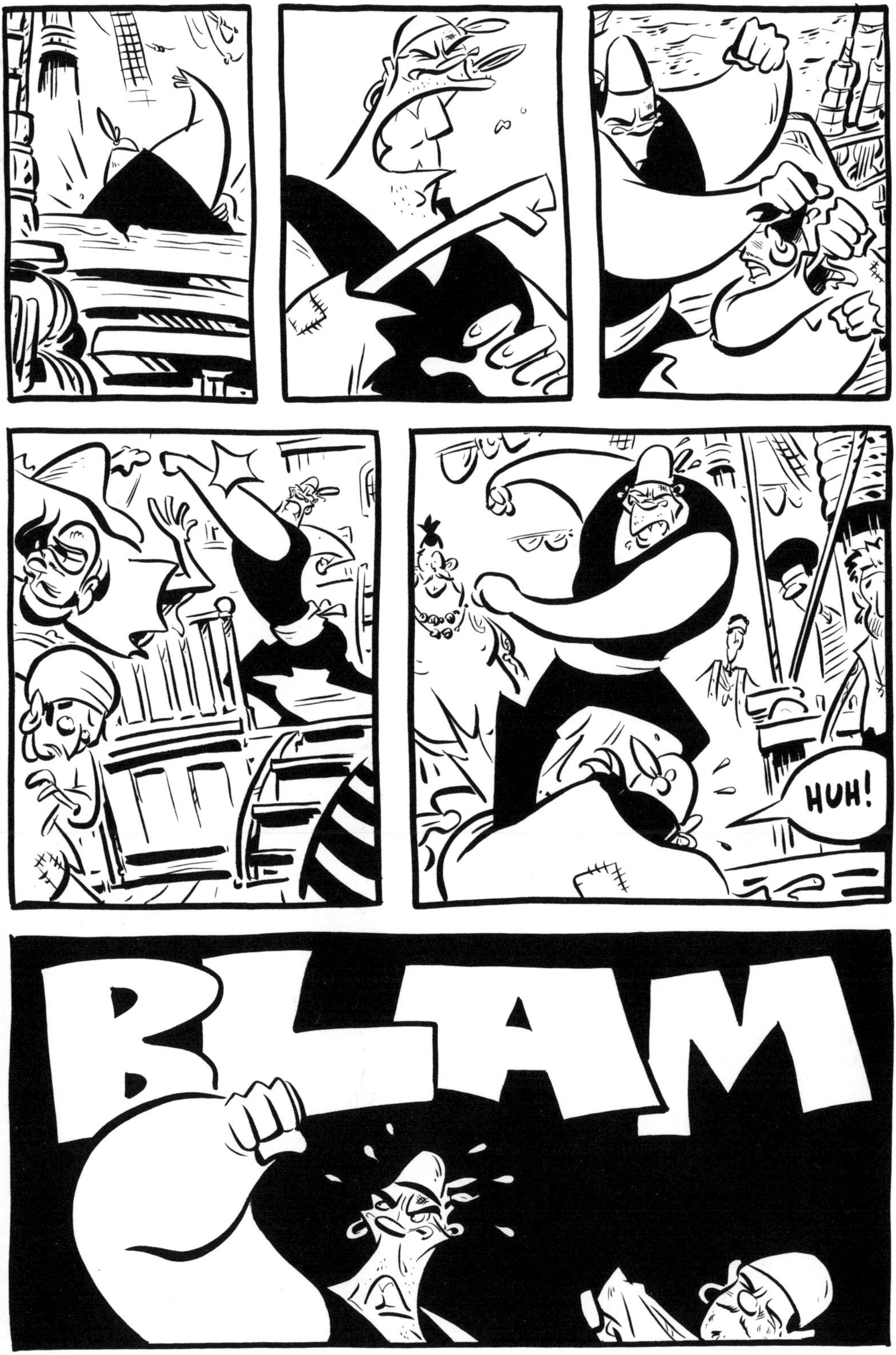
HUH!
BLAM

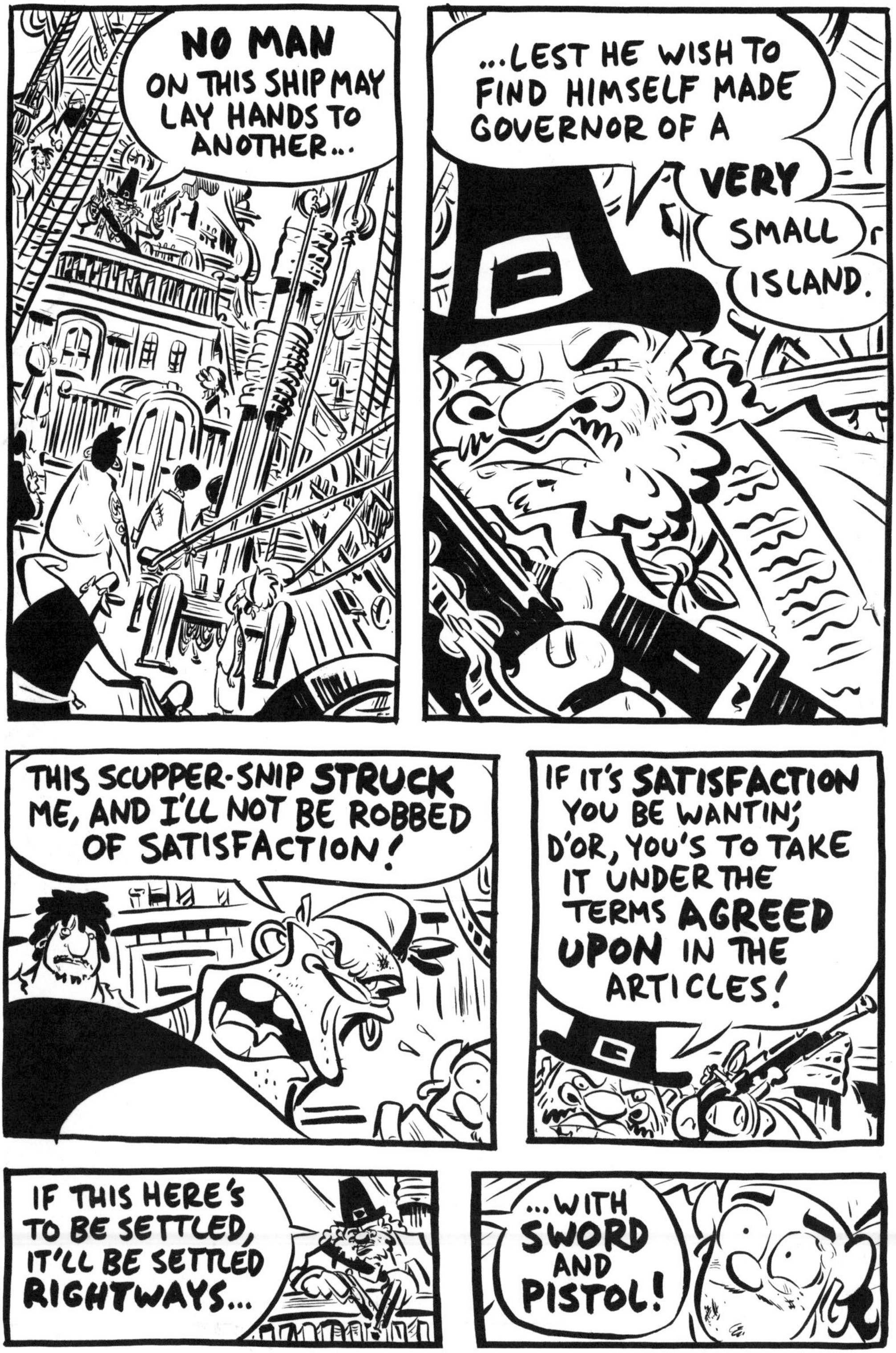
NO MAN
ON THIS SHIP MAY
LAY HANDS TO
ANOTHER...
...LEST HE WISH TO
FIND HIMSELF MADE
GOVERNOR OF A
VERY
SMALL
ISLAND.
THIS SCUPPER-SNIP STRUCK
ME, AND I'LL NOT BE ROBBED
OF SATISFACTION!
IF IT'S SATISFACTION
YOU BE WANTIN',
D'OR, YOU'S TO TAKE
IT UNDER THE
TERMS AGREED
UPON IN THE
ARTICLES!
IF THIS HERE'S
TO BE SETTLED,
IT'LL BE SETTLED
RIGHTWAYS...
...WITH
SWORD
AND
PISTOL!

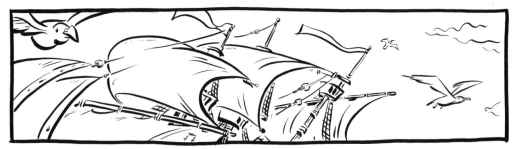

HMF.

BARELY ENOUGH LAND TO SURVIVE A GOAT, BUT IT'LL SERVE OUR ENDS.

CUT SAIL AND LAY ANCHOR!

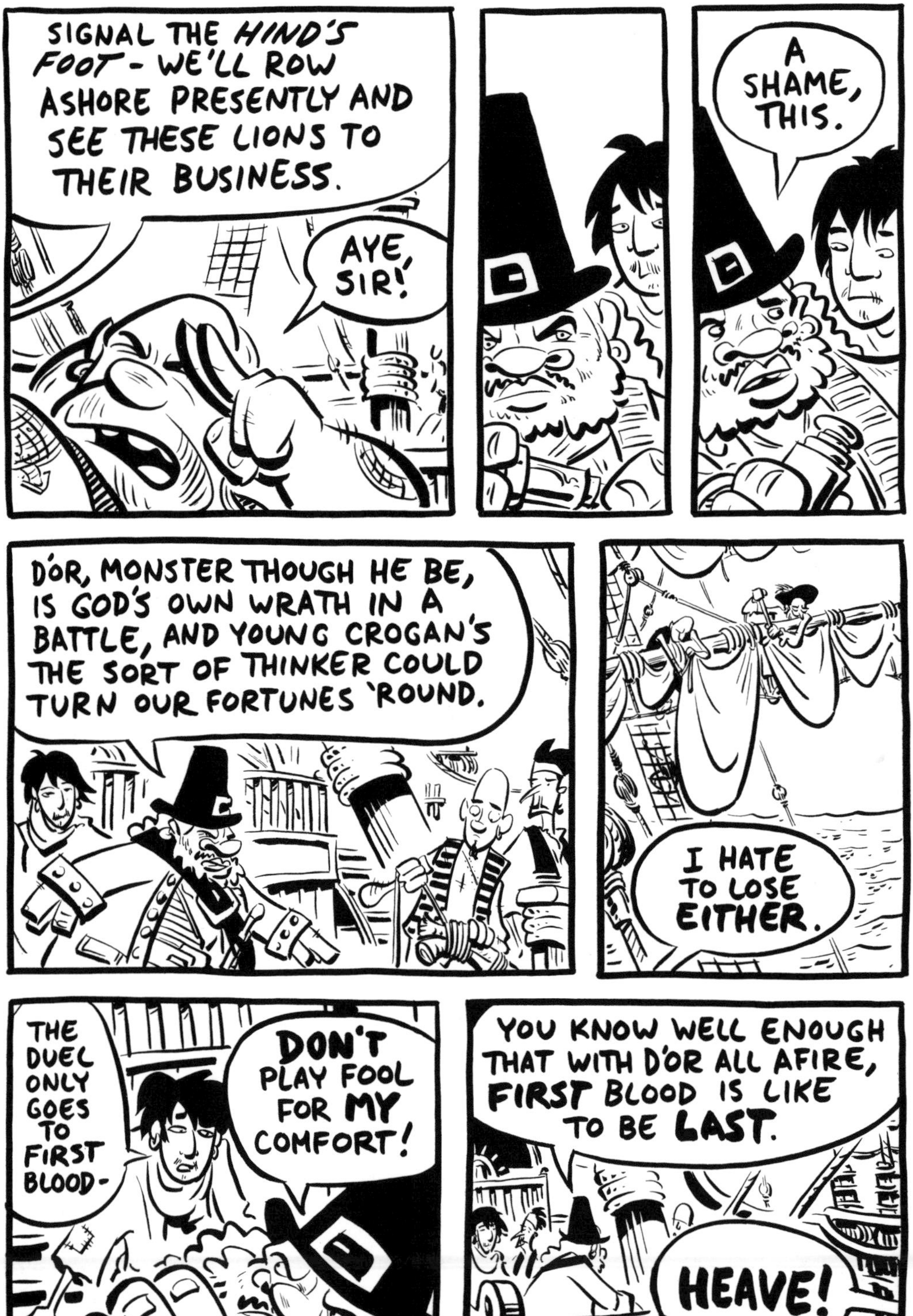
SIGNAL THE *HIND'S FOOT* - WE'LL ROW ASHORE PRESENTLY AND SEE THESE LIONS TO THEIR BUSINESS.
AYE, SIR!
A SHAME, THIS.
D'OR, MONSTER THOUGH HE BE, IS GOD'S OWN WRATH IN A BATTLE, AND YOUNG CROGAN'S THE SORT OF THINKER COULD TURN OUR FORTUNES 'ROUND.
I HATE TO LOSE **EITHER**.
THE DUEL ONLY GOES TO FIRST BLOOD-
DON'T PLAY FOOL FOR **MY** COMFORT!
YOU KNOW WELL ENOUGH THAT WITH D'OR ALL AFIRE, **FIRST** BLOOD IS LIKE TO BE **LAST**.
HEAVE!

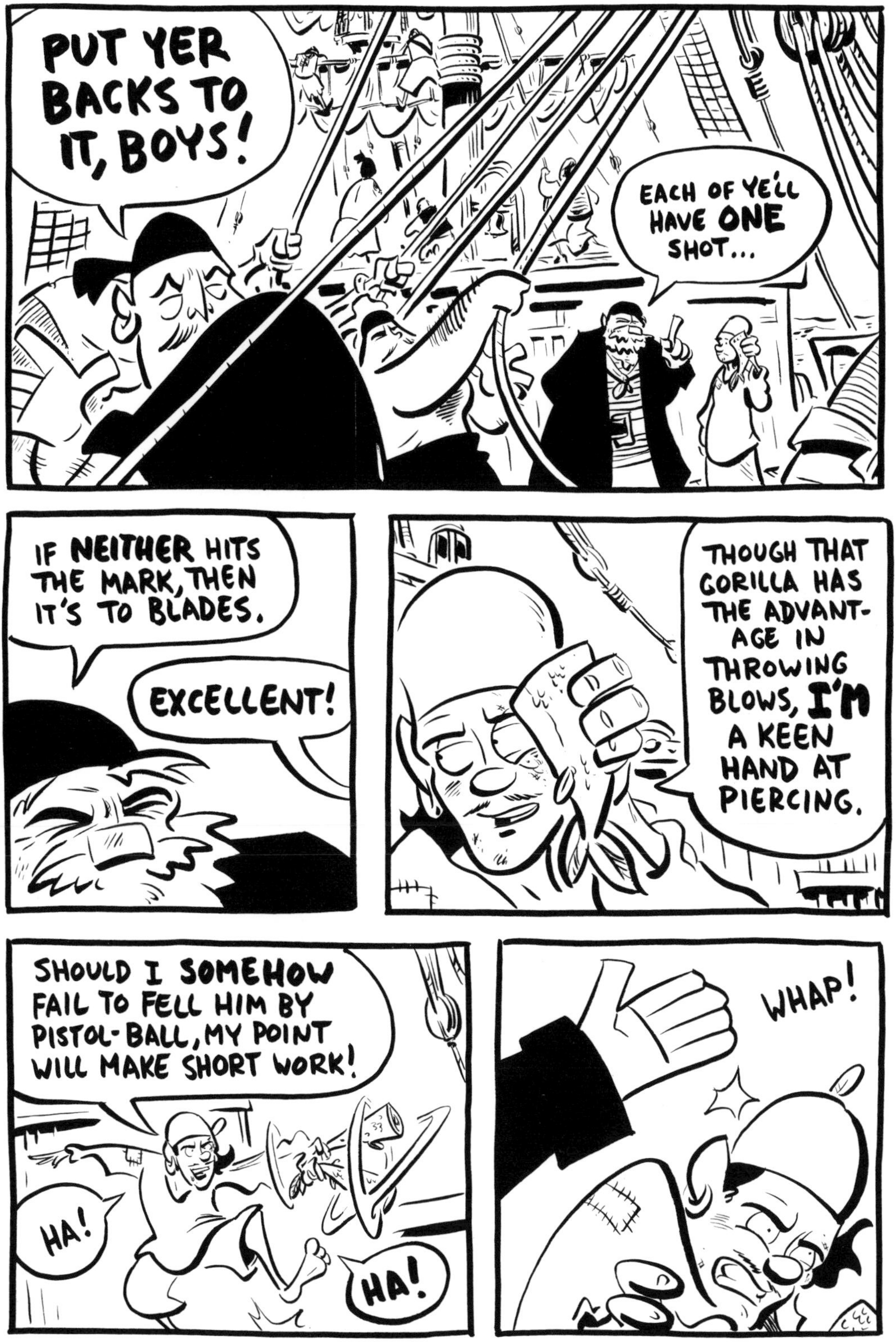
PUT YER BACKS TO IT, BOYS!
EACH OF YE'LL HAVE ONE SHOT...
IF NEITHER HITS THE MARK, THEN IT'S TO BLADES.
EXCELLENT!
THOUGH THAT GORILLA HAS THE ADVANT-AGE IN THROWING BLOWS, I'M A KEEN HAND AT PIERCING.
SHOULD I SOMEHOW FAIL TO FELL HIM BY PISTOL-BALL, MY POINT WILL MAKE SHORT WORK!
HA!
HA!
WHAP!

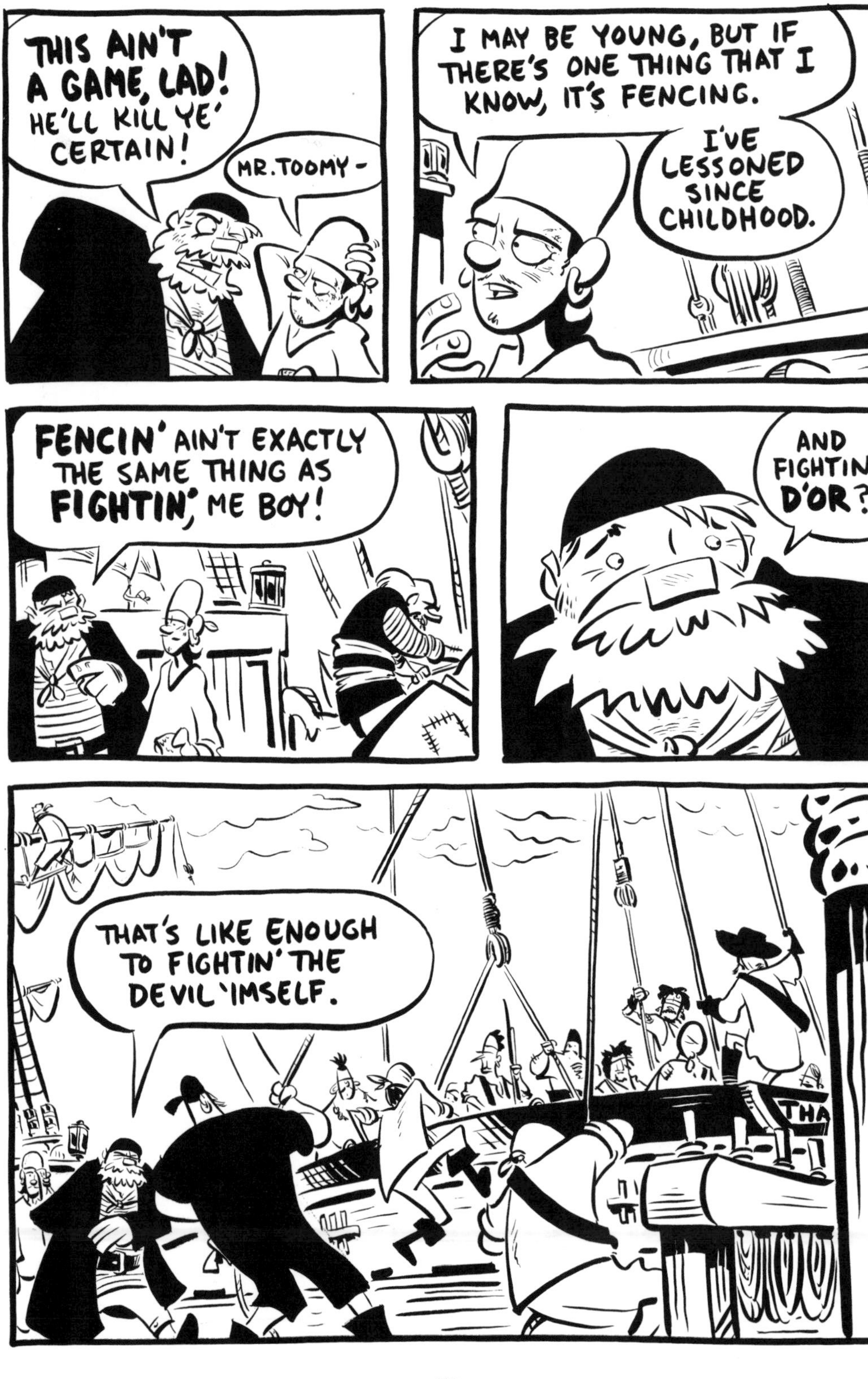
THIS AIN'T A GAME, LAD! HE'LL KILL YE' CERTAIN!
MR. TOOMY -
I MAY BE YOUNG, BUT IF THERE'S ONE THING THAT I KNOW, IT'S FENCING.
I'VE LESSONED SINCE CHILDHOOD.
FENCIN' AIN'T EXACTLY THE SAME THING AS FIGHTIN', ME BOY!
AND FIGHTIN' D'OR?
THAT'S LIKE ENOUGH TO FIGHTIN' THE DEVIL 'IMSELF.
THA

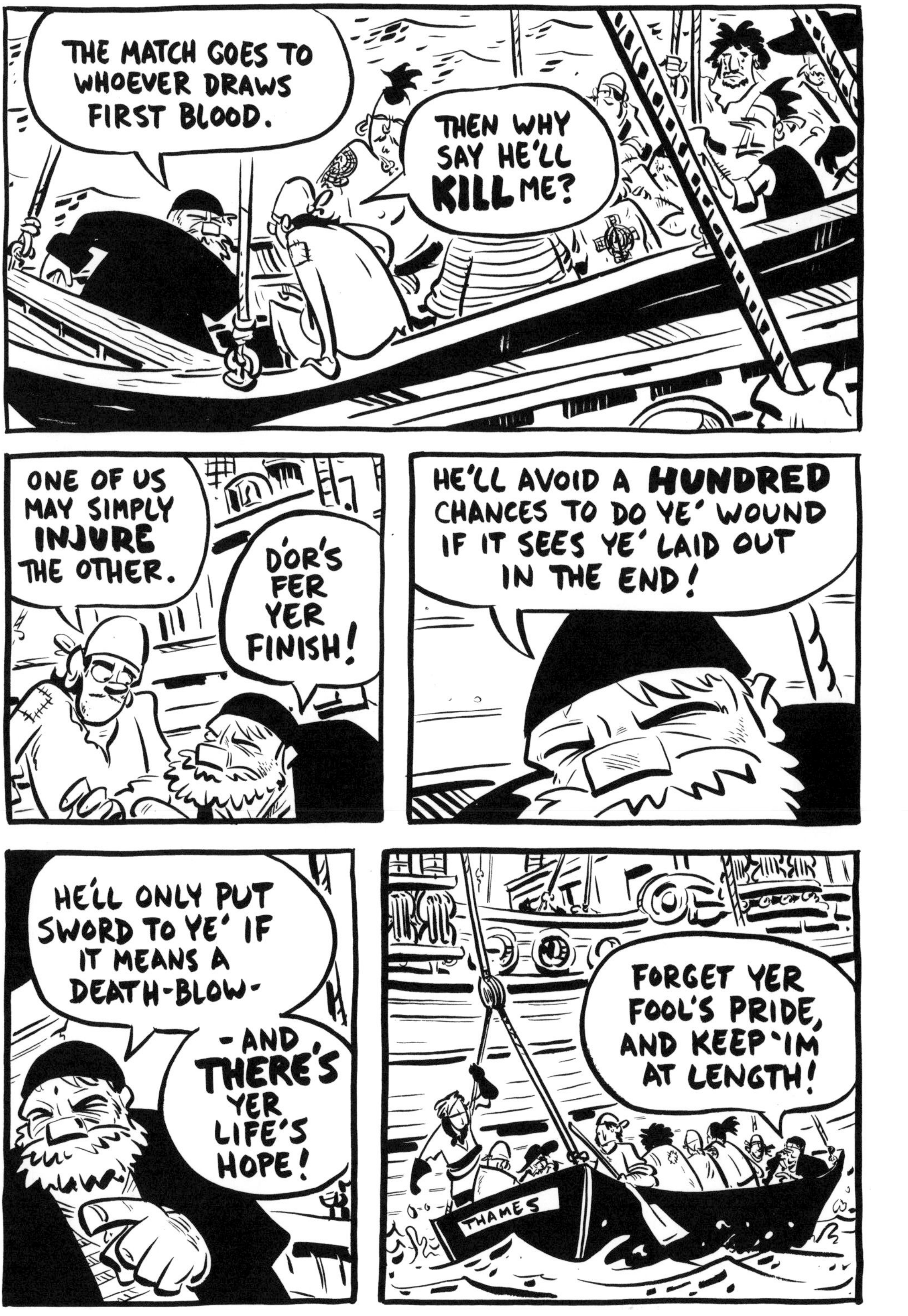
THE MATCH GOES TO WHOEVER DRAWS FIRST BLOOD.
THEN WHY SAY HE'LL KILL ME?
ONE OF US MAY SIMPLY INJURE THE OTHER.
D'OR'S FER YER FINISH!
HE'LL AVOID A HUNDRED CHANCES TO DO YE' WOUND IF IT SEES YE' LAID OUT IN THE END!
HE'LL ONLY PUT SWORD TO YE' IF IT MEANS A DEATH-BLOW-
-AND THERE'S YER LIFE'S HOPE!
FORGET YER FOOL'S PRIDE, AND KEEP 'IM AT LENGTH!
THAMES

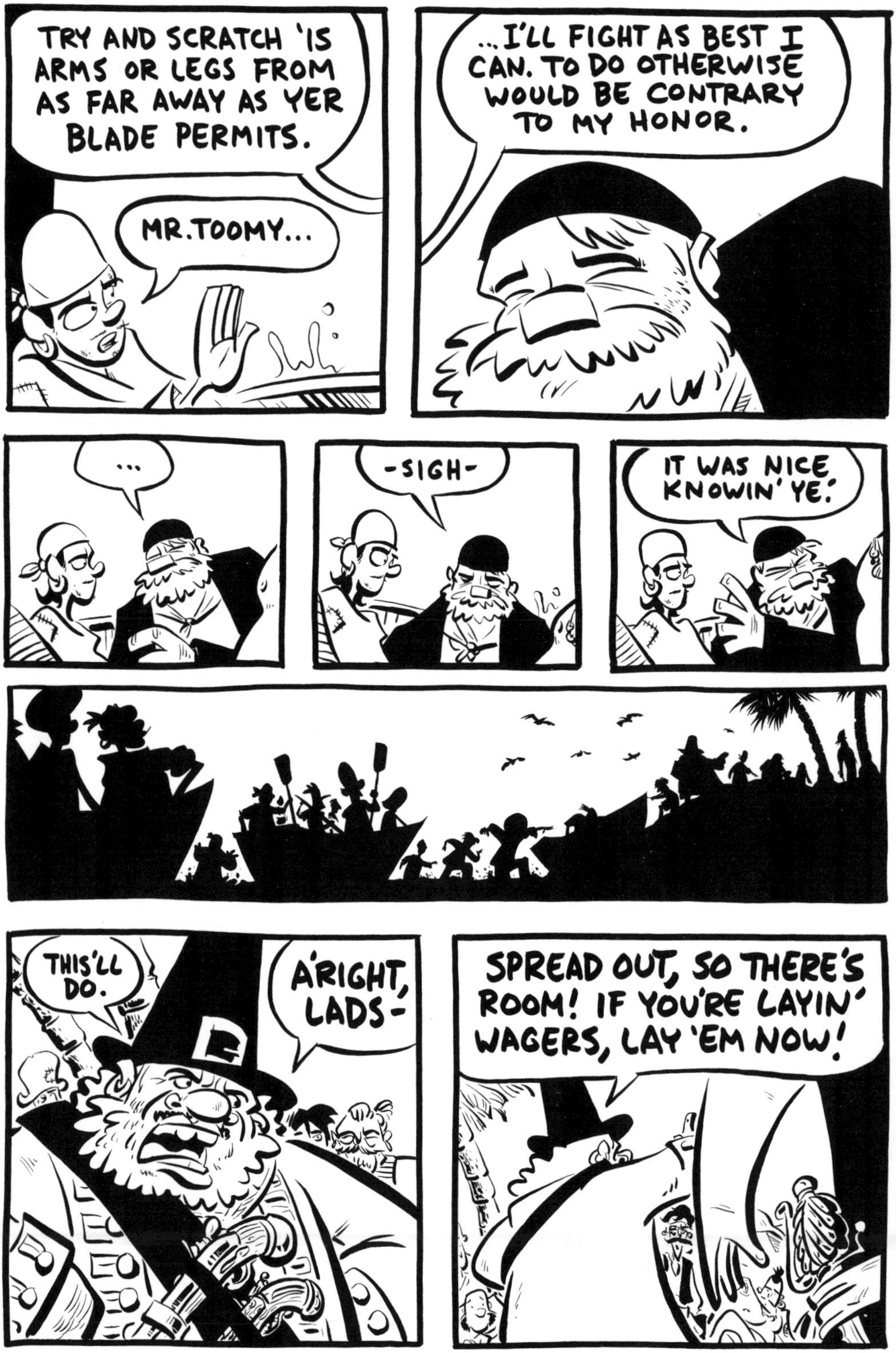
TRY AND SCRATCH 'IS ARMS OR LEGS FROM AS FAR AWAY AS YER BLADE PERMITS.
MR. TOOMY...
...I'LL FIGHT AS BEST I CAN. TO DO OTHERWISE WOULD BE CONTRARY TO MY HONOR.
...
-SIGH-
IT WAS NICE KNOWIN' YE.
THIS'LL DO.
A'RIGHT, LADS-
SPREAD OUT, SO THERE'S ROOM! IF YOU'RE LAYIN' WAGERS, LAY 'EM NOW!

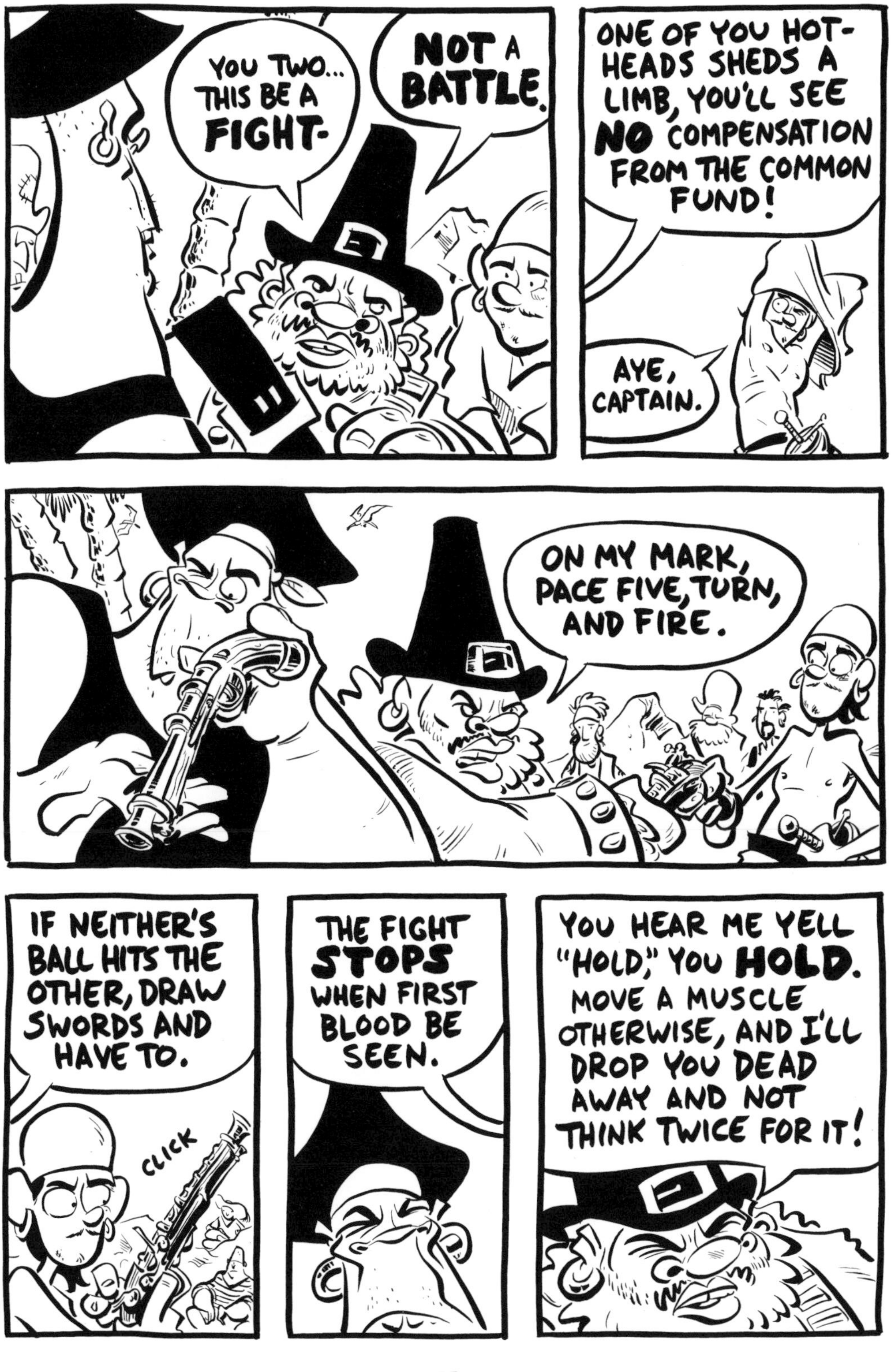
YOU TWO... THIS BE A FIGHT-
NOT A BATTLE.
ONE OF YOU HOT-HEADS SHEDS A LIMB, YOU'LL SEE NO COMPENSATION FROM THE COMMON FUND!
AYE, CAPTAIN.
ON MY MARK, PACE FIVE, TURN, AND FIRE.
IF NEITHER'S BALL HITS THE OTHER, DRAW SWORDS AND HAVE TO.
CLICK
THE FIGHT STOPS WHEN FIRST BLOOD BE SEEN.
YOU HEAR ME YELL "HOLD," YOU HOLD. MOVE A MUSCLE OTHERWISE, AND I'LL DROP YOU DEAD AWAY AND NOT THINK TWICE FOR IT!

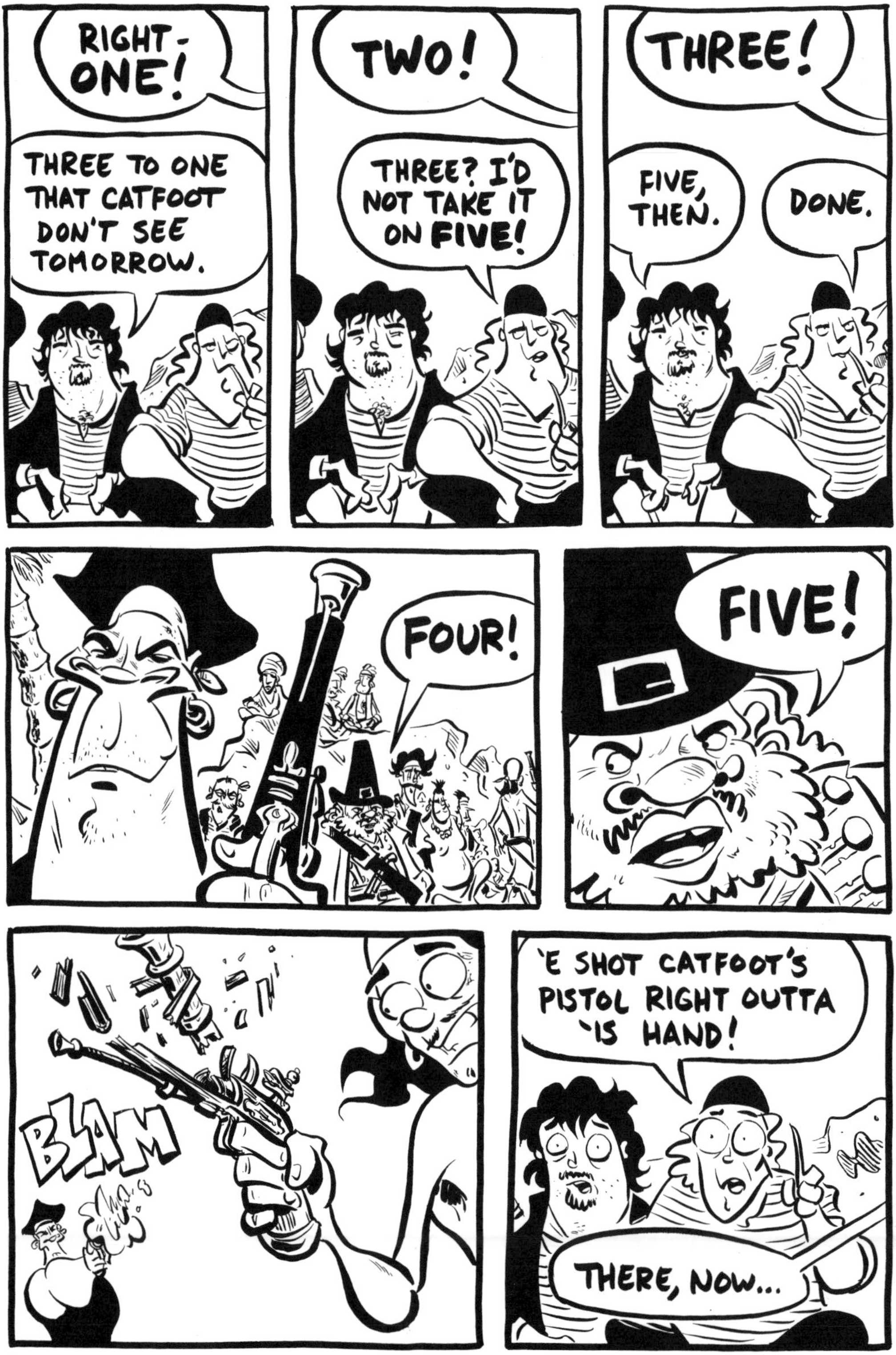
RIGHT-
ONE!
THREE TO ONE THAT CATFOOT DON'T SEE TOMORROW.
TWO!
THREE? I'D NOT TAKE IT ON FIVE!
THREE!
FIVE, THEN.
DONE.
FOUR!
FIVE!
BLAM
'E SHOT CATFOOT'S PISTOL RIGHT OUTTA 'IS HAND!
THERE, NOW...

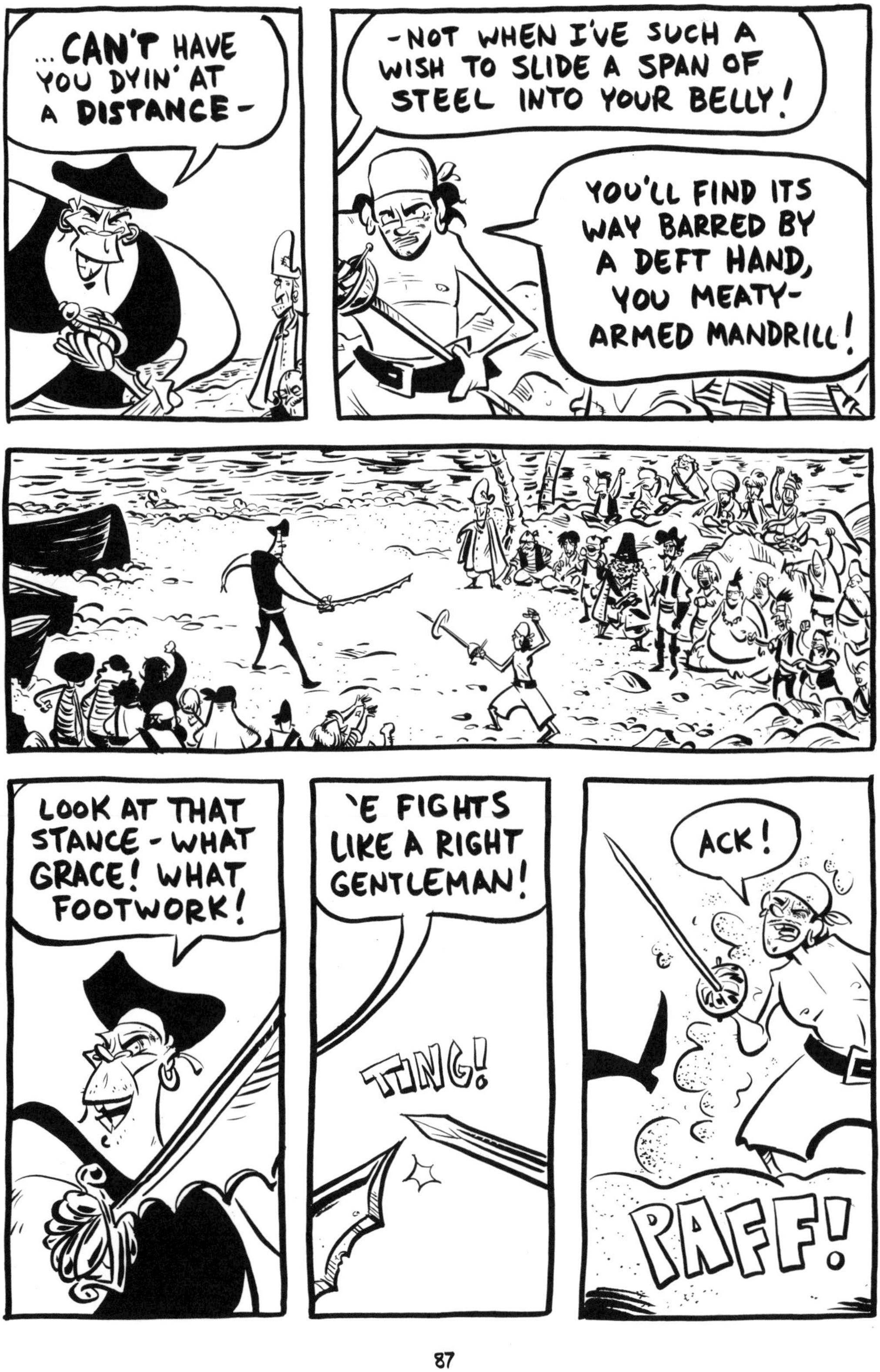
...CAN'T HAVE YOU DYIN' AT A DISTANCE-
-NOT WHEN I'VE SUCH A WISH TO SLIDE A SPAN OF STEEL INTO YOUR BELLY!
YOU'LL FIND ITS WAY BARRED BY A DEFT HAND, YOU MEATY-ARMED MANDRILL!
LOOK AT THAT STANCE - WHAT GRACE! WHAT FOOTWORK!
`E FIGHTS LIKE A RIGHT GENTLEMAN!
TING!
ACK!
PAFF!

THE BOY'S
LOST HIS
FORM-D'OR'S
PUSHING
HIM BACK!

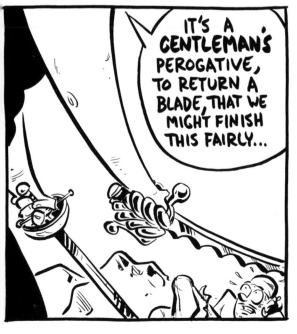

IT'S A GENTLEMAN'S PEROGATIVE, TO RETURN A BLADE, THAT WE MIGHT FINISH THIS FAIRLY...

THANKFULLY, I'VE **NO** SUCH ILLUSIONS AS TO **MY** CHARACTER!

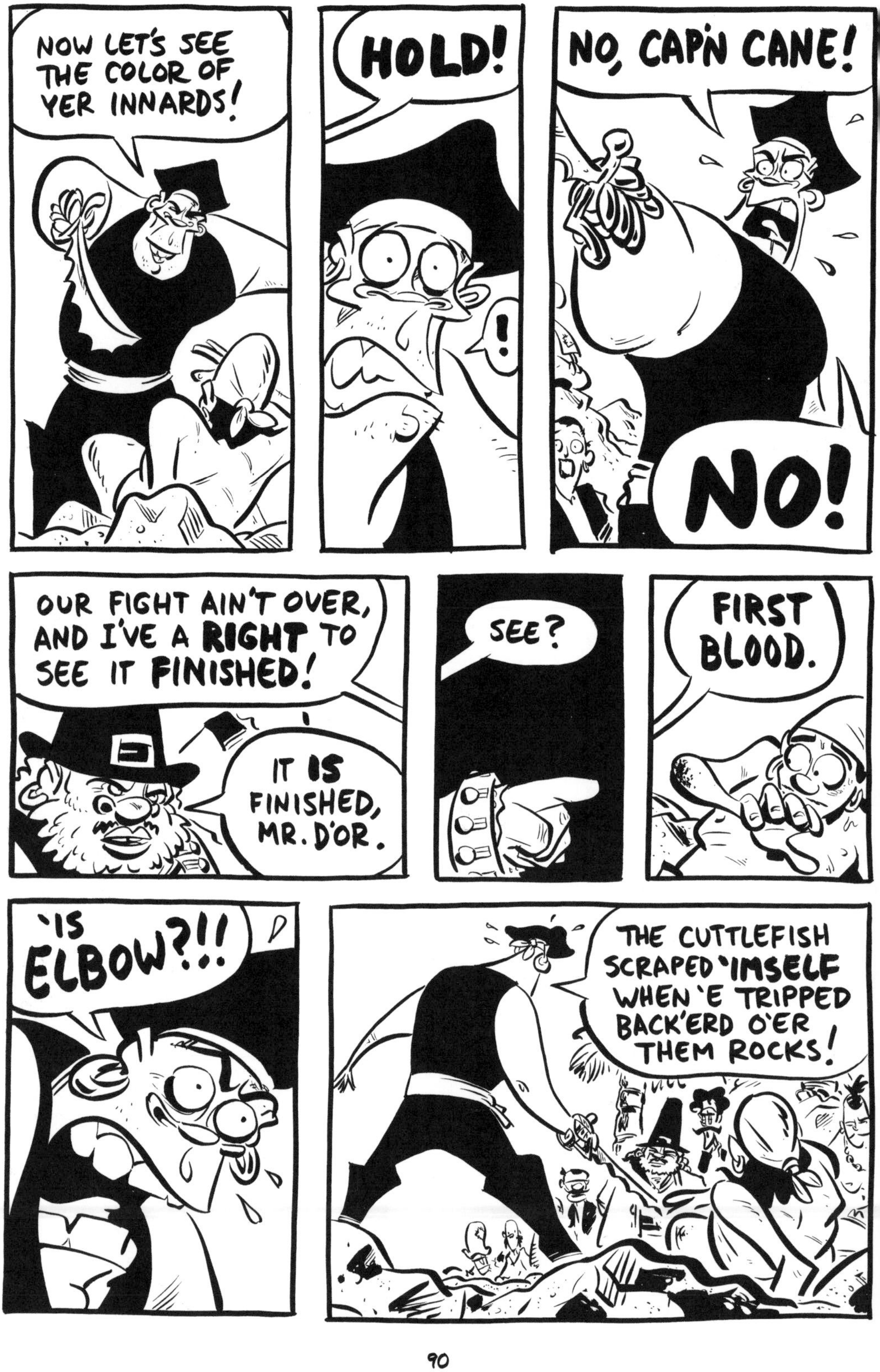
NOW LET'S SEE THE COLOR OF YER INNARDS!
HOLD!
!
NO, CAP'N CANE!
NO!
OUR FIGHT AIN'T OVER, AND I'VE A RIGHT TO SEE IT FINISHED!
IT IS FINISHED, MR. D'OR.
SEE?
FIRST BLOOD.
`IS ELBOW?!!
THE CUTTLEFISH SCRAPED 'IMSELF WHEN 'E TRIPPED BACK'ERD O'ER THEM ROCKS!

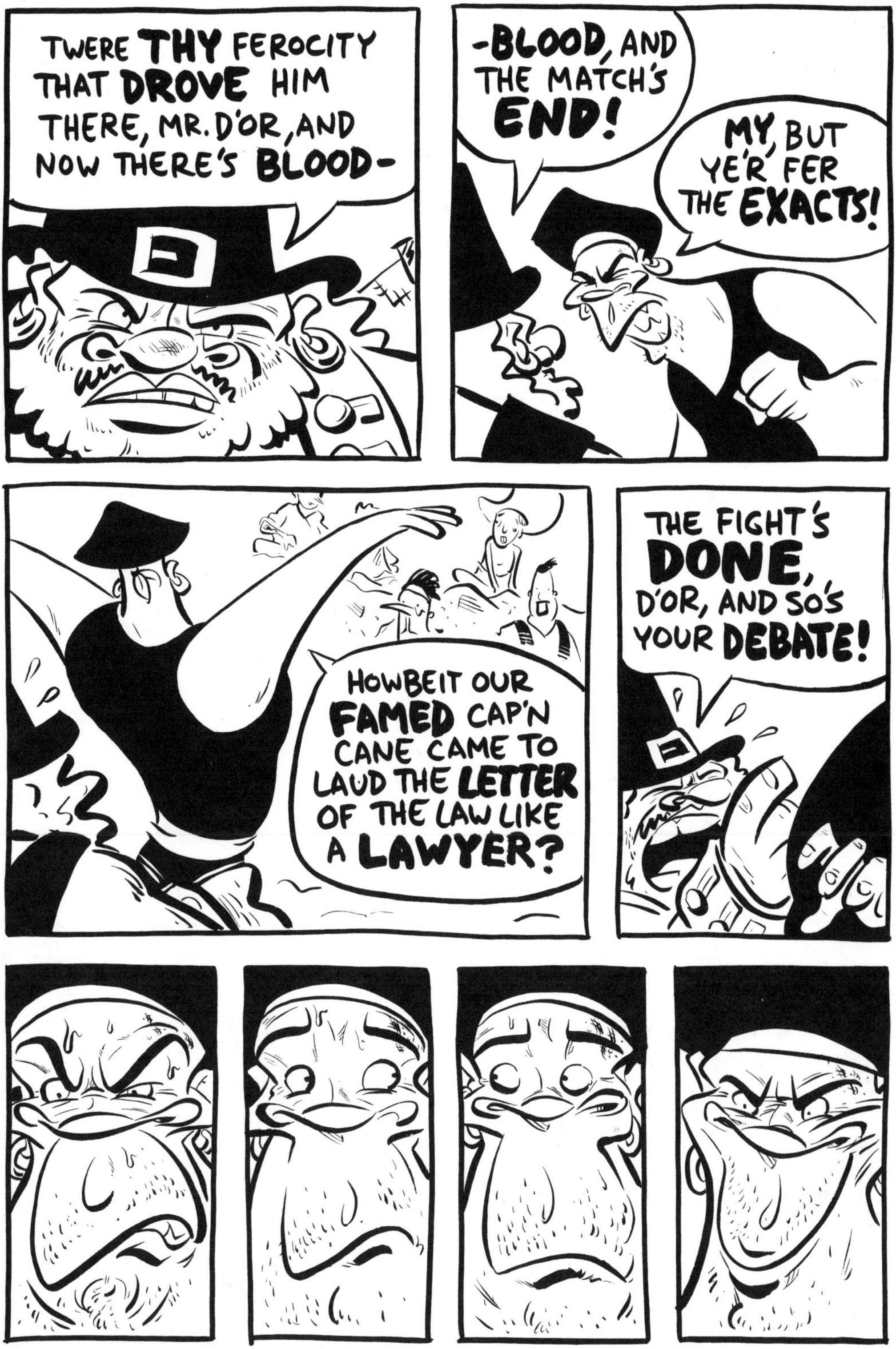
TWERE THY FEROCITY THAT DROVE HIM THERE, MR. D'OR, AND NOW THERE'S BLOOD-
-BLOOD, AND THE MATCH'S END!
MY, BUT YE'R FER THE EXACTS!
HOWBEIT OUR FAMED CAP'N CANE CAME TO LAUD THE LETTER OF THE LAW LIKE A LAWYER?
THE FIGHT'S DONE, D'OR, AND SO'S YOUR DEBATE!

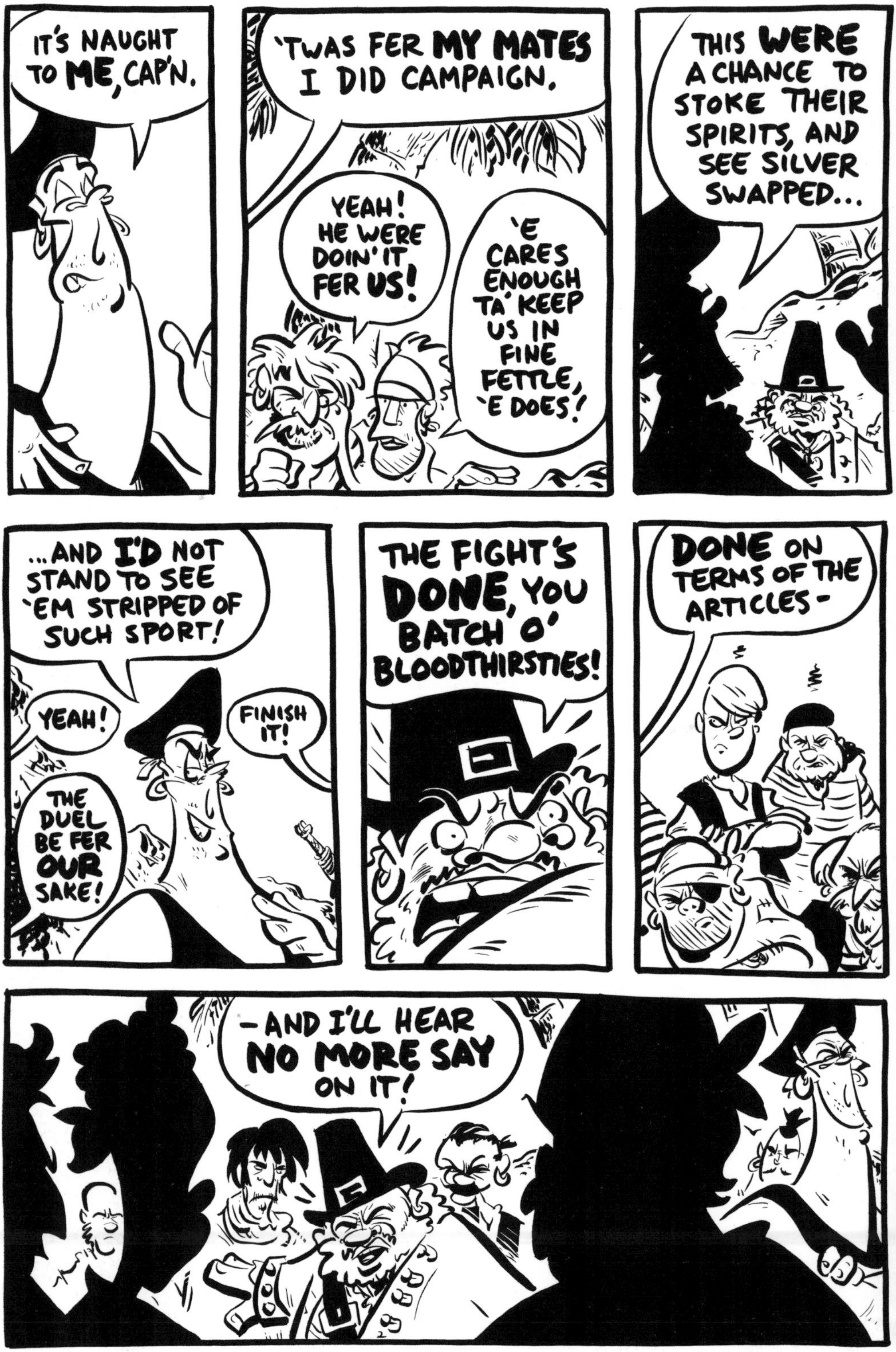
IT'S NAUGHT TO ME, CAP'N.
'TWAS FER MY MATES I DID CAMPAIGN.
YEAH! HE WERE DOIN' IT FER US!
'E CARES ENOUGH TA' KEEP US IN FINE FETTLE, 'E DOES!
THIS WERE A CHANCE TO STOKE THEIR SPIRITS, AND SEE SILVER SWAPPED...
...AND I'D NOT STAND TO SEE 'EM STRIPPED OF SUCH SPORT!
YEAH!
FINISH IT!
THE DUEL BE FER OUR SAKE!
THE FIGHT'S DONE, YOU BATCH O' BLOODTHIRSTIES!
DONE ON TERMS OF THE ARTICLES-
-AND I'LL HEAR NO MORE SAY ON IT!

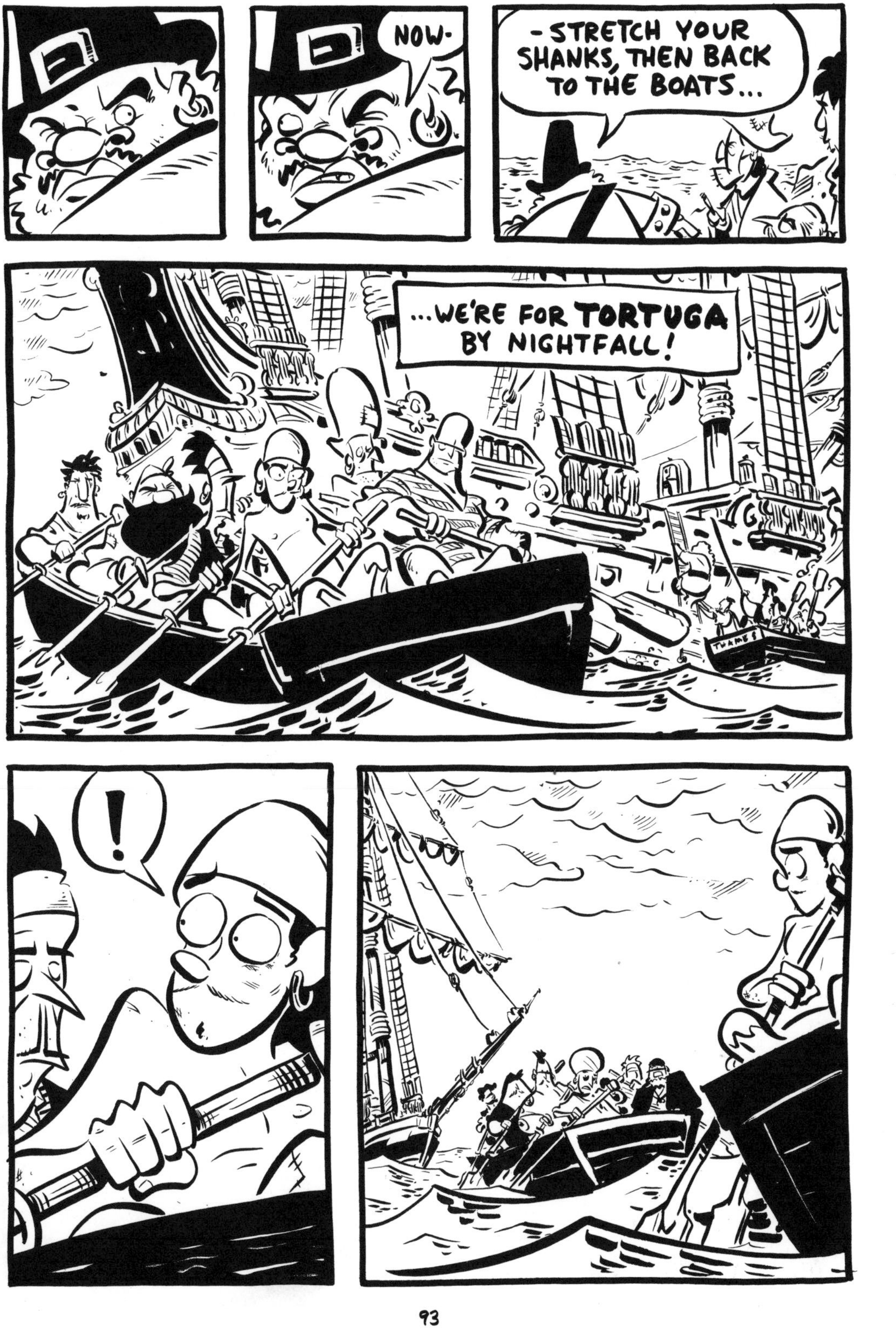
NOW-
-STRETCH YOUR SHANKS, THEN BACK TO THE BOATS...
...WE'RE FOR TORTUGA BY NIGHTFALL!
THAMES
!

TOOMY... STALEY...

ARE THEY TO SAIL ON THE *HIND'S FOOT?*

HA!

YE DIDN'T THINK CAP'N CANE'D LEAVE YER LOT **TOGETHER**, DID 'YE?

A **HANDFUL** OF GREENLEGS WE CAN KEEP EYE TO, BUT IF YOU PRESSERS STAYED **TOGETHER**, YOU MIGHT BE WONT TO **PLOT** ON US...

...CUT OUR THROATS IN OUR **SLEEP!**

BETTER YOU'S AIN'T GOT THE TEMPTATION!

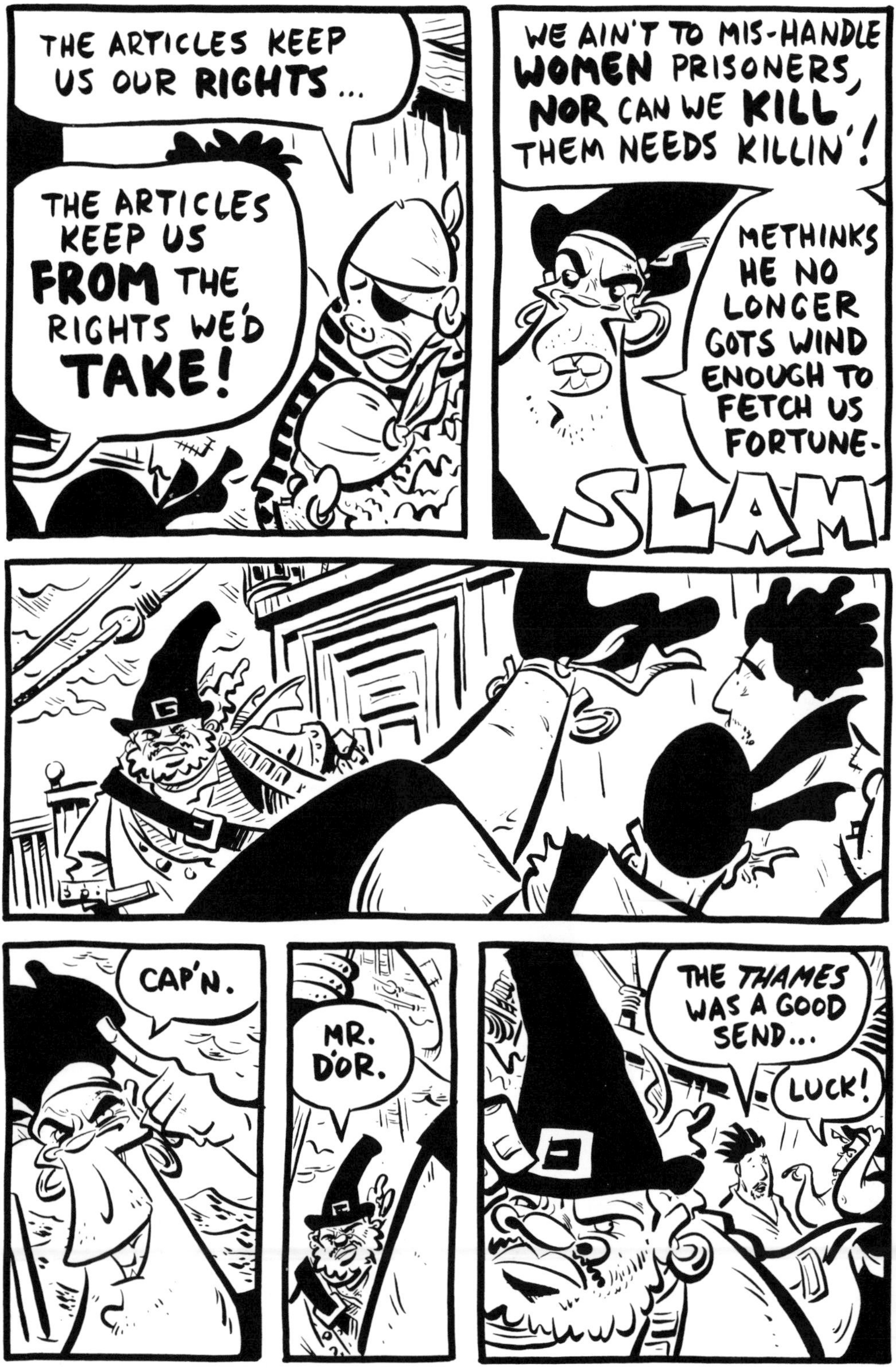
THE ARTICLES KEEP US OUR RIGHTS...
THE ARTICLES KEEP US FROM THE RIGHTS WE'D TAKE!
WE AIN'T TO MIS-HANDLE WOMEN PRISONERS, NOR CAN WE KILL THEM NEEDS KILLIN'!
METHINKS HE NO LONGER GOTS WIND ENOUGH TO FETCH US FORTUNE-
SLAM
CAP'N.
MR. D'OR.
THE THAMES WAS A GOOD SEND...
LUCK!

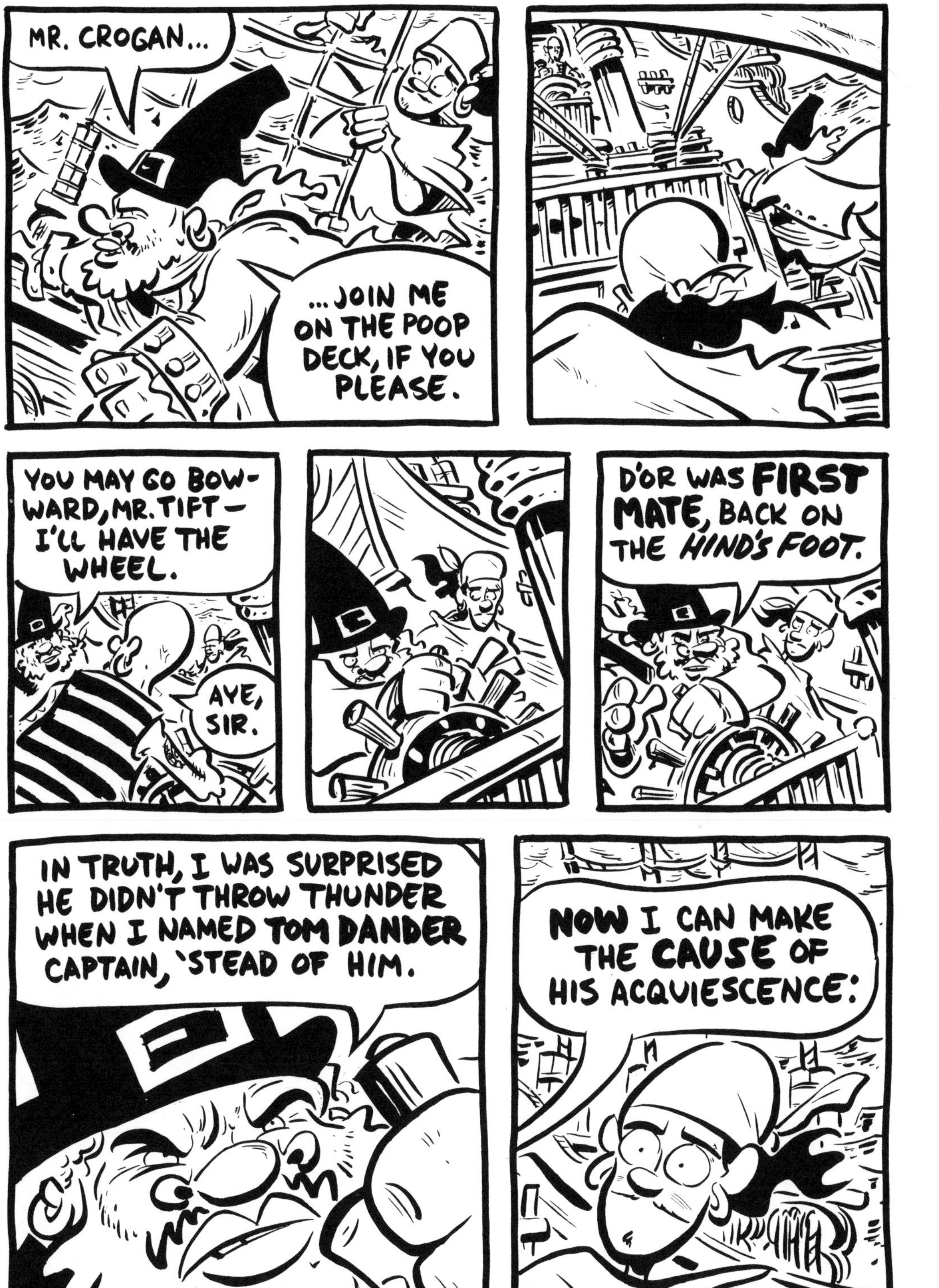
MR. CROGAN...
...JOIN ME ON THE POOP DECK, IF YOU PLEASE.
YOU MAY GO BOW-WARD, MR. TIFT— I'LL HAVE THE WHEEL.
AYE, SIR.
D'OR WAS FIRST MATE, BACK ON THE HIND'S FOOT.
IN TRUTH, I WAS SURPRISED HE DIDN'T THROW THUNDER WHEN I NAMED TOM DANDER CAPTAIN, 'STEAD OF HIM.
NOW I CAN MAKE THE CAUSE OF HIS ACQUIESCENCE:

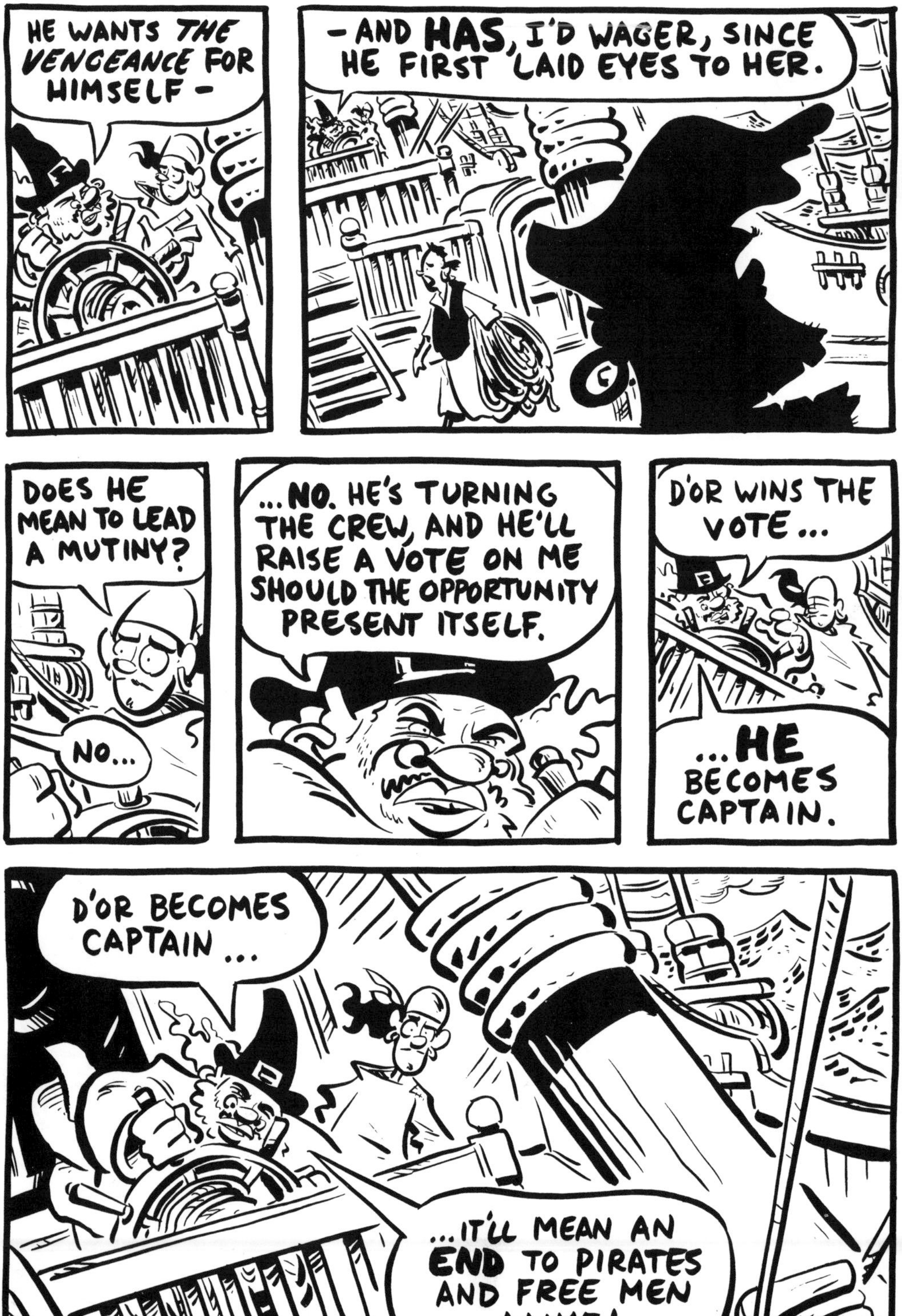
HE WANTS *THE VENGEANCE* FOR HIMSELF -
- AND **HAS**, I'D WAGER, SINCE HE FIRST LAID EYES TO HER.
DOES HE MEAN TO LEAD A MUTINY?
NO...
... **NO**. HE'S TURNING THE CREW, AND HE'LL RAISE A VOTE ON ME SHOULD THE OPPORTUNITY PRESENT ITSELF.
D'OR WINS THE VOTE...
... **HE** BECOMES CAPTAIN.
D'OR BECOMES CAPTAIN...
...IT'LL MEAN AN **END** TO PIRATES AND FREE MEN ALIKE!

I DON'T UNDERSTAND.

THE **RULES** BY WHICH WE GOVERN OURSELVES ALLOW US TO SURVIVE AND PROSPER.

WE **SPARE** SHIPS IF THEY YIELD WITHOUT FIGHTING— WE LEAVE WOMEN UNMOLESTED—

—WE ATTACK NEITHER EACH OTHER **OR** THE **FRENCH**, AS THEY GIVE US SAFE PORT AND PASSAGE!

AND IF D'OR WERE CAPTAIN?

HE'S MADE CLEAR MANY A TIME THAT HE HAS NO USE FOR SUCH CIVILITIES.

THINK ON IT!

WERE WE TO SLAUGHTER EVERY SHIP WE CAME ACROSS, THEN EACH SHIP WE HOVE NEAR WOULD FIGHT LIKE THE DEVIL— JUST TO KEEP LIVE.

WE START ON THE FRENCH, WE'LL FIND **NO** FRIENDLY PORT!

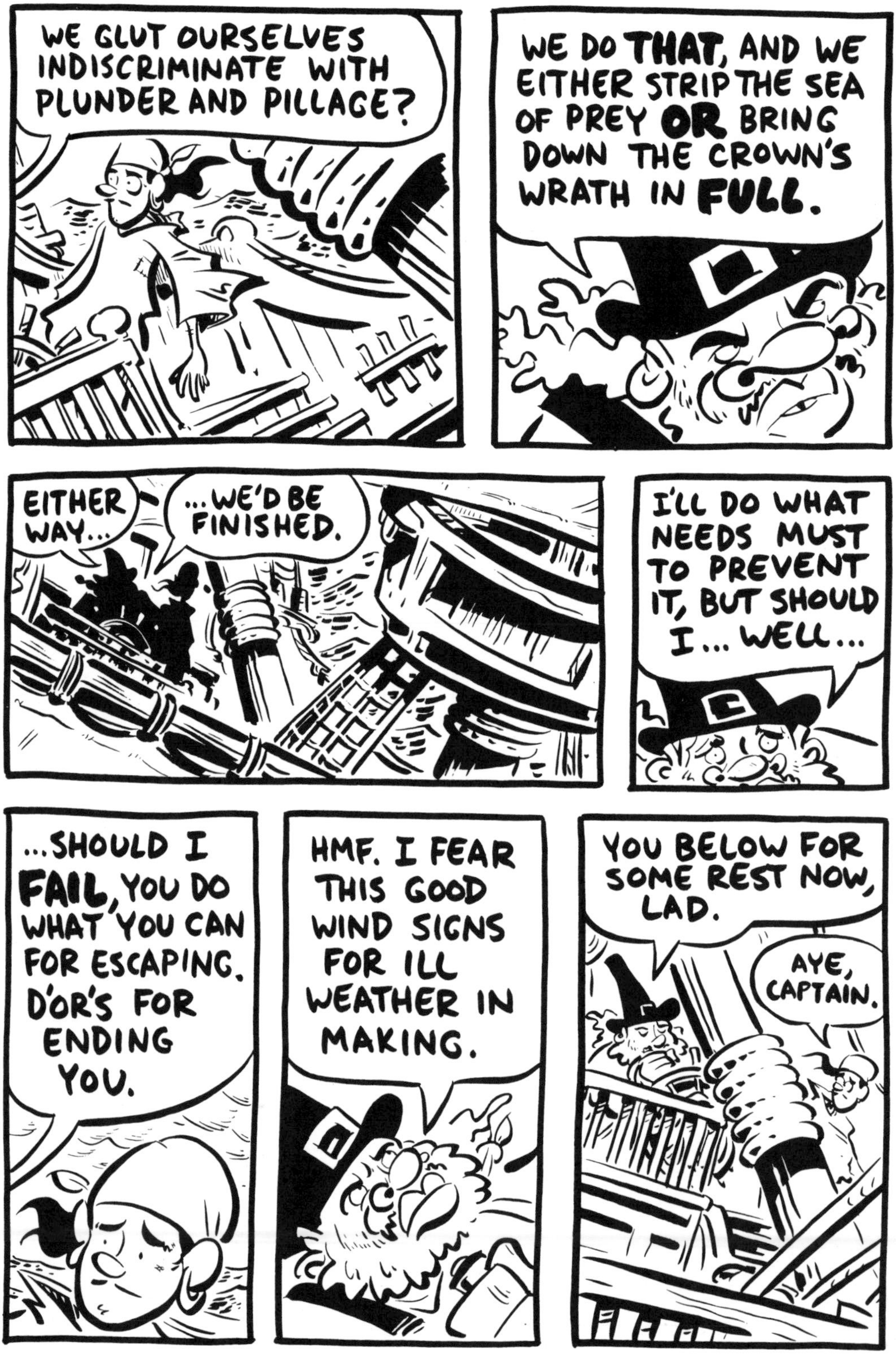
WE GLUT OURSELVES INDISCRIMINATE WITH PLUNDER AND PILLAGE?
WE DO THAT, AND WE EITHER STRIP THE SEA OF PREY OR BRING DOWN THE CROWN'S WRATH IN FULL.
EITHER WAY...
...WE'D BE FINISHED.
I'LL DO WHAT NEEDS MUST TO PREVENT IT, BUT SHOULD I... WELL...
...SHOULD I FAIL, YOU DO WHAT YOU CAN FOR ESCAPING. D'OR'S FOR ENDING YOU.
HMF. I FEAR THIS GOOD WIND SIGNS FOR ILL WEATHER IN MAKING.
YOU BELOW FOR SOME REST NOW, LAD.
AYE, CAPTAIN.

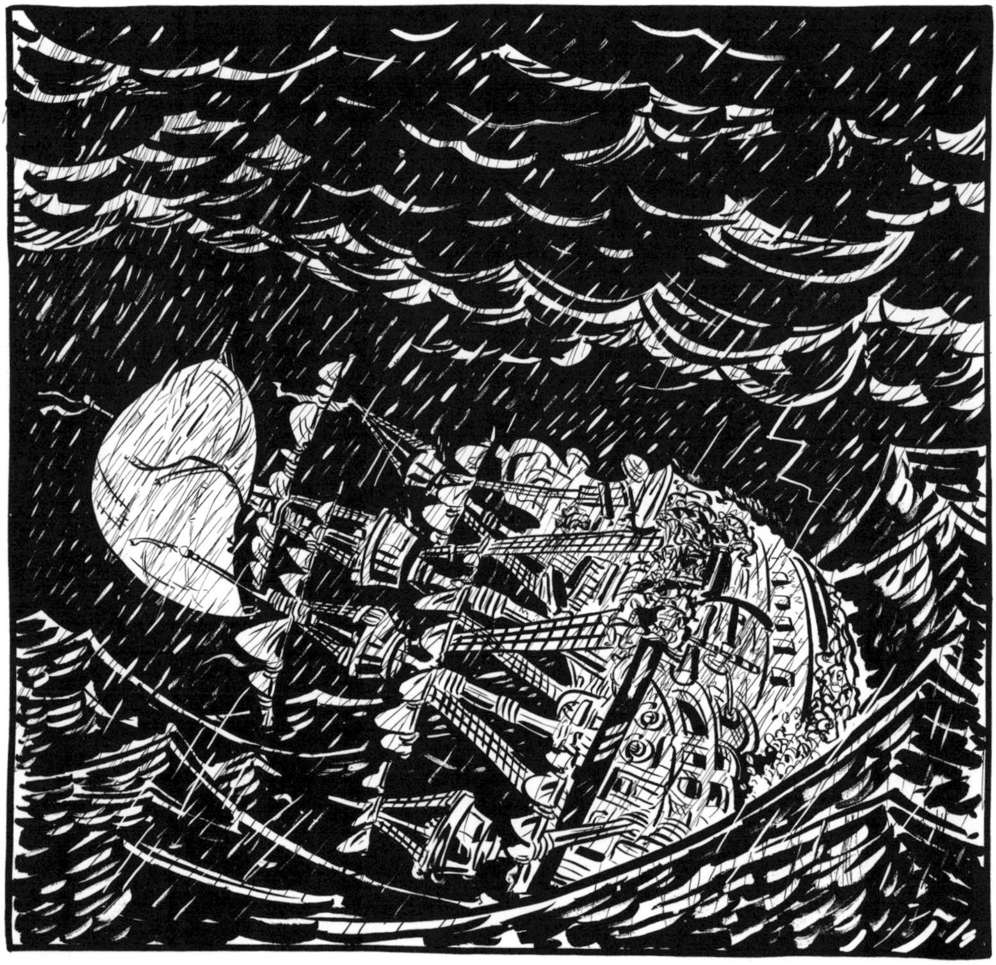

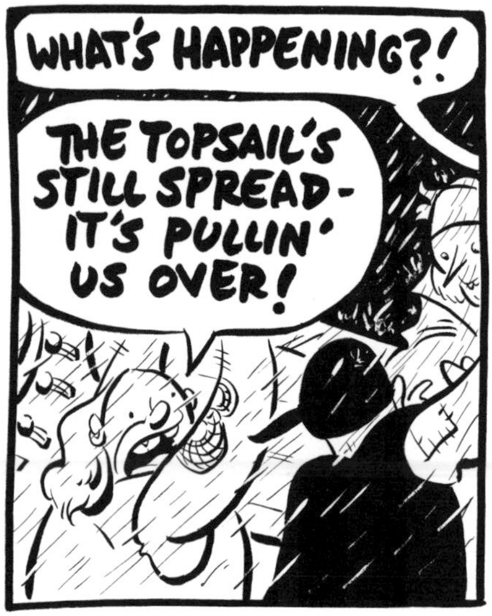
WHAT'S HAPPENING?!
THE TOPSAIL'S STILL SPREAD- IT'S PULLIN' US OVER!

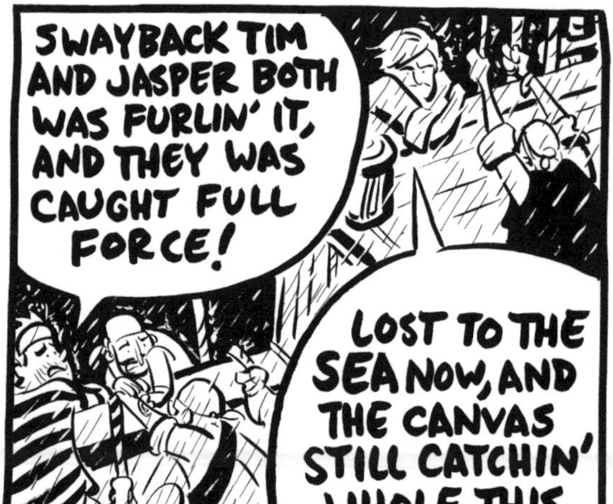
SWAYBACK TIM AND JASPER BOTH WAS FURLIN' IT, AND THEY WAS CAUGHT FULL FORCE!
LOST TO THE SEA NOW, AND THE CANVAS STILL CATCHIN' WHOLE THIS GALE!

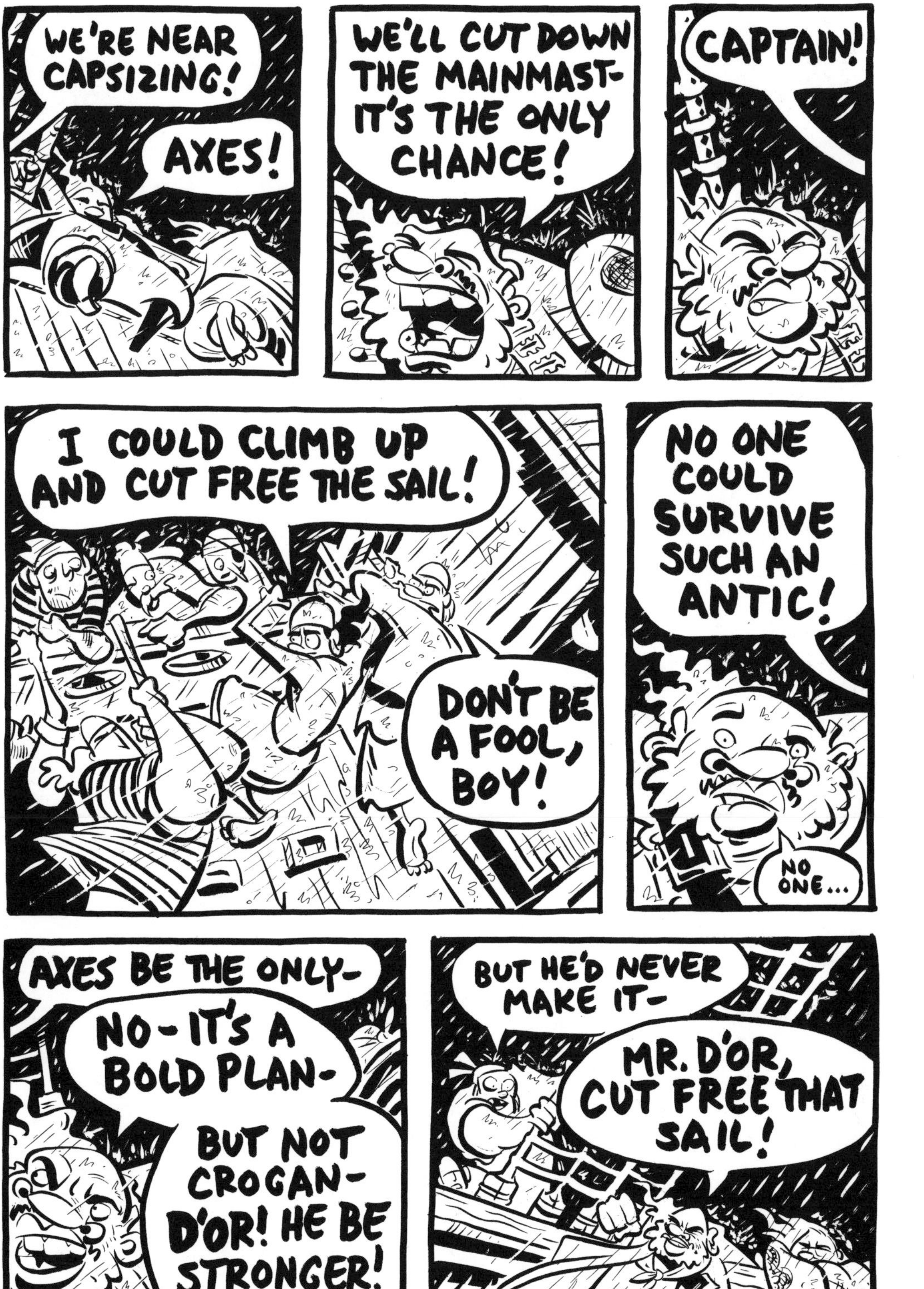
WE'RE NEAR CAPSIZING!
AXES!
WE'LL CUT DOWN THE MAINMAST- IT'S THE ONLY CHANCE!
CAPTAIN!
I COULD CLIMB UP AND CUT FREE THE SAIL!
DON'T BE A FOOL, BOY!
NO ONE COULD SURVIVE SUCH AN ANTIC!
NO ONE...
AXES BE THE ONLY-
NO- IT'S A BOLD PLAN-
BUT NOT CROGAN-D'OR! HE BE STRONGER!
BUT HE'D NEVER MAKE IT-
MR. D'OR, CUT FREE THAT SAIL!

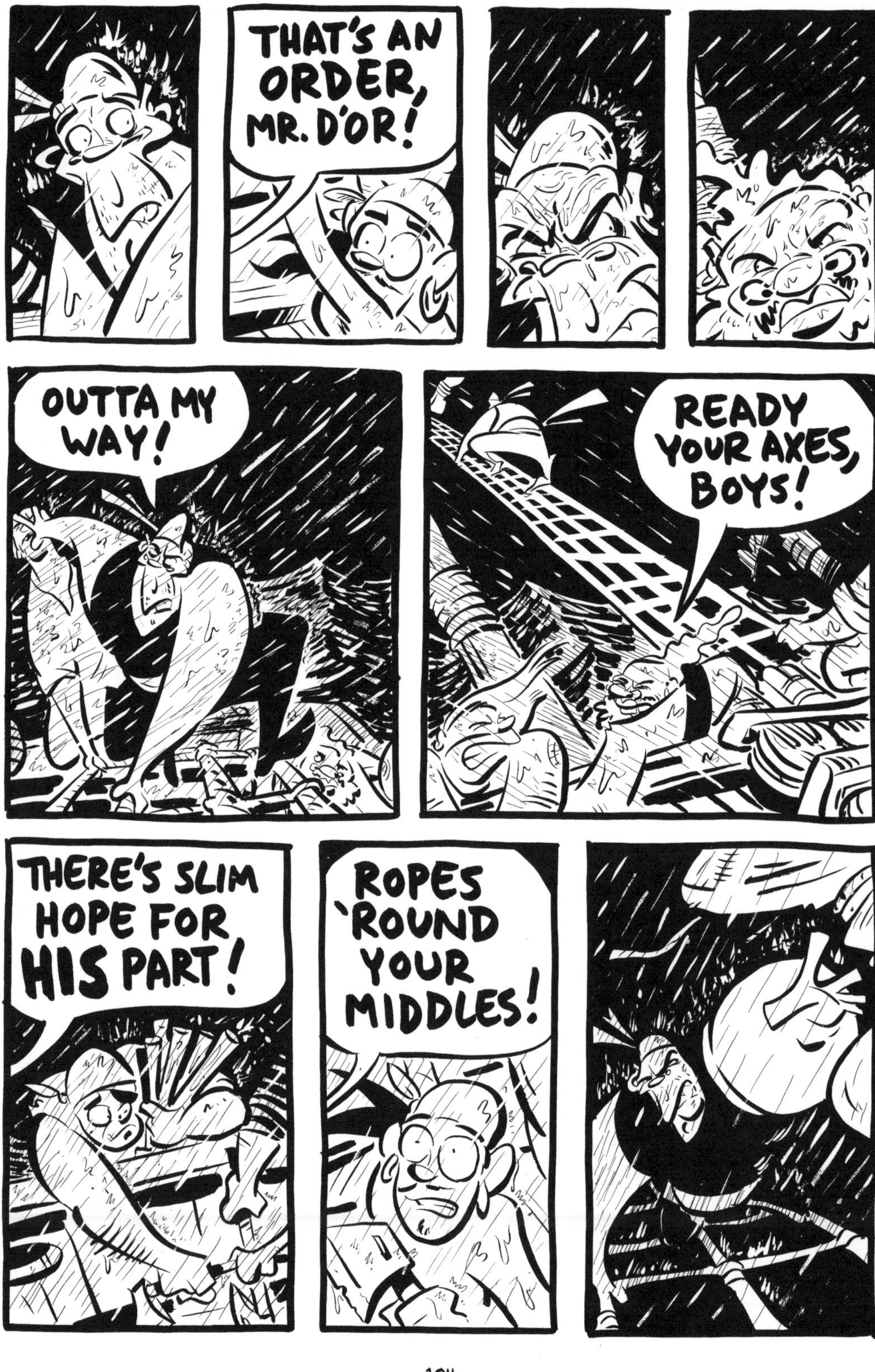
THAT'S AN ORDER, MR. D'OR!
OUTTA MY WAY!
READY YOUR AXES, BOYS!
THERE'S SLIM HOPE FOR HIS PART!
ROPES 'ROUND YOUR MIDDLES!

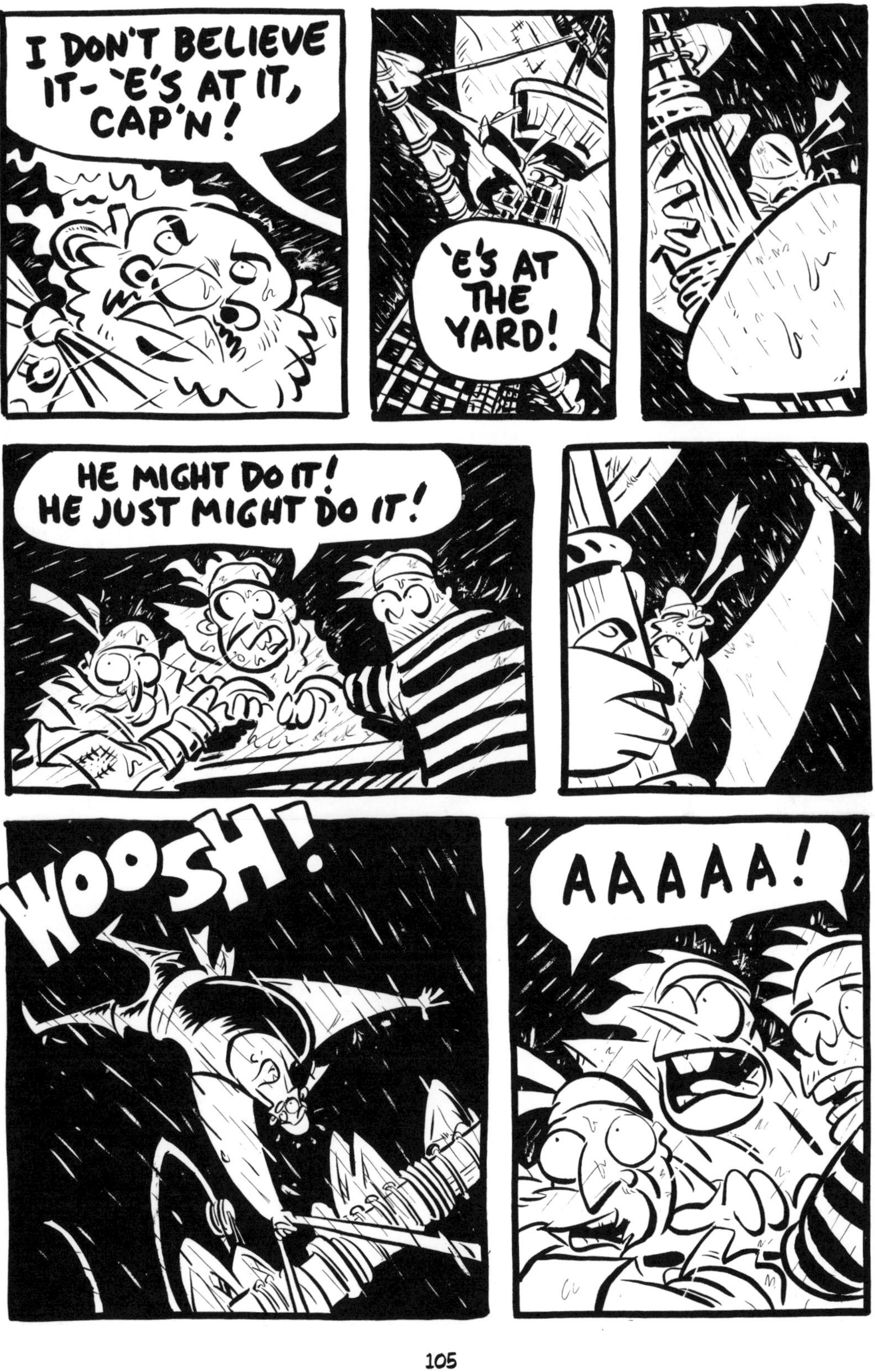
I DON'T BELIEVE IT- `E'S AT IT, CAP'N!
`E'S AT THE YARD!
HE MIGHT DO IT! HE JUST MIGHT DO IT!
WOOSH!
AAAAA!

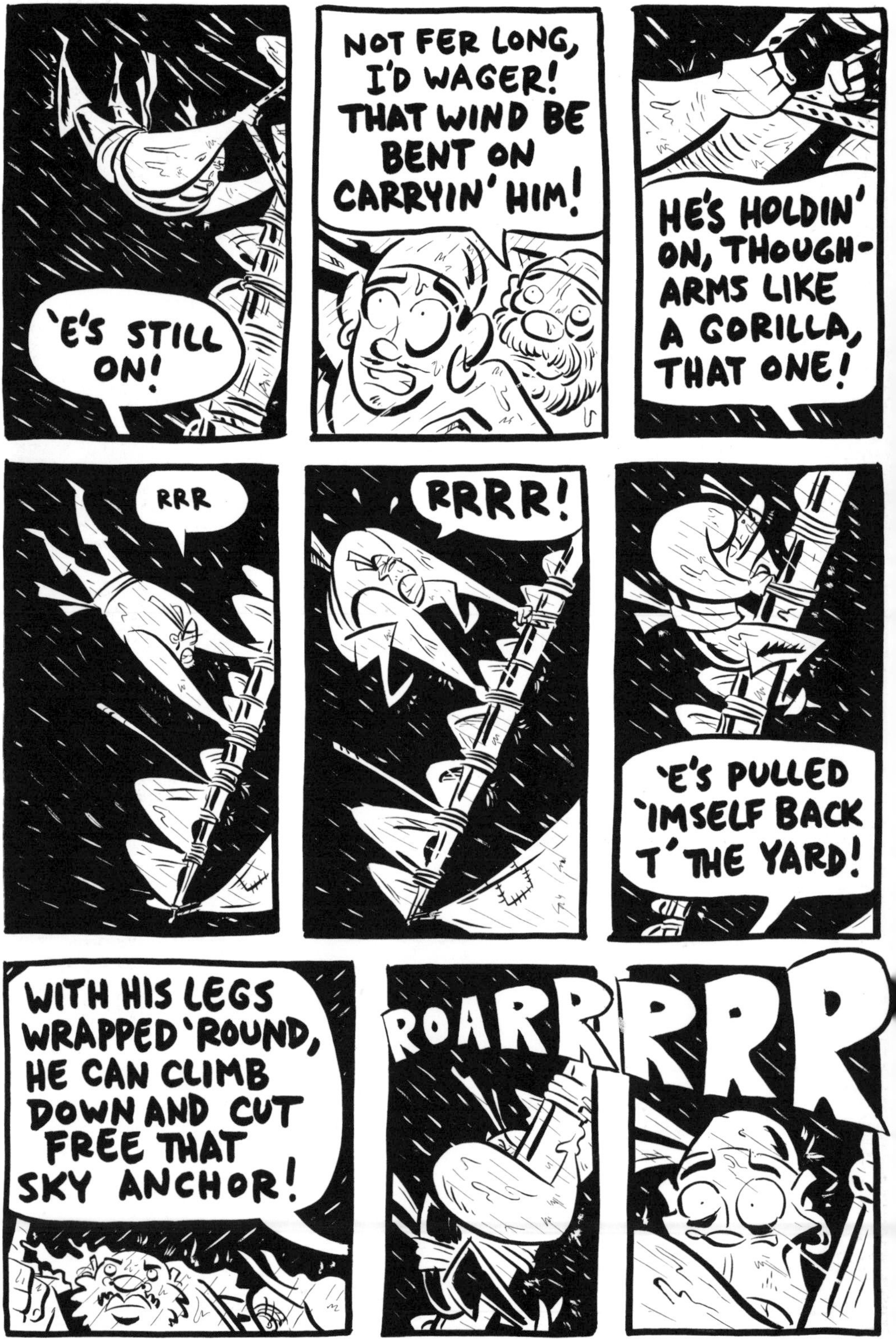
`E'S STILL ON!
NOT FER LONG, I'D WAGER! THAT WIND BE BENT ON CARRYIN' HIM!
HE'S HOLDIN' ON, THOUGH- ARMS LIKE A GORILLA, THAT ONE!
RRR
RRRR!
`E'S PULLED `IMSELF BACK T' THE YARD!
WITH HIS LEGS WRAPPED 'ROUND, HE CAN CLIMB DOWN AND CUT FREE THAT SKY ANCHOR!
ROARRRRR

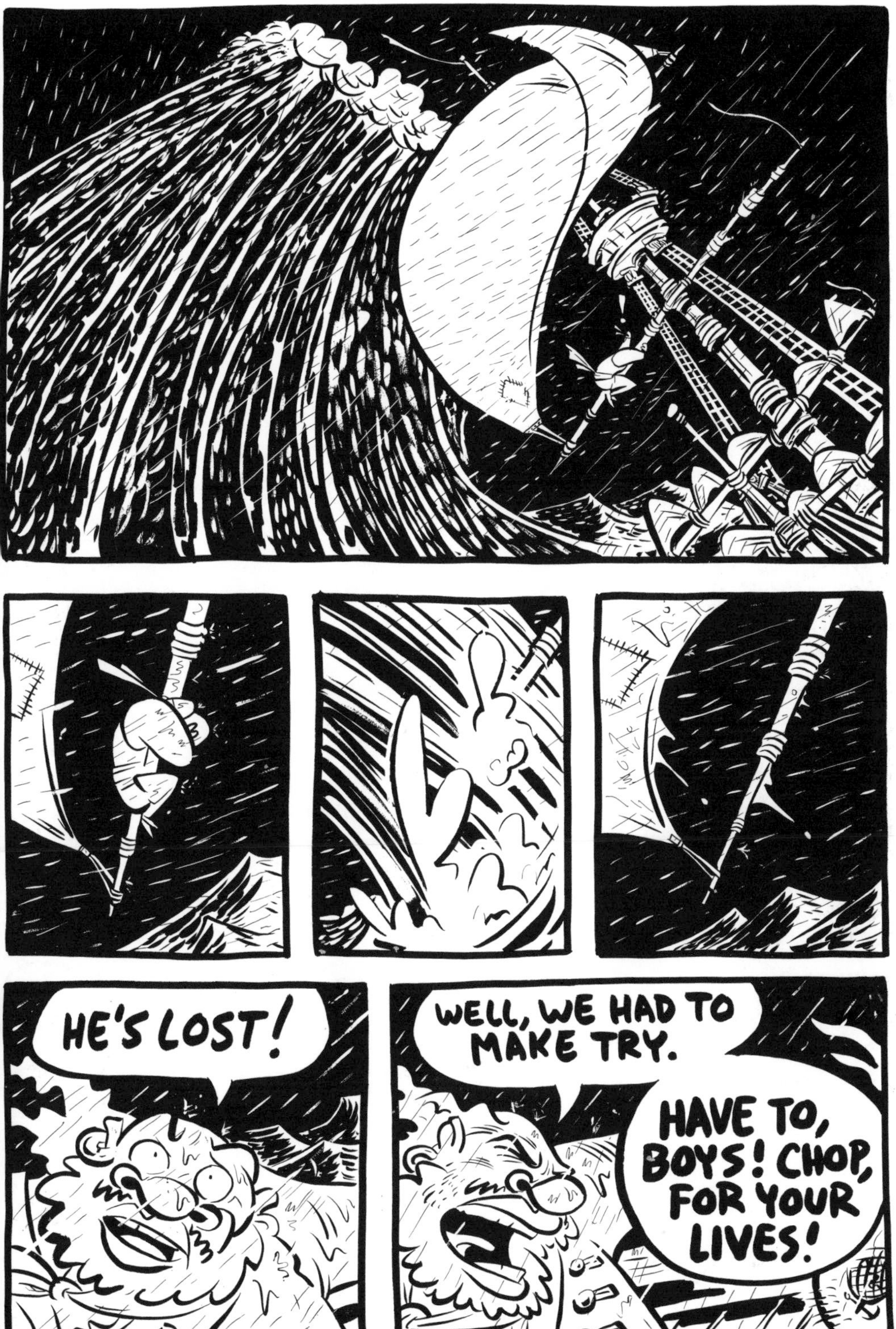
HE'S LOST!
WELL, WE HAD TO MAKE TRY.
HAVE TO, BOYS! CHOP, FOR YOUR LIVES!

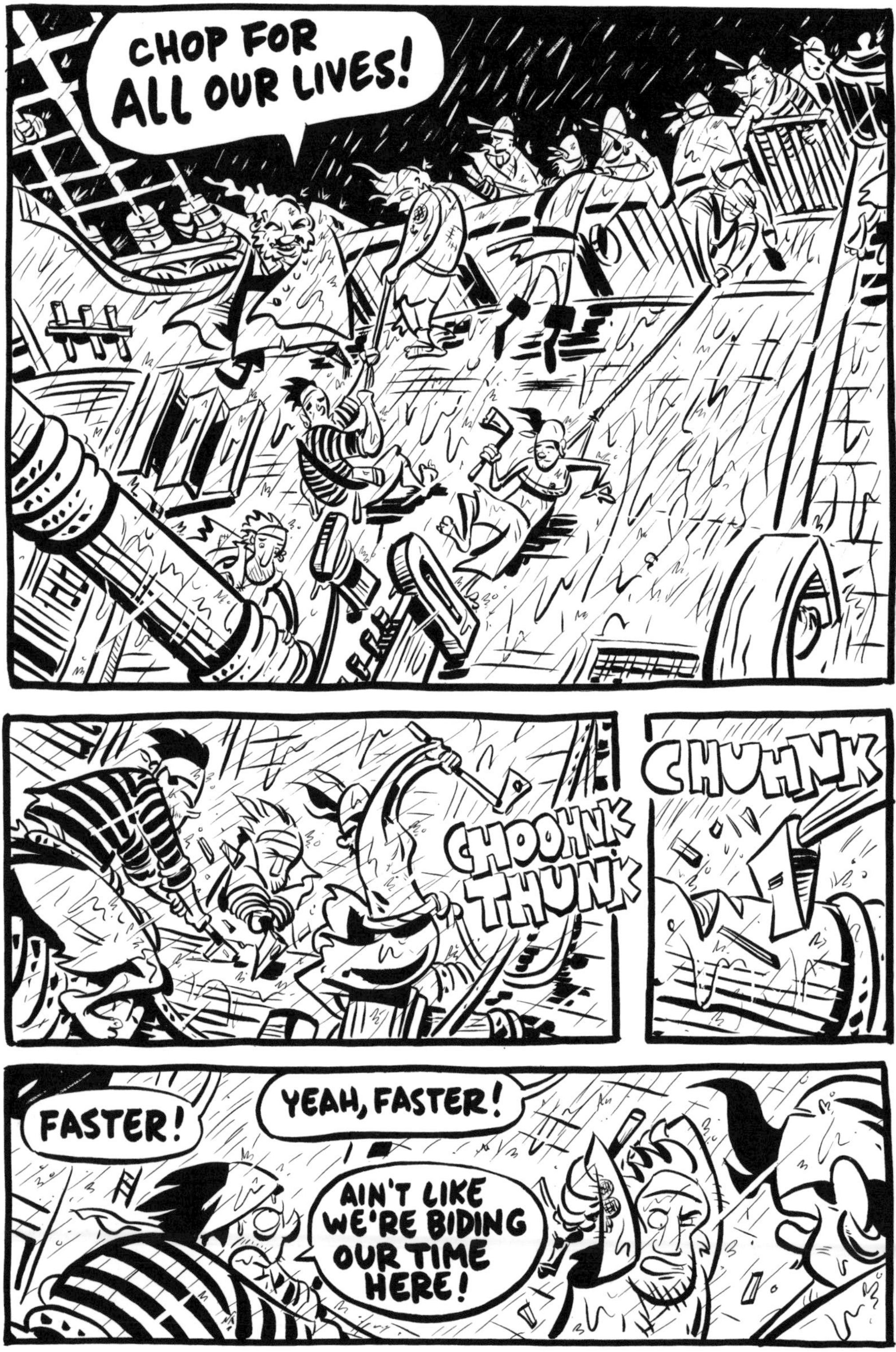
CHOP FOR ALL OUR LIVES!
CHOOHNK
THUNK
CHUHNK
FASTER!
YEAH, FASTER!
AIN'T LIKE WE'RE BIDING OUR TIME HERE!

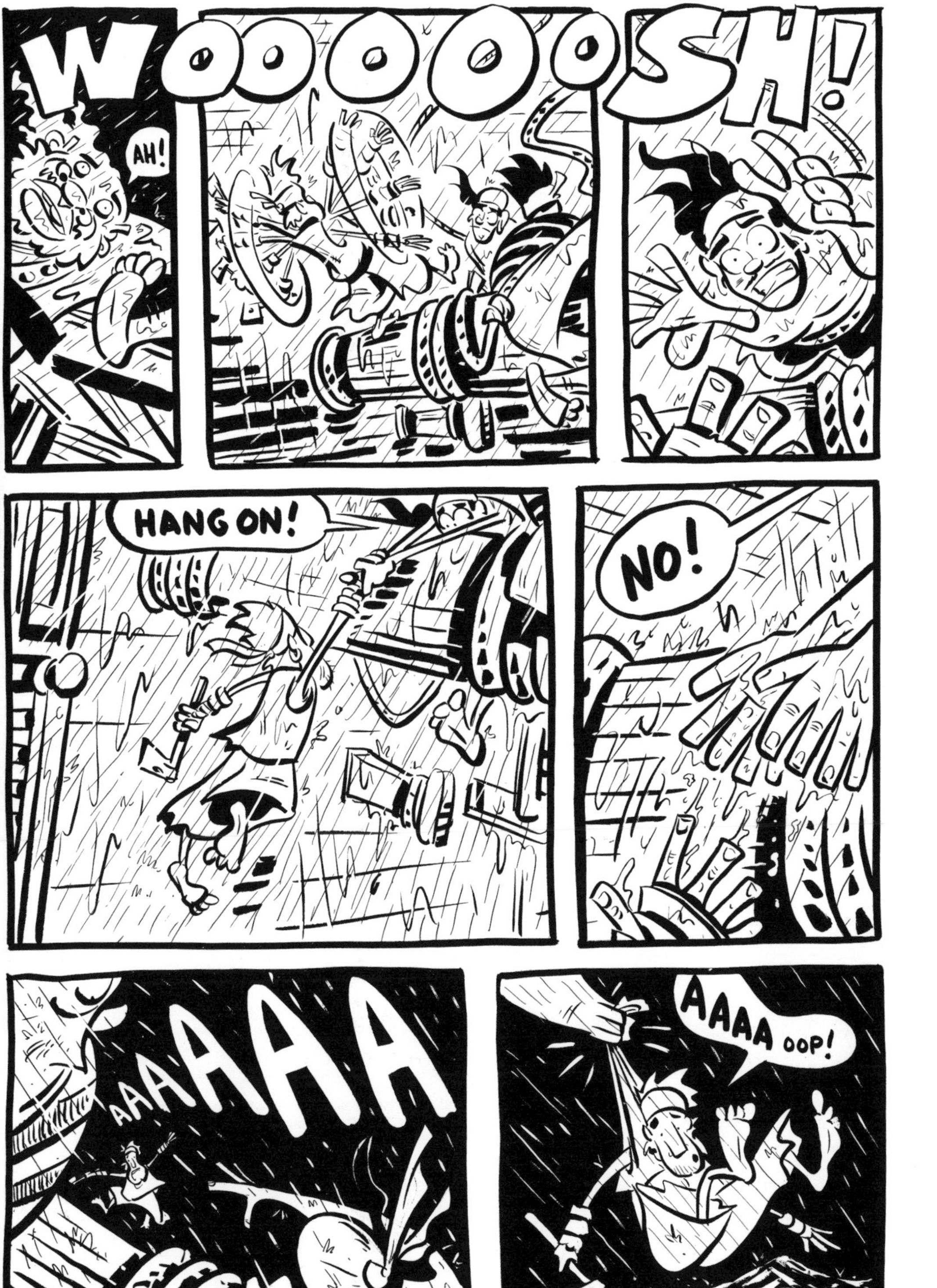
WOOOOOSH!
AH!
HANG ON!
NO!
AAAAAA
AAAA OOP!

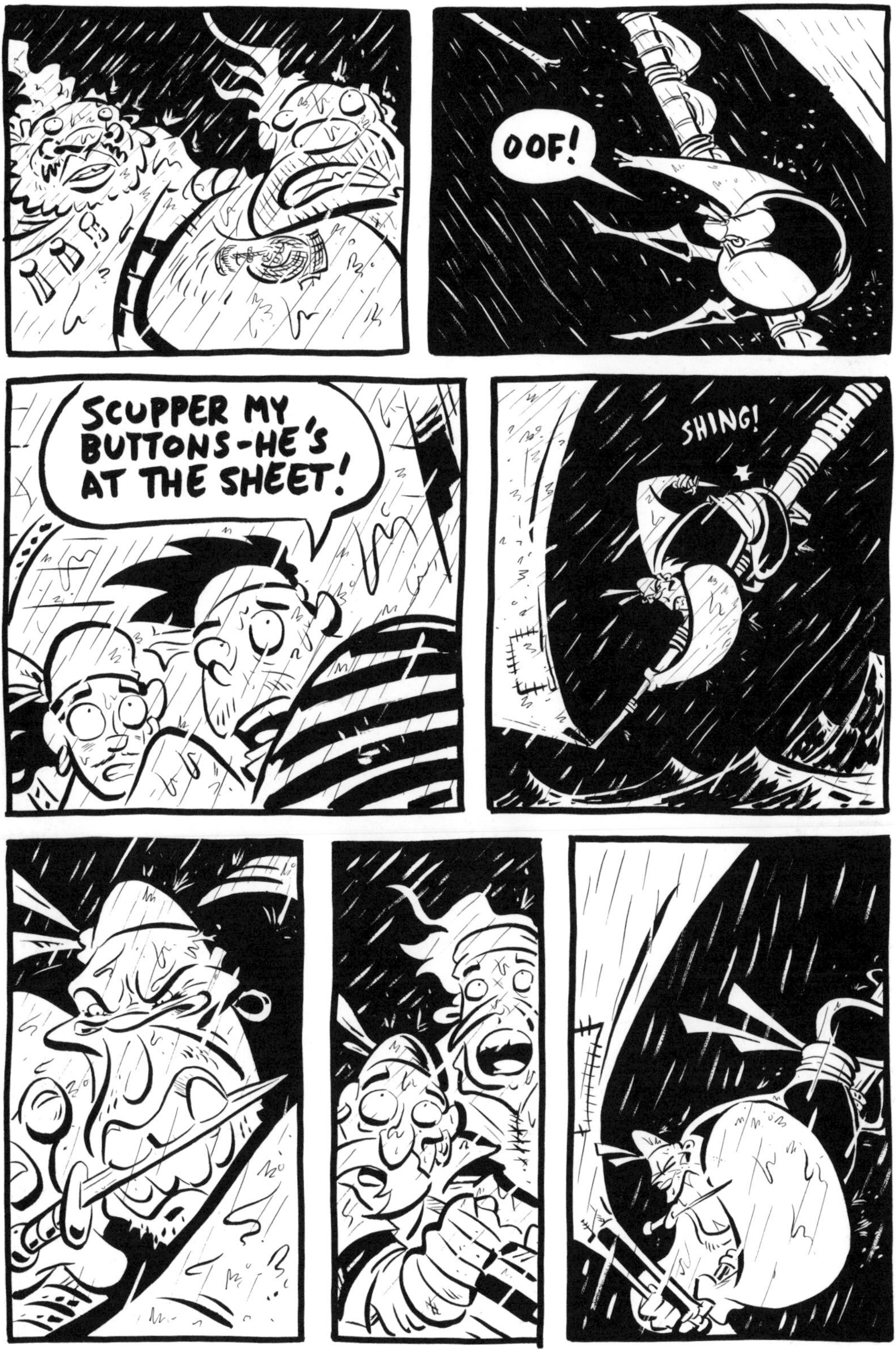
OOF!
SCUPPER MY BUTTONS-HE'S AT THE SHEET!
SHING!

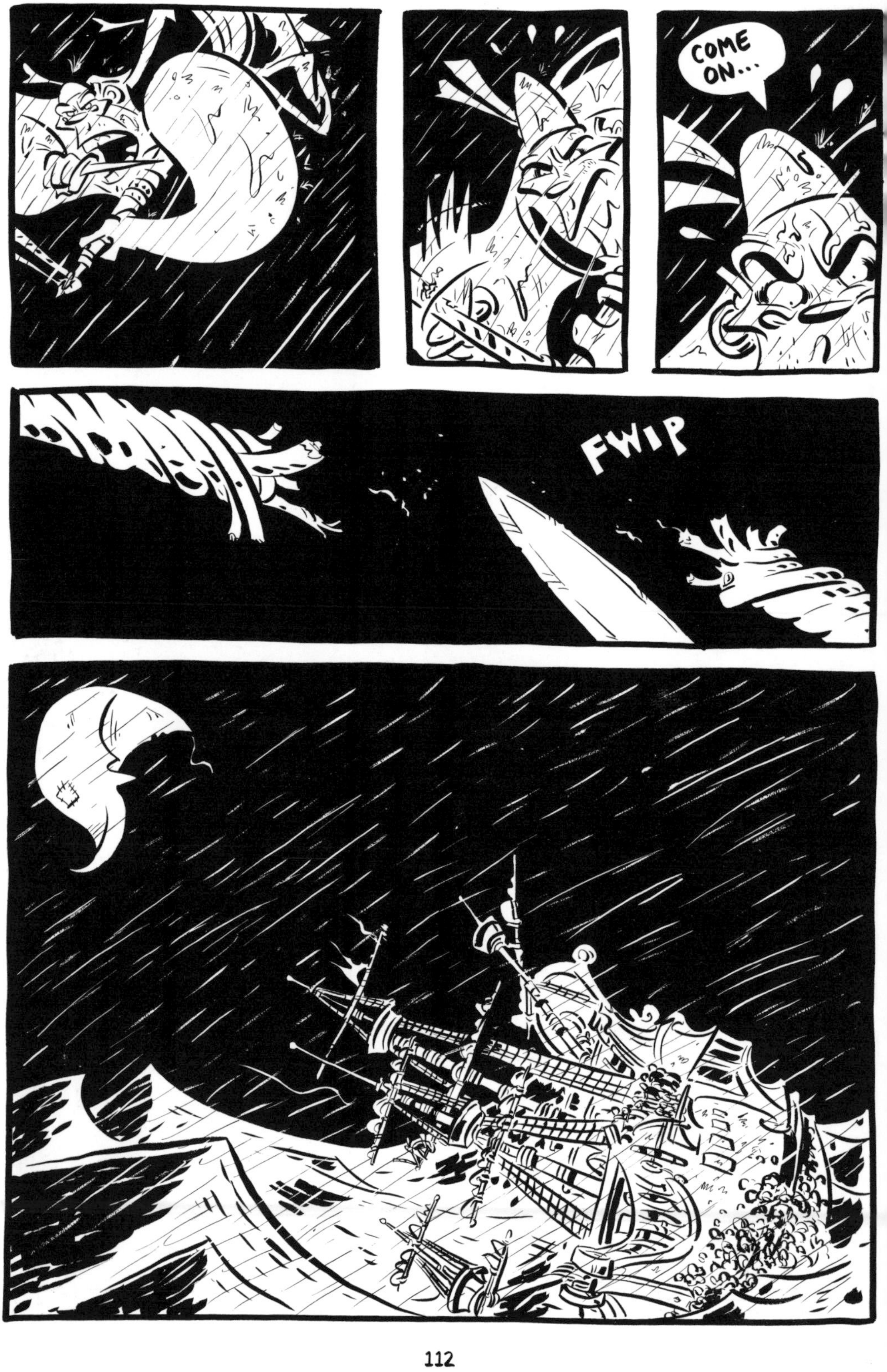
COME ON...
FWIP

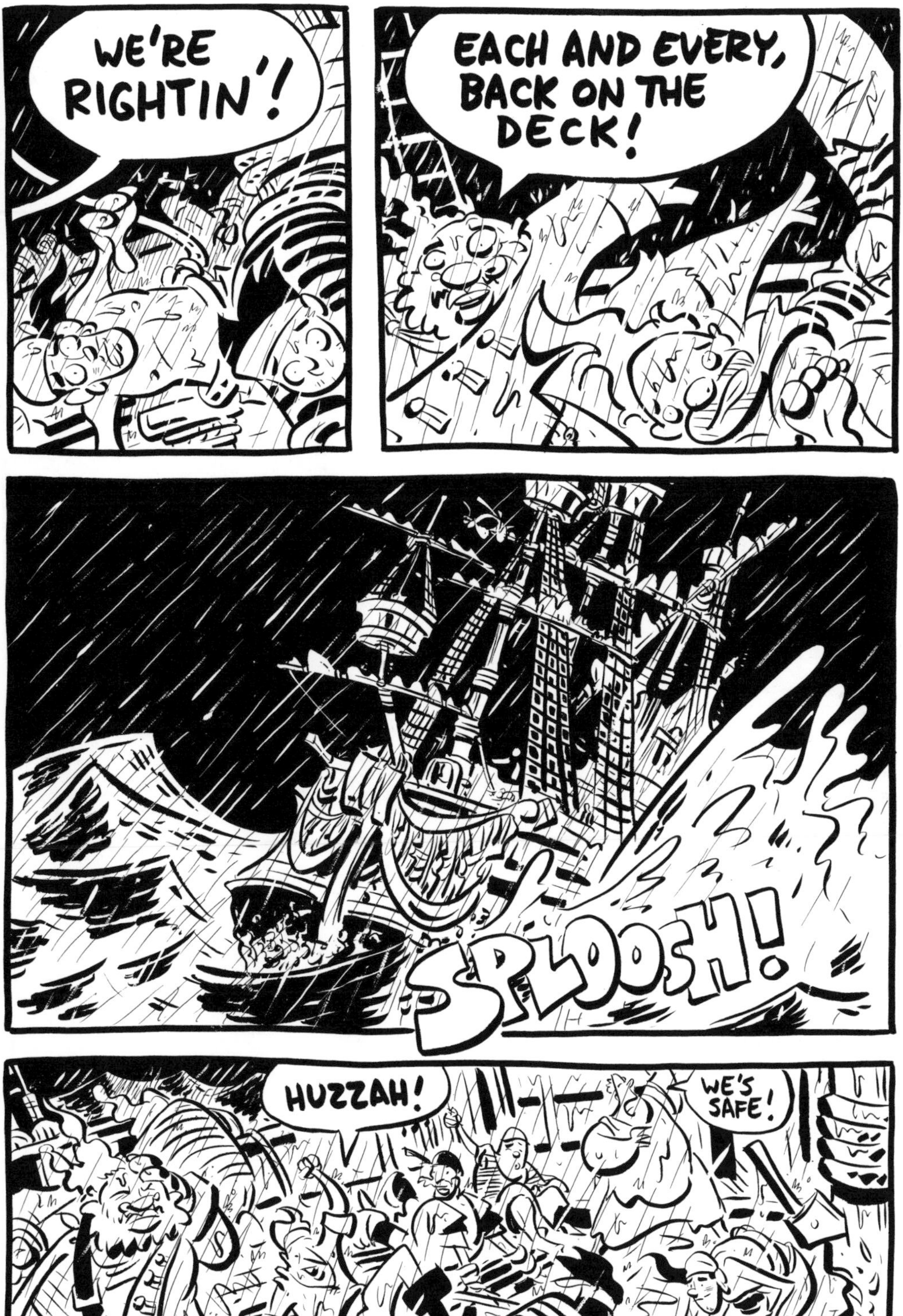
WE'RE RIGHTIN'!
EACH AND EVERY, BACK ON THE DECK!
SPLOOSH!
HUZZAH!
WE'S SAFE!

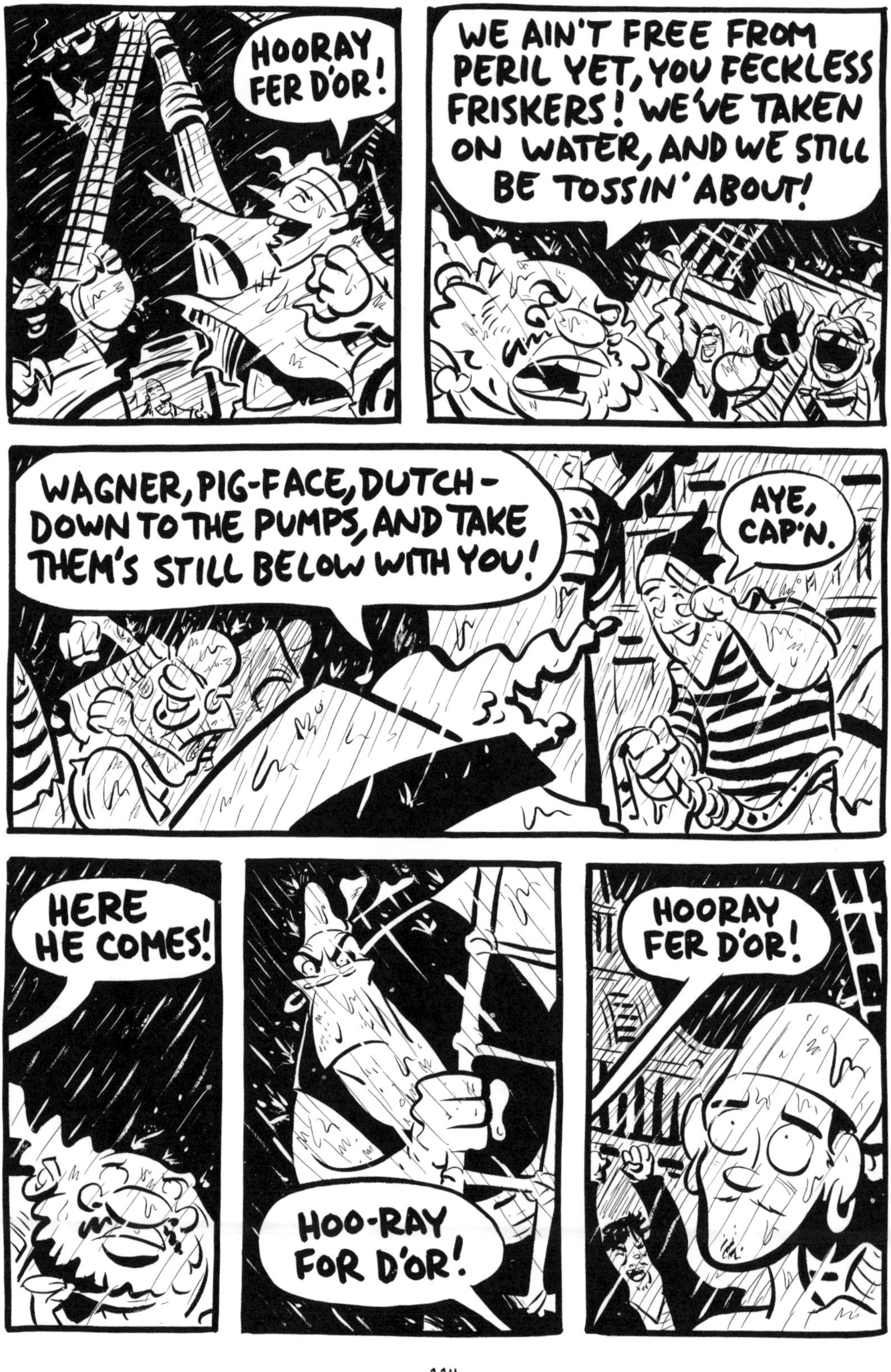
HOORAY FER D'OR!
WE AIN'T FREE FROM PERIL YET, YOU FECKLESS FRISKERS! WE'VE TAKEN ON WATER, AND WE STILL BE TOSSIN' ABOUT!
WAGNER, PIG-FACE, DUTCH- DOWN TO THE PUMPS, AND TAKE THEM'S STILL BELOW WITH YOU!
AYE, CAP'N.
HERE HE COMES!
HOO-RAY FOR D'OR!
HOORAY FER D'OR!

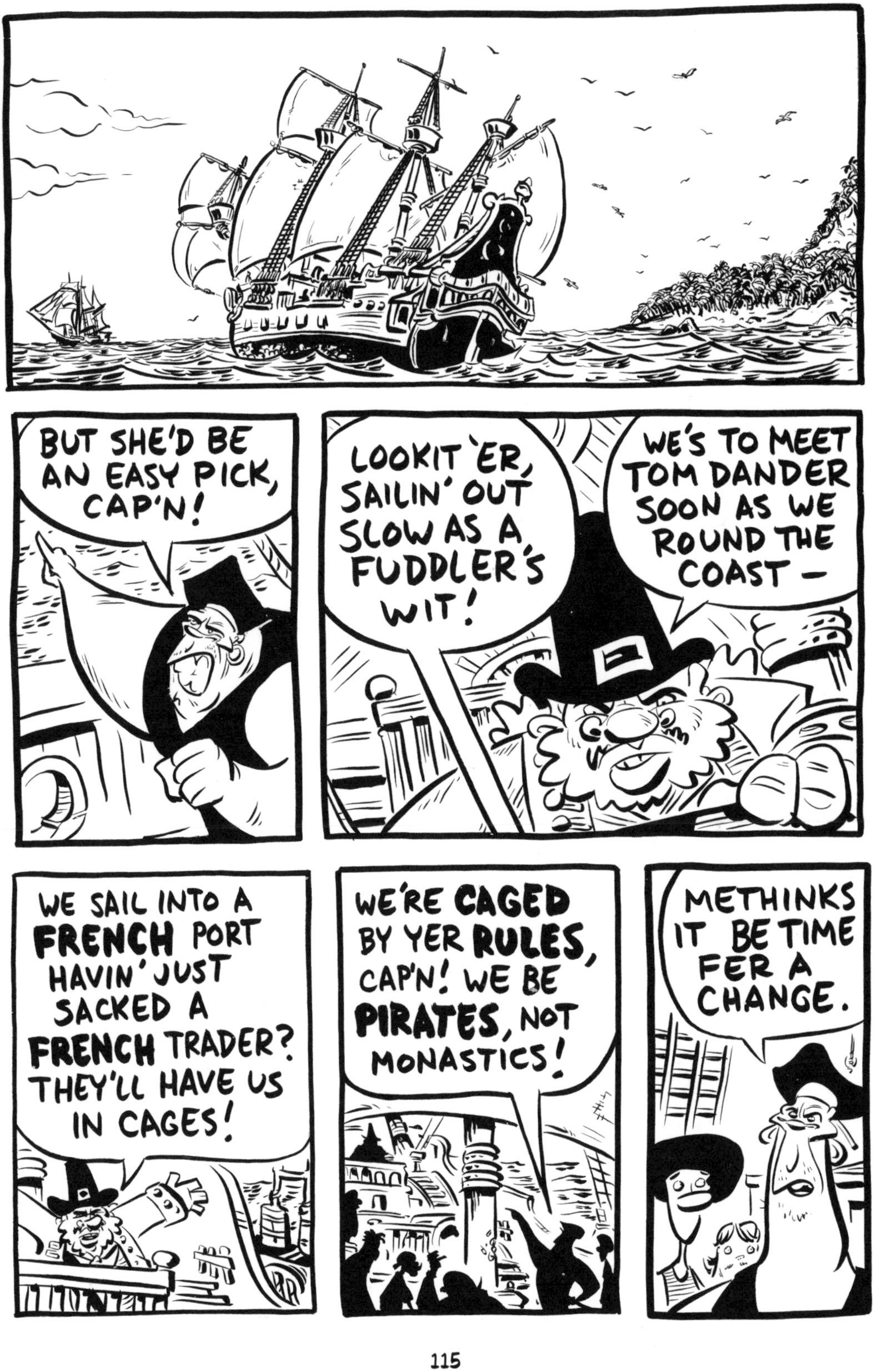
BUT SHE'D BE AN EASY PICK, CAP'N!
LOOKIT 'ER, SAILIN' OUT SLOW AS A FUDDLER'S WIT!
WE'S TO MEET TOM DANDER SOON AS WE ROUND THE COAST —
WE SAIL INTO A **FRENCH** PORT HAVIN' JUST SACKED A **FRENCH** TRADER? THEY'LL HAVE US IN CAGES!
WE'RE **CAGED** BY YER **RULES**, CAP'N! WE BE **PIRATES**, NOT MONASTICS!
METHINKS IT BE TIME FER A CHANGE.

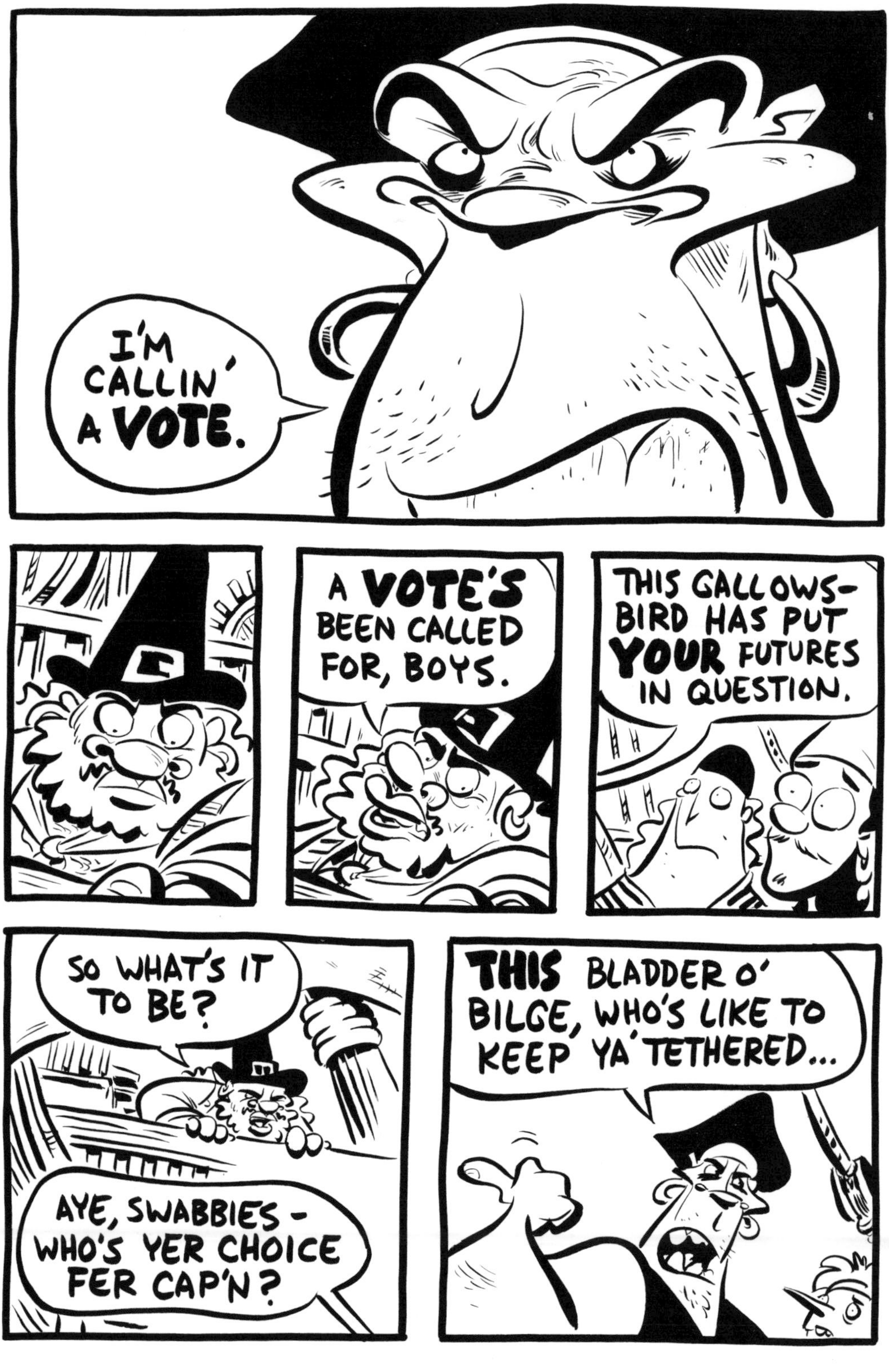
I'M CALLIN' A VOTE.
A VOTE'S BEEN CALLED FOR, BOYS.
THIS GALLOWS-BIRD HAS PUT YOUR FUTURES IN QUESTION.
SO WHAT'S IT TO BE?
AYE, SWABBIES - WHO'S YER CHOICE FER CAP'N?
THIS BLADDER O' BILGE, WHO'S LIKE TO KEEP YA' TETHERED...

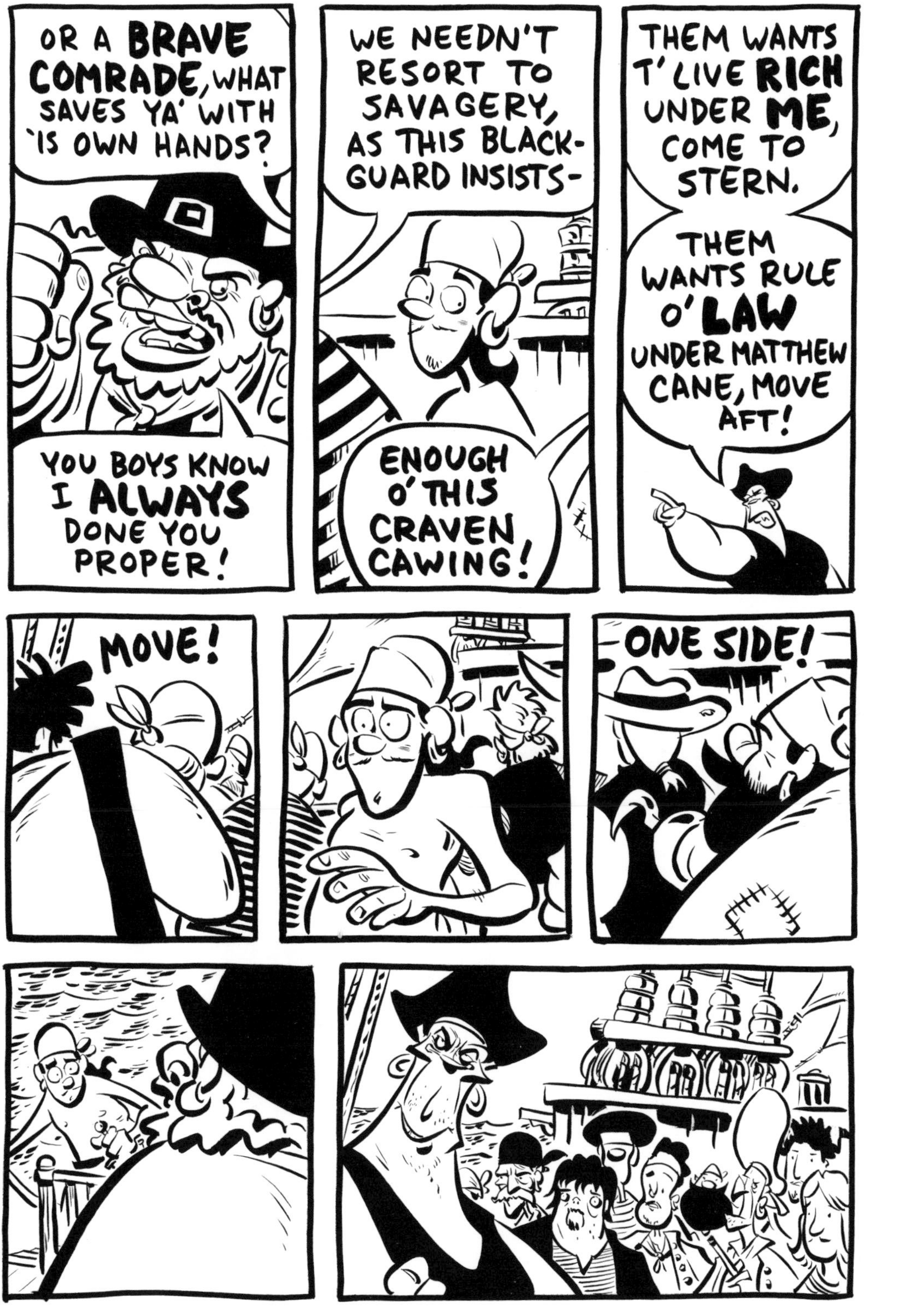
OR A BRAVE COMRADE, WHAT SAVES YA' WITH 'IS OWN HANDS?
YOU BOYS KNOW I ALWAYS DONE YOU PROPER!
WE NEEDN'T RESORT TO SAVAGERY, AS THIS BLACK-GUARD INSISTS-
ENOUGH O' THIS CRAVEN CAWING!
THEM WANTS T' LIVE RICH UNDER ME, COME TO STERN.
THEM WANTS RULE O' LAW UNDER MATTHEW CANE, MOVE AFT!
MOVE!
ONE SIDE!

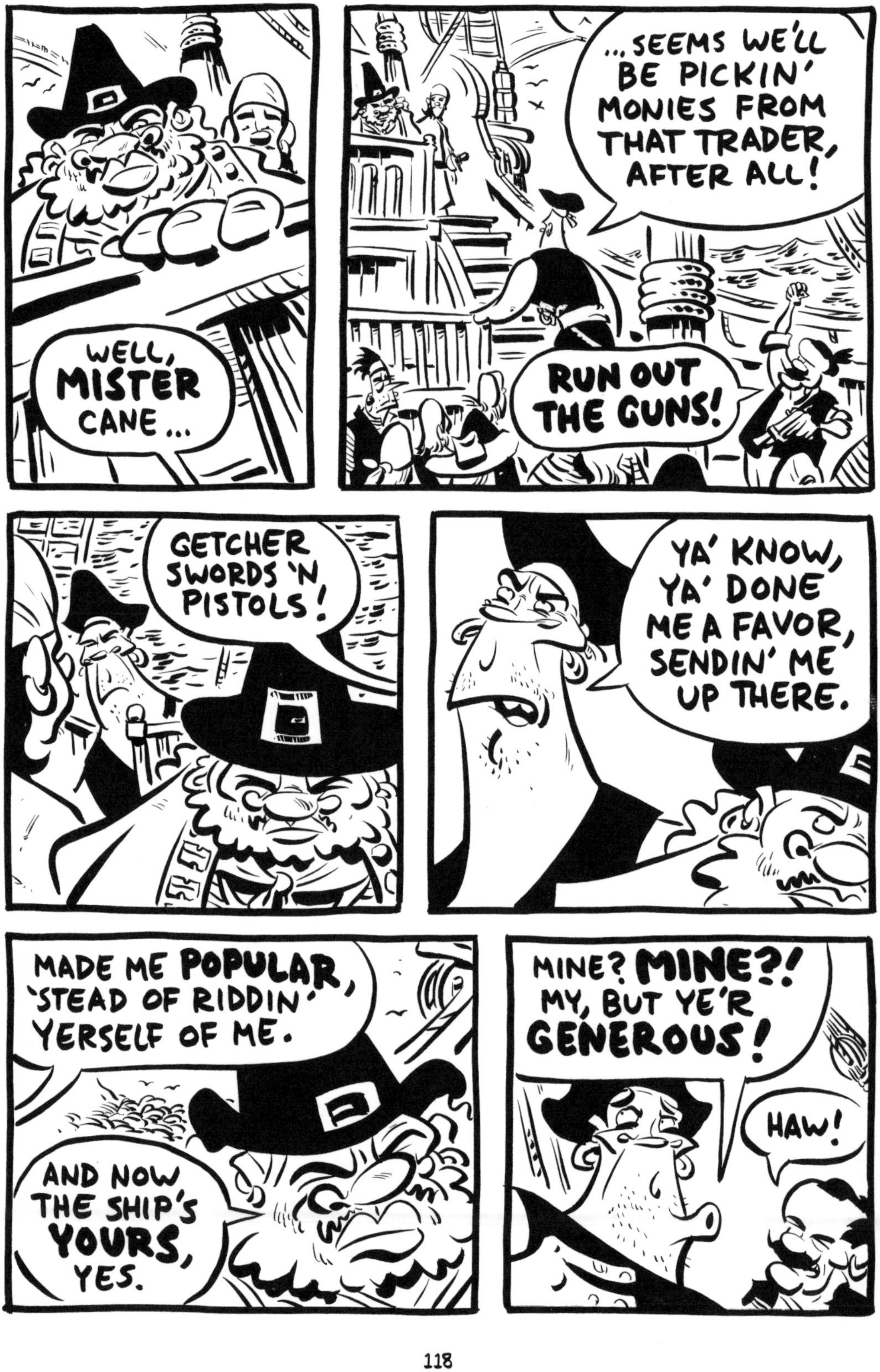
WELL, MISTER CANE...
...SEEMS WE'LL BE PICKIN' MONIES FROM THAT TRADER, AFTER ALL!
RUN OUT THE GUNS!
GETCHER SWORDS 'N PISTOLS!
YA' KNOW, YA' DONE ME A FAVOR, SENDIN' ME UP THERE.
MADE ME POPULAR, 'STEAD OF RIDDIN' YERSELF OF ME.
AND NOW THE SHIP'S YOURS, YES.
MINE? MINE?! MY, BUT YE'R GENEROUS!
HAW!

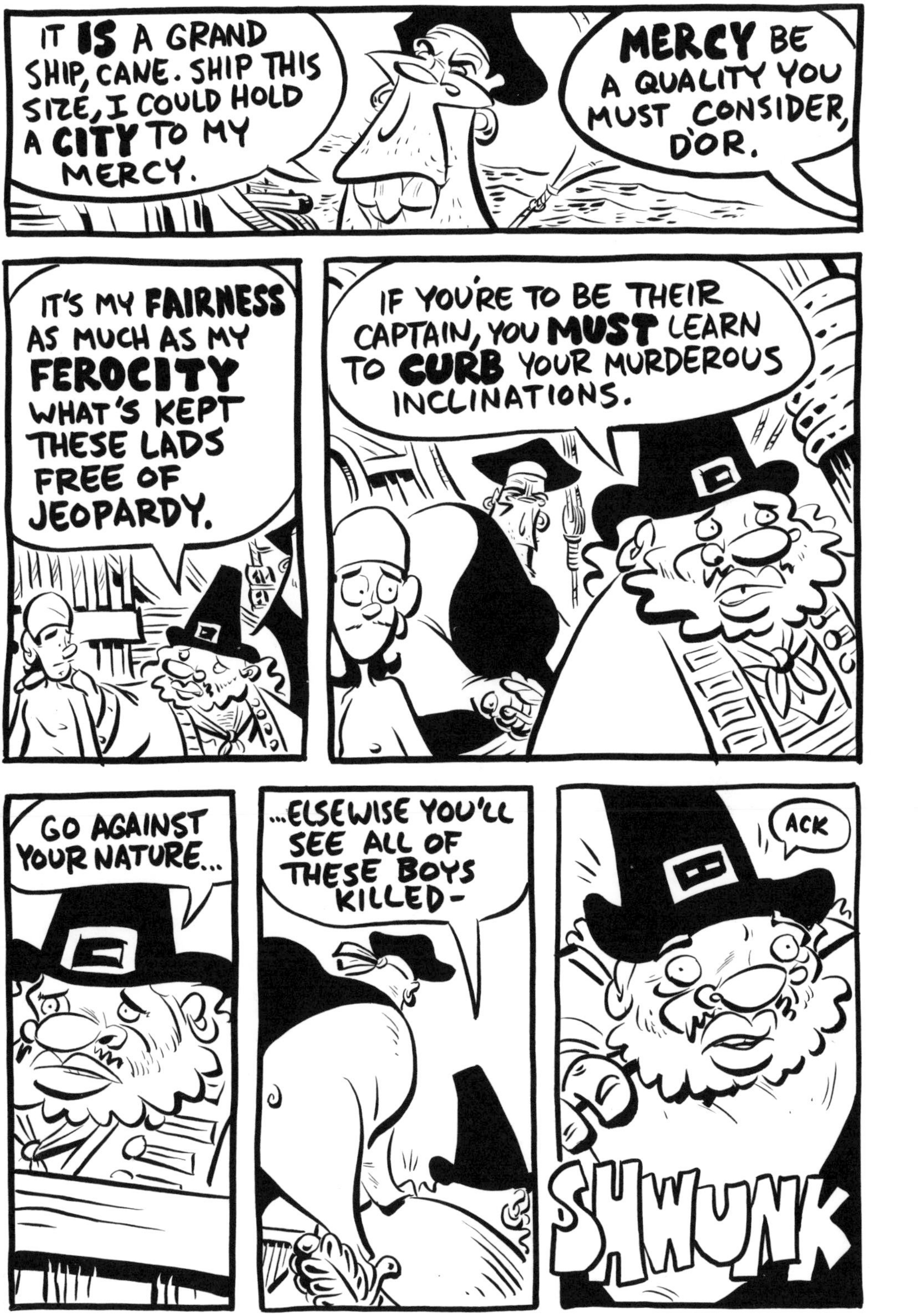
IT **IS** A GRAND SHIP, CANE. SHIP THIS SIZE, I COULD HOLD A **CITY** TO MY MERCY.
MERCY BE A QUALITY YOU MUST CONSIDER, D'OR.
IT'S MY **FAIRNESS** AS MUCH AS MY **FEROCITY** WHAT'S KEPT THESE LADS FREE OF JEOPARDY.
IF YOU'RE TO BE THEIR CAPTAIN, YOU **MUST** LEARN TO **CURB** YOUR MURDEROUS INCLINATIONS.
GO AGAINST YOUR NATURE...
...ELSEWISE YOU'LL SEE ALL OF THESE BOYS KILLED-
ACK
SHWUNK

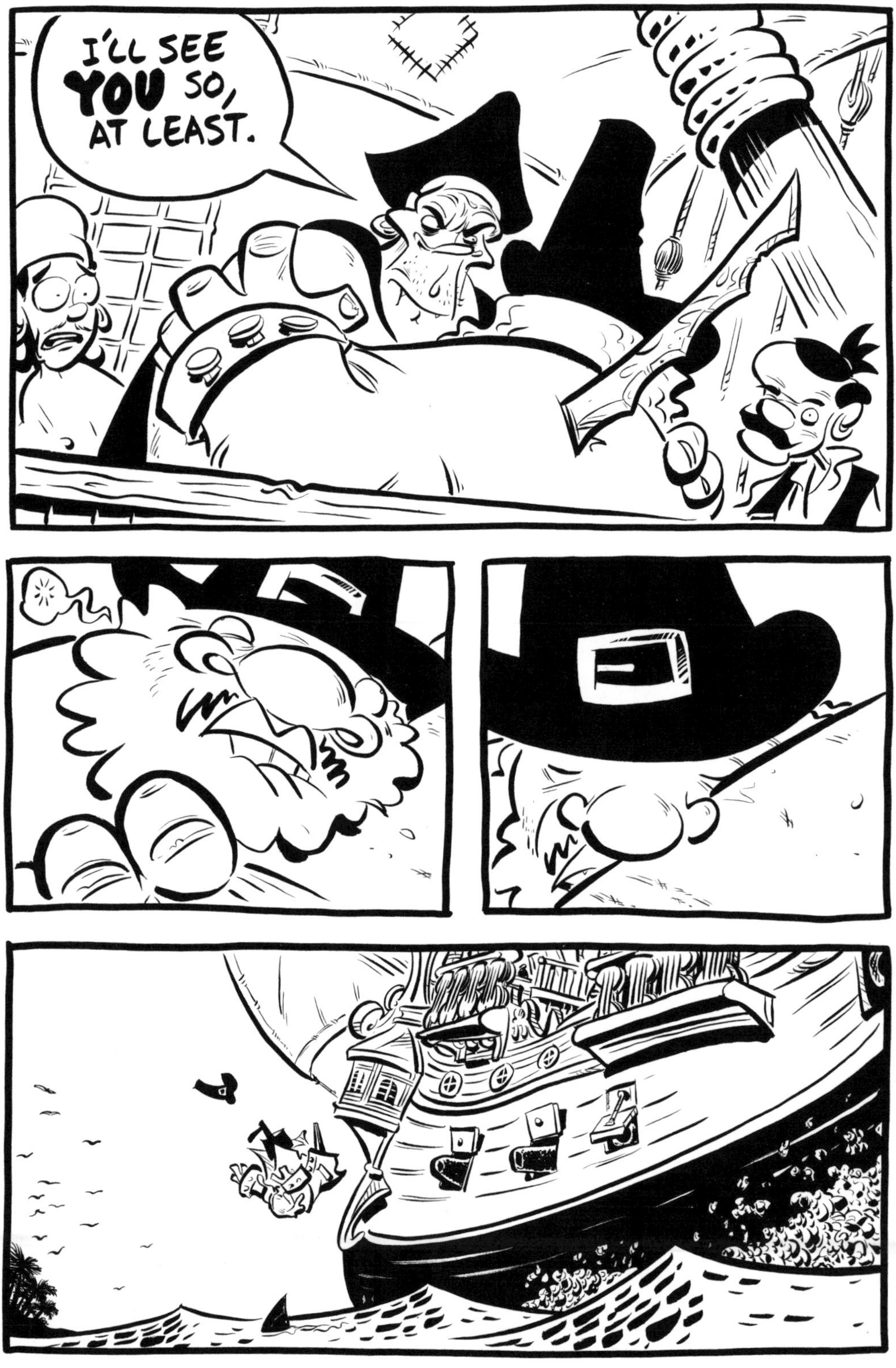
I'LL SEE
YOU SO,
AT LEAST.

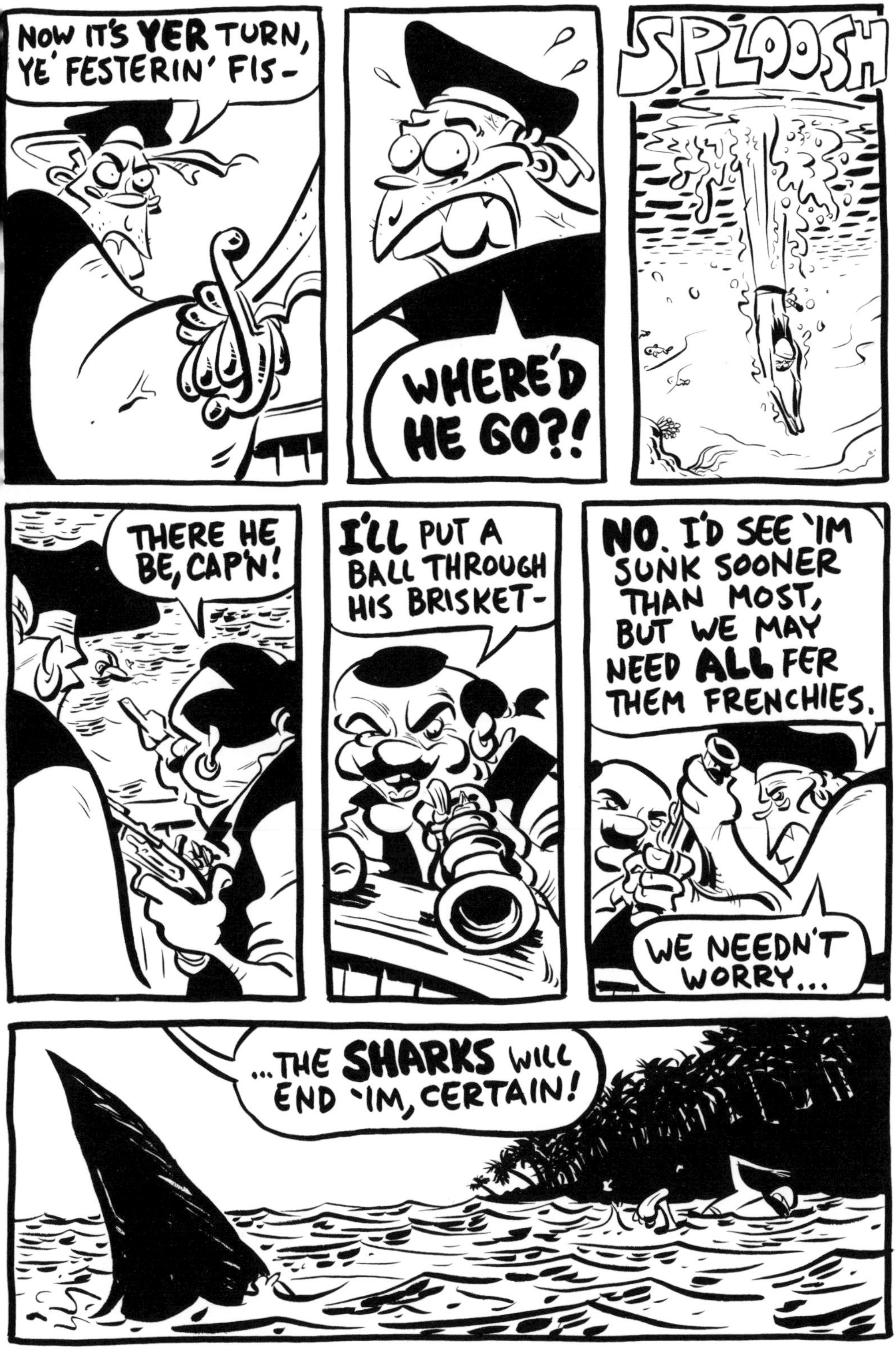
NOW IT'S YER TURN, YE' FESTERIN' FIS-
WHERE'D HE GO?!
SPLOOSH
THERE HE BE, CAP'N!
I'LL PUT A BALL THROUGH HIS BRISKET-
NO. I'D SEE 'IM SUNK SOONER THAN MOST, BUT WE MAY NEED ALL FER THEM FRENCHIES.
WE NEEDN'T WORRY...
...THE SHARKS WILL END 'IM, CERTAIN!

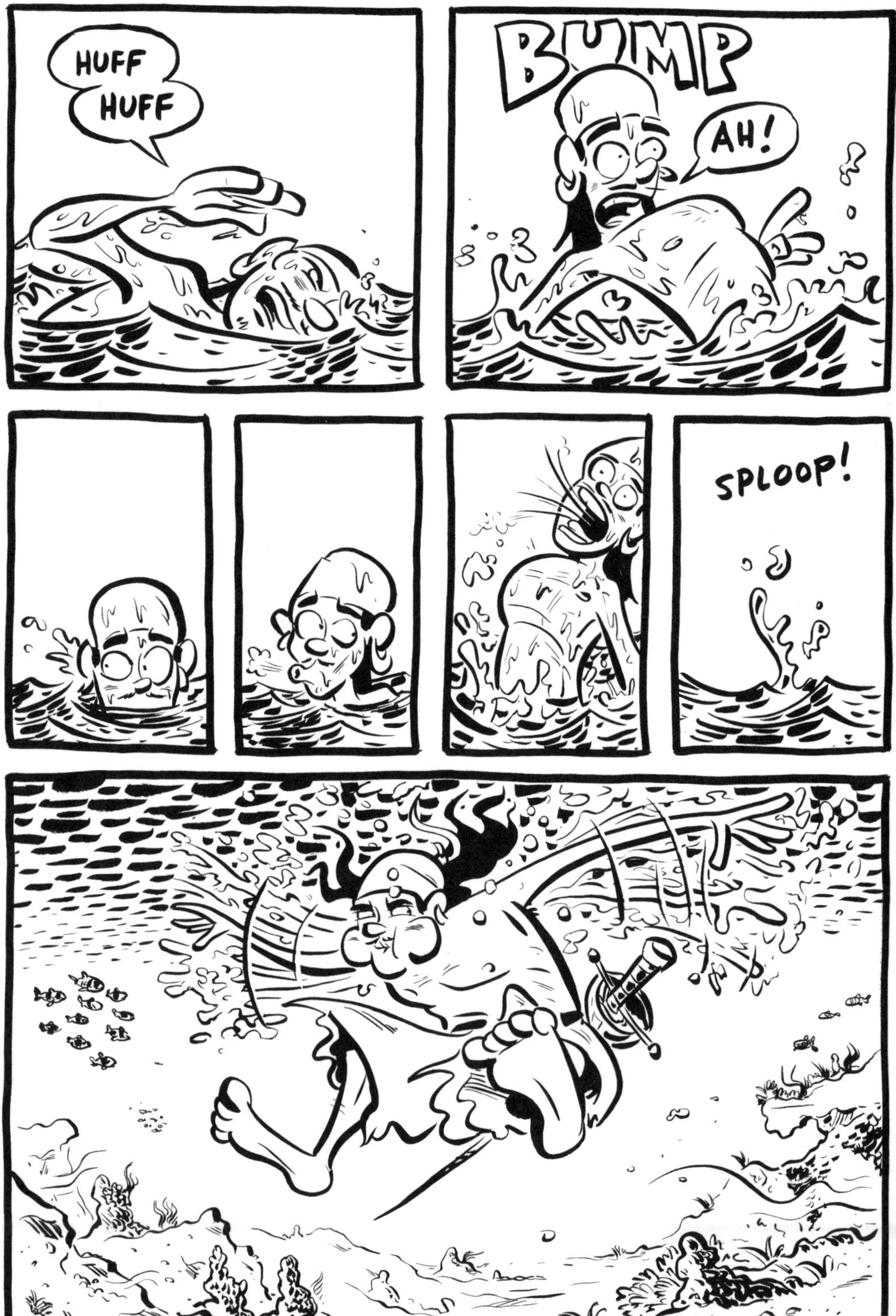
HUFF
HUFF
BUMP
AH!
SPLOOP!

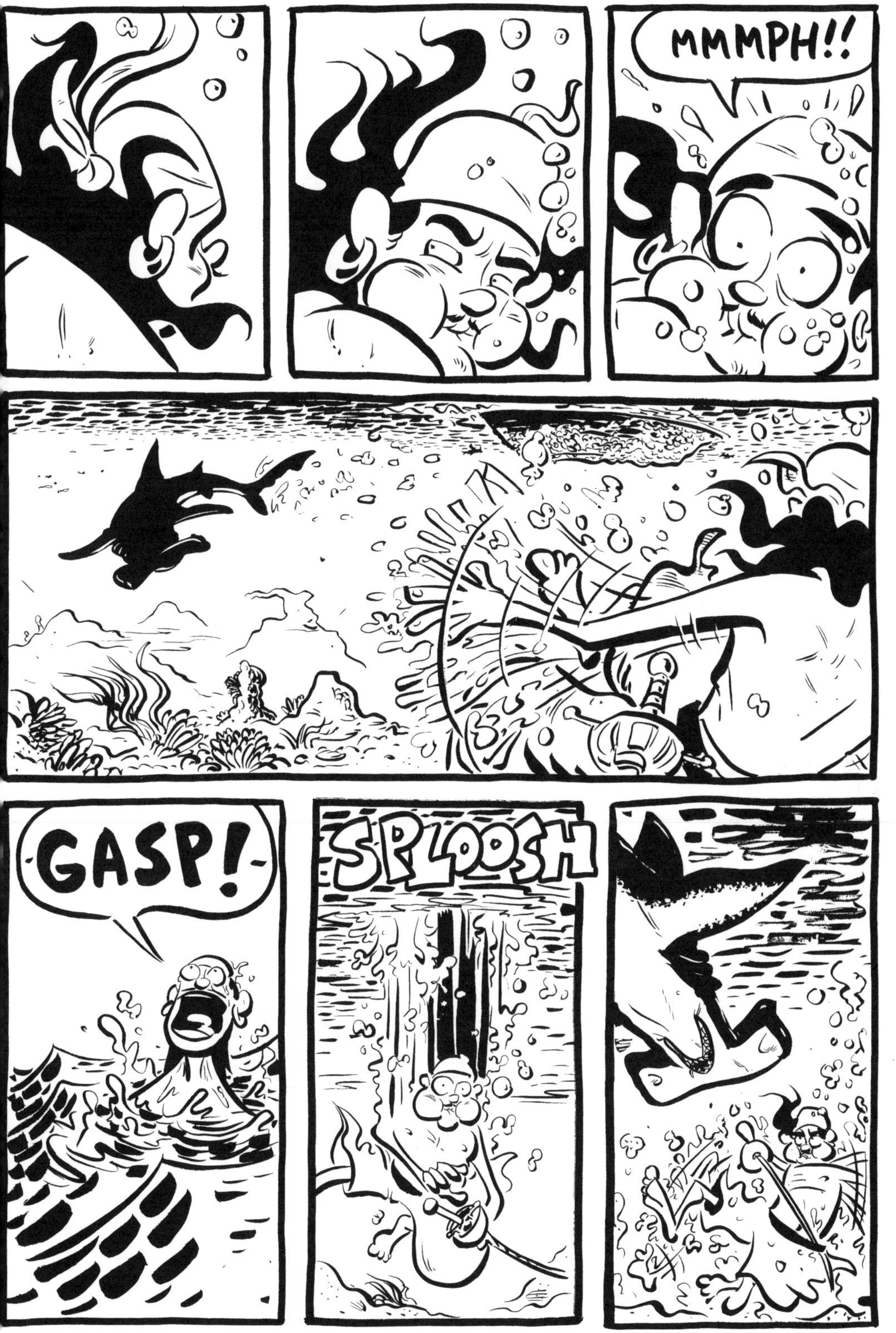
MMMPH!!
GASP!
SPLOOSH

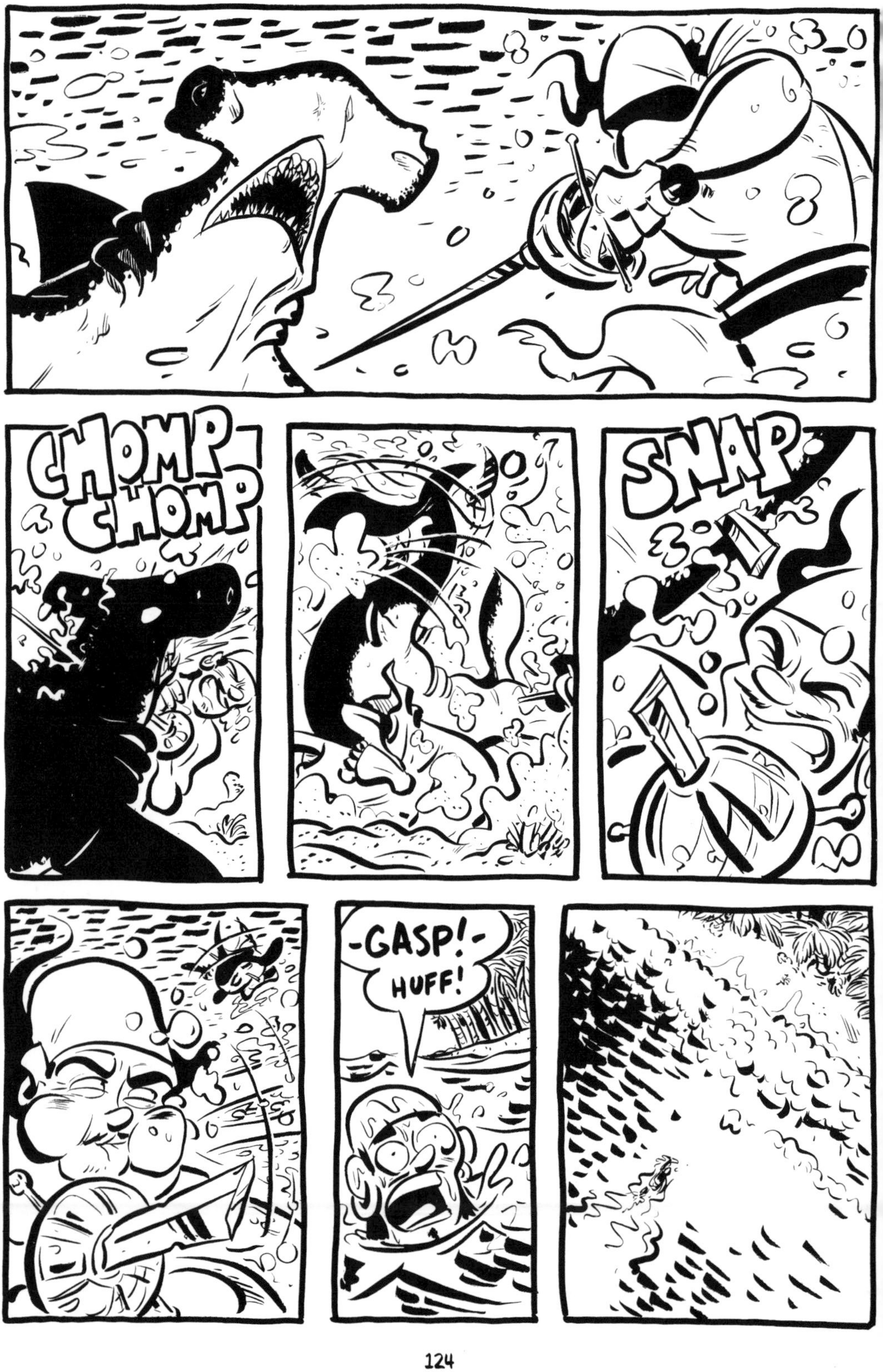
CHOMP
CHOMP
SNAP
-GASP!-
HUFF!

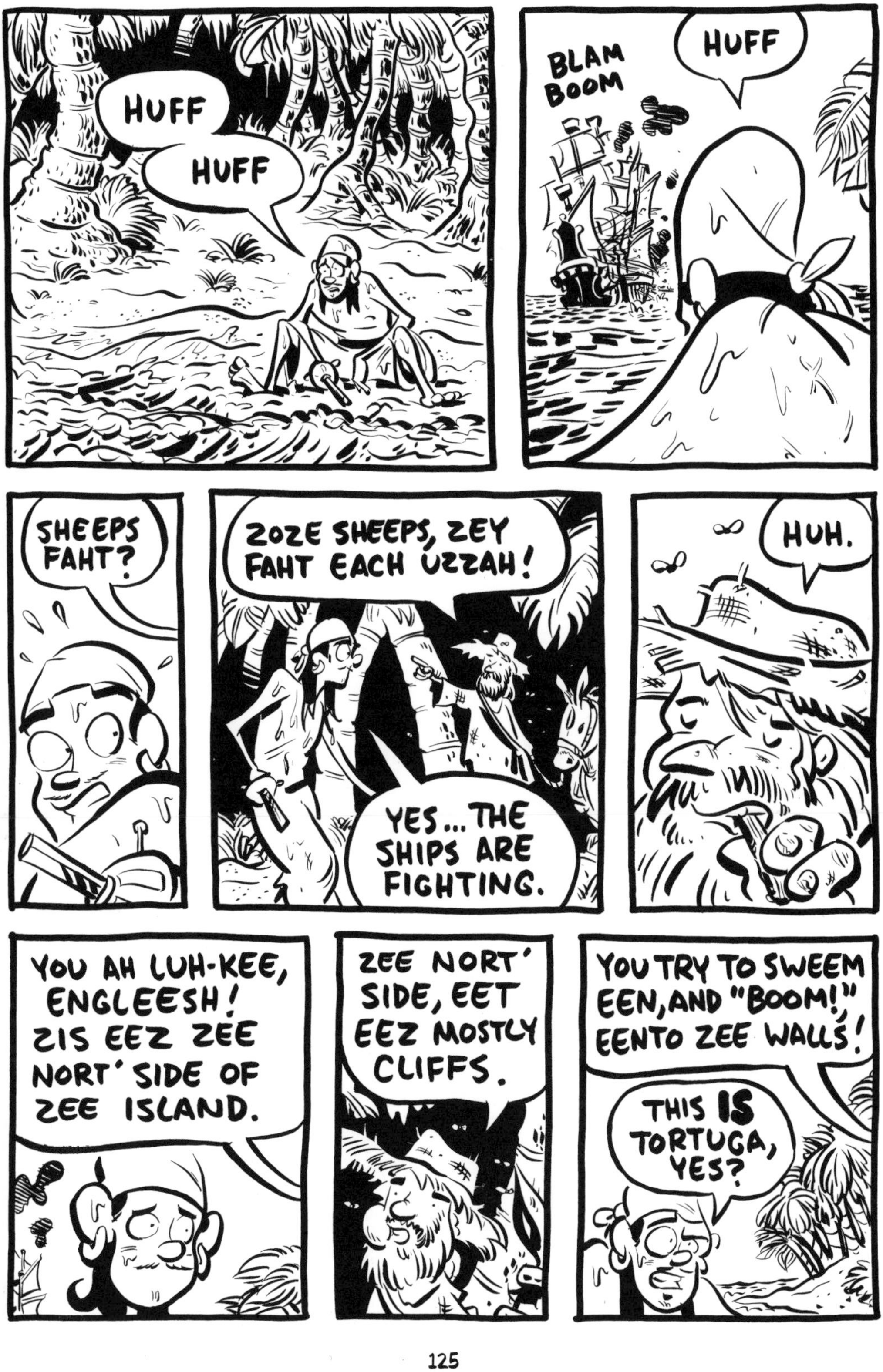
HUFF
HUFF
BLAM
BOOM
HUFF
SHEEPS FAHT?
ZOZE SHEEPS, ZEY FAHT EACH UZZAH!
YES... THE SHIPS ARE FIGHTING.
HUH.
YOU AH LUH-KEE, ENGLEESH! ZIS EEZ ZEE NORT' SIDE OF ZEE ISLAND.
ZEE NORT' SIDE, EET EEZ MOSTLY CLIFFS.
YOU TRY TO SWEEM EEN, AND "BOOM!" EENTO ZEE WALLS!
THIS **IS** TORTUGA, YES?

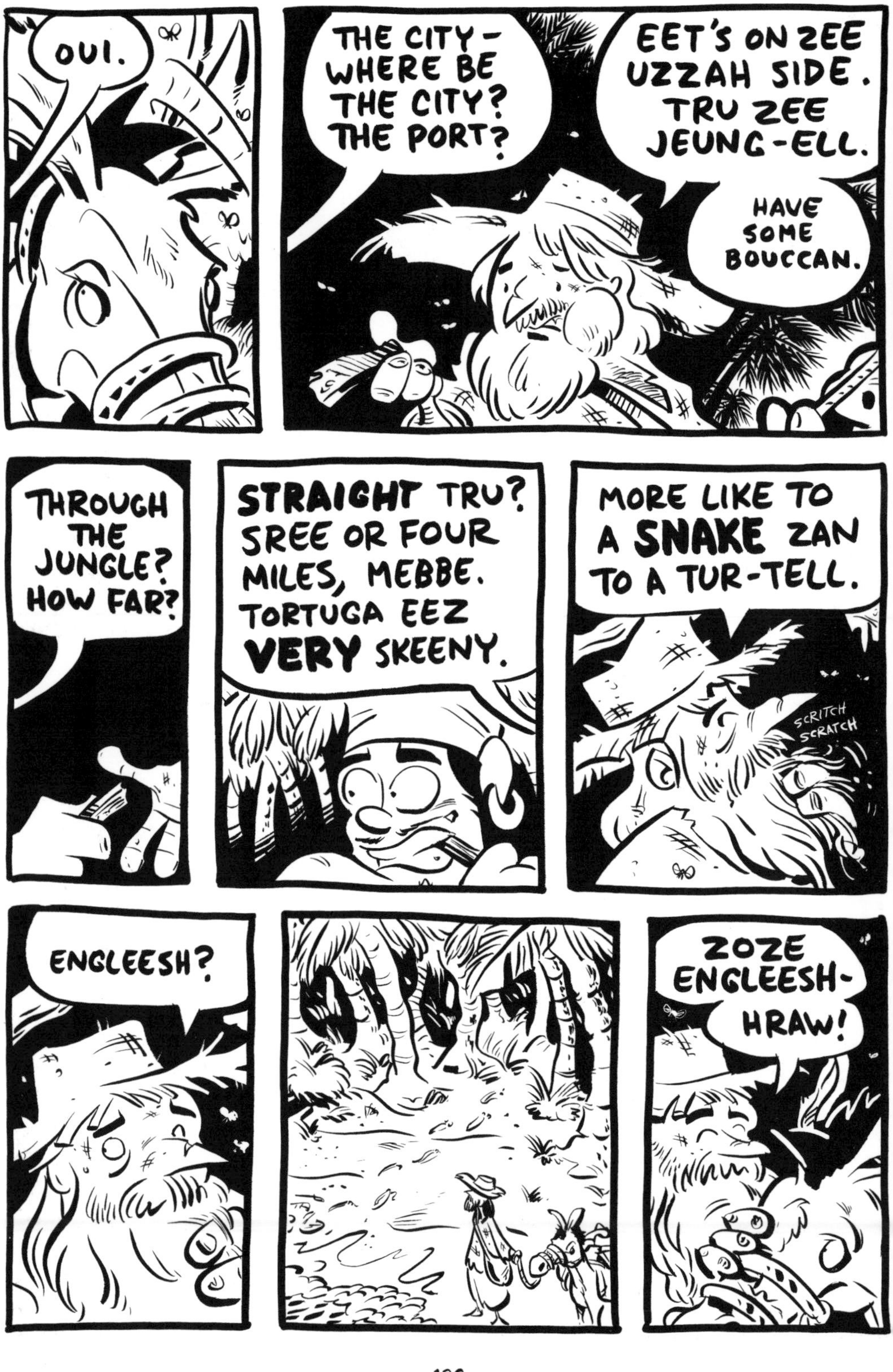
OUI.
THE CITY- WHERE BE THE CITY? THE PORT?
EET'S ON ZEE UZZAH SIDE. TRU ZEE JEUNG-ELL.
HAVE SOME BOUCCAN.
THROUGH THE JUNGLE? HOW FAR?
STRAIGHT TRU? SREE OR FOUR MILES, MEBBE. TORTUGA EEZ VERY SKEENY.
MORE LIKE TO A SNAKE ZAN TO A TUR-TELL.
SCRITCH SCRATCH
ENGLEESH?
ZOZE ENGLEESH- HRAW!

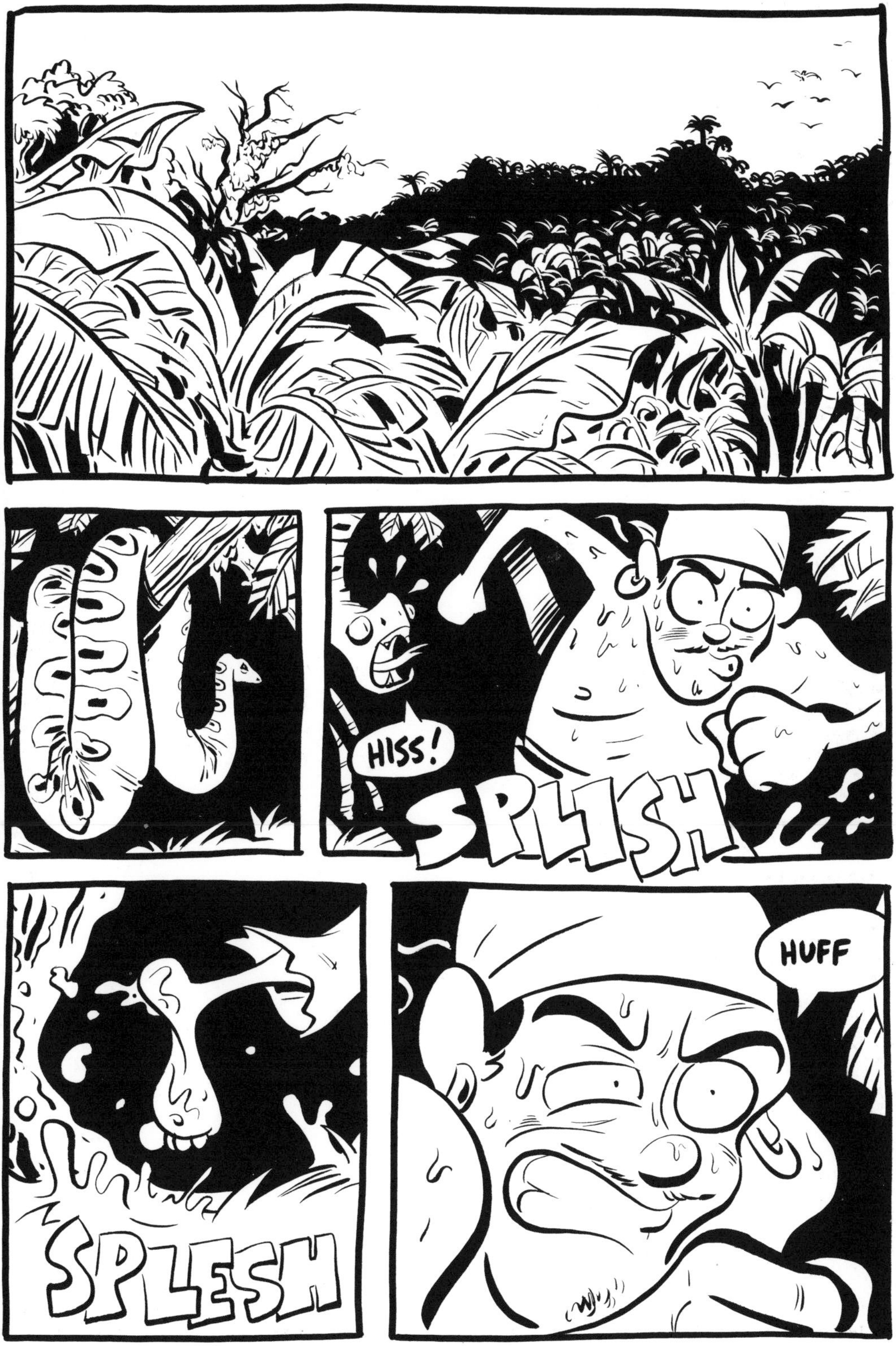
HISS!
SPLISH
SPLESH
HUFF

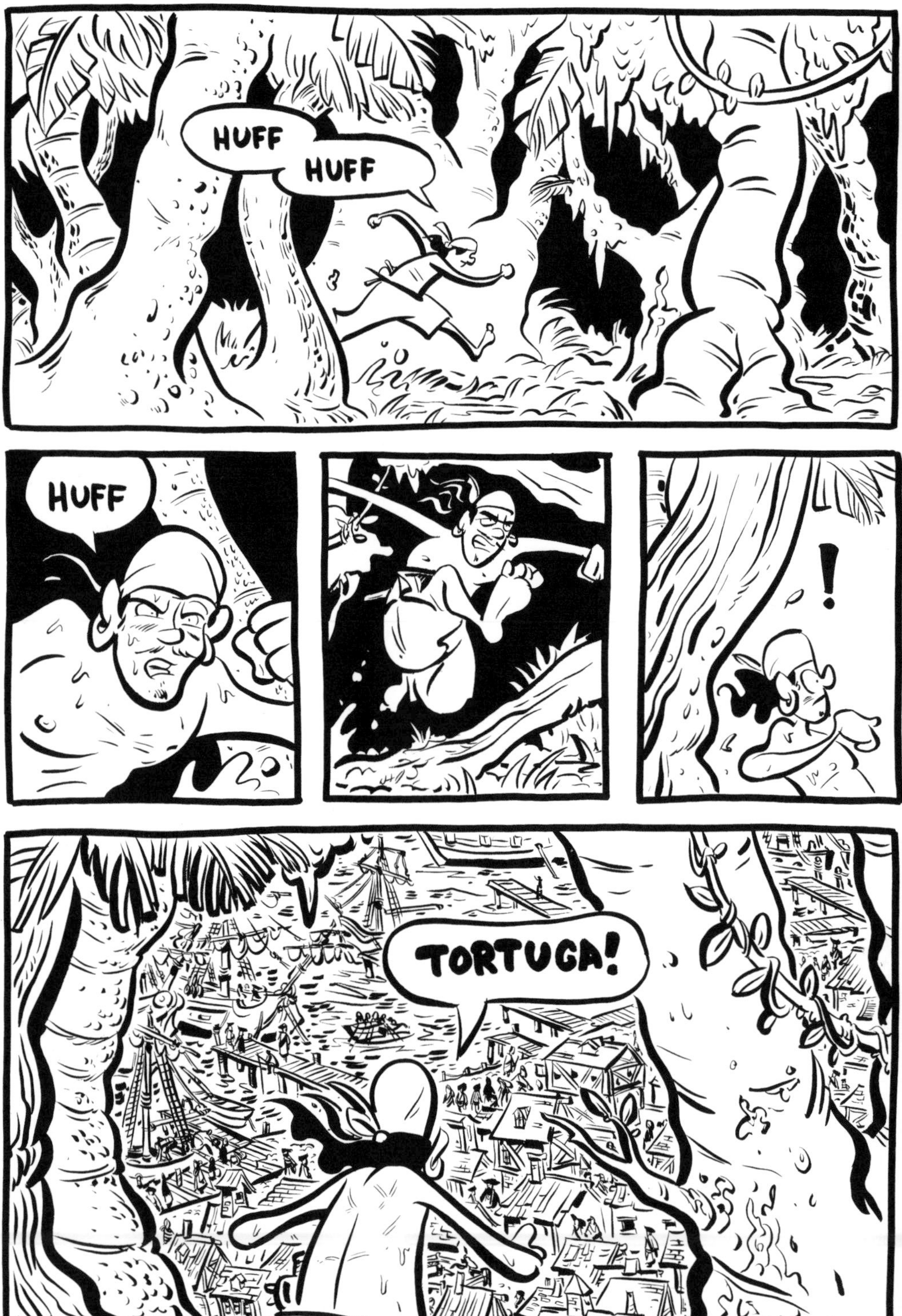
HUFF
HUFF
HUFF
!
TORTUGA!

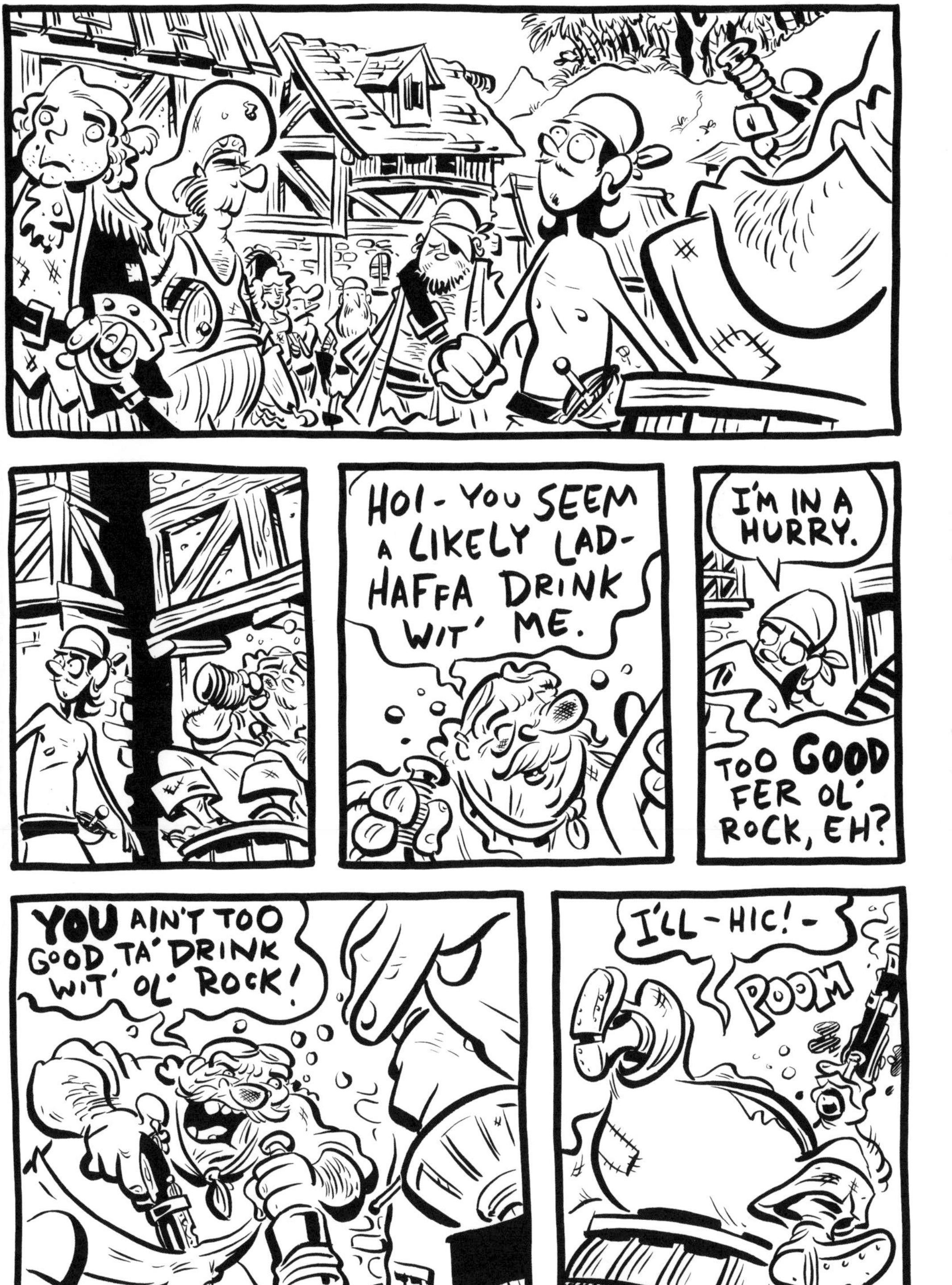

HOI - YOU SEEM A LIKELY LAD- HAFFA DRINK WIT' ME.
I'M IN A HURRY.
TOO GOOD FER OL' ROCK, EH?
YOU AIN'T TOO GOOD TA' DRINK WIT' OL' ROCK!
I'LL - HIC! -
POOM

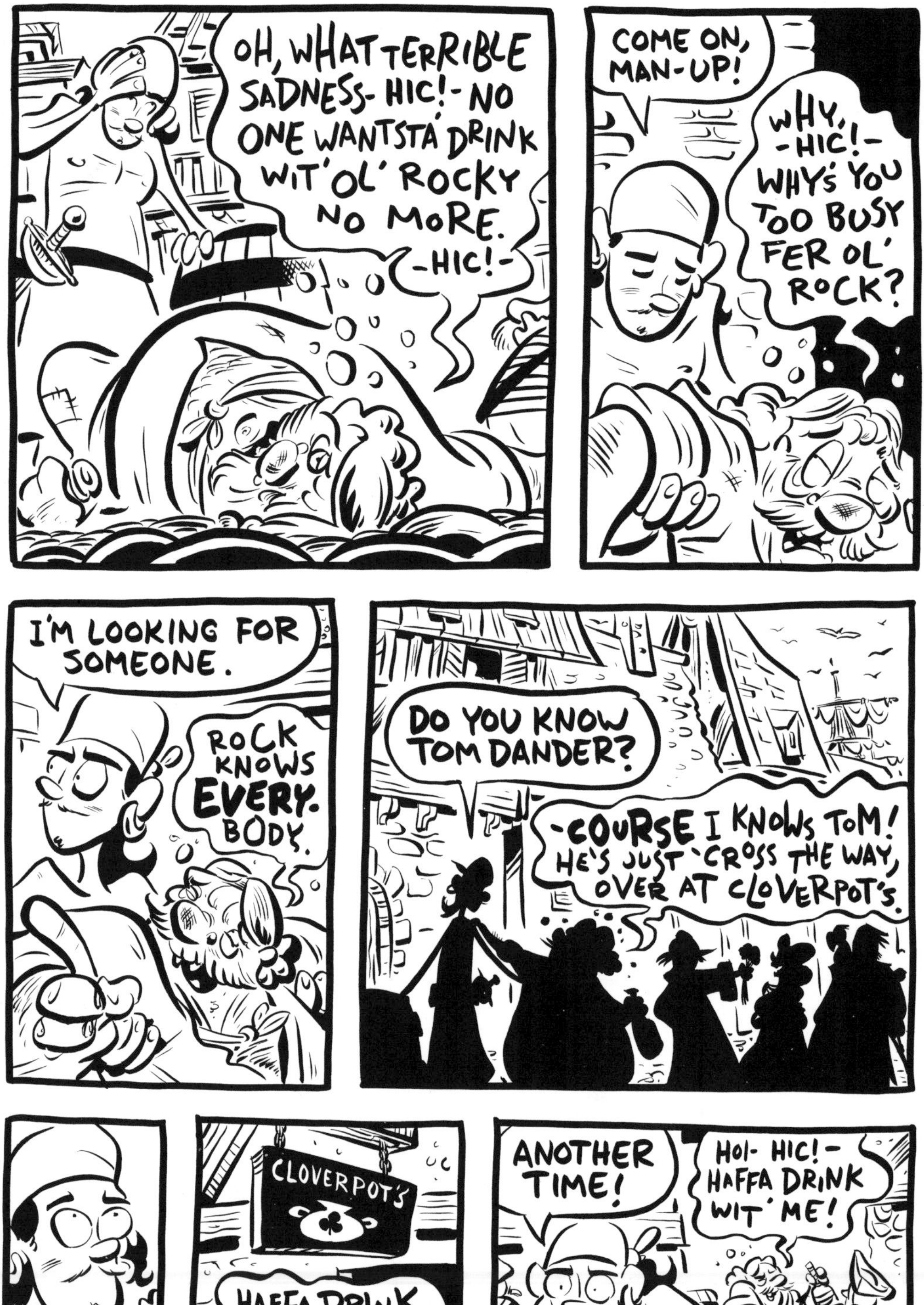
OH, WHAT TERRIBLE SADNESS- HIC! - NO ONE WANTSTA' DRINK WIT' OL' ROCKY NO MORE.
-HIC!-
COME ON, MAN-UP!
WHY, -HIC!- WHY'S YOU TOO BUSY FER OL' ROCK?
I'M LOOKING FOR SOMEONE.
ROCK KNOWS EVERY-BODY.
DO YOU KNOW TOM DANDER?
-COURSE I KNOWS TOM! HE'S JUST 'CROSS THE WAY, OVER AT CLOVERPOT'S.
CLOVERPOT'S
HAFFA DRINK WIT' ME.
ANOTHER TIME!
HOI- HIC! - HAFFA DRINK WIT' ME!

HOLD, THERE.

THIS HERE BE A **CHOICE** ESTABLISHMENT, AND **YOU** LOOK THE PAUPER.

'LESS YE'R CARRYIN' PURSE, FIND YER LIBATIONS ELSEWHERES.

I JUST NEED TO SPEAK WITH SOMEONE INSIDE.

I THINK NOT.

MOVE ALONG, LITTLE FRIEND, OR I'LL BREAK YER ARMS.

I'M NOT LEAVING.

ERACK

GOOD.

TOM DANDER—BE HE HERE?

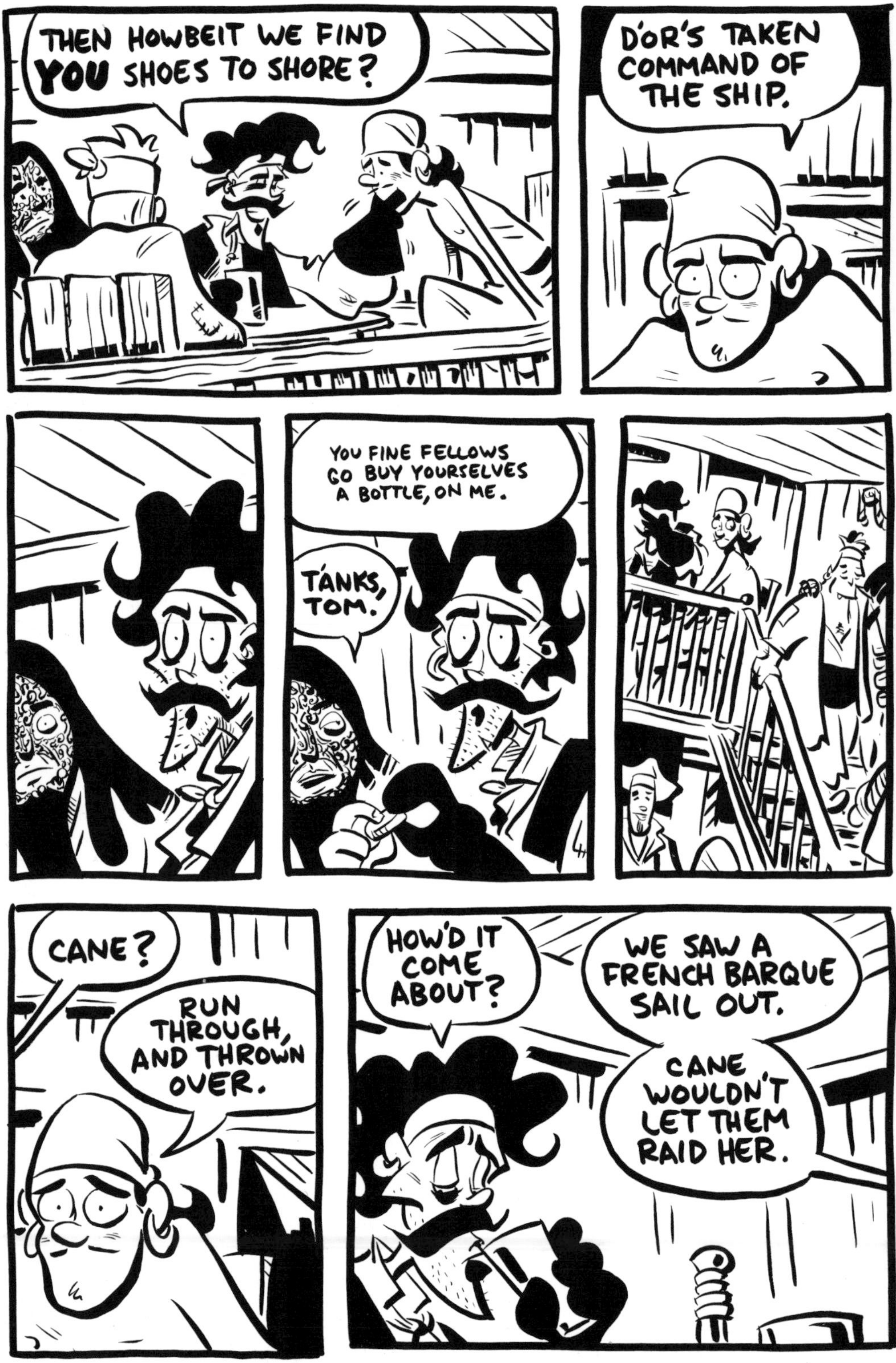
THEN HOWBEIT WE FIND **YOU** SHOES TO SHORE?
D'OR'S TAKEN COMMAND OF THE SHIP.
YOU FINE FELLOWS GO BUY YOURSELVES A BOTTLE, ON ME.
TANKS, TOM.
CANE?
RUN THROUGH, AND THROWN OVER.
HOW'D IT COME ABOUT?
WE SAW A FRENCH BARQUE SAIL OUT.
CANE WOULDN'T LET THEM RAID HER.

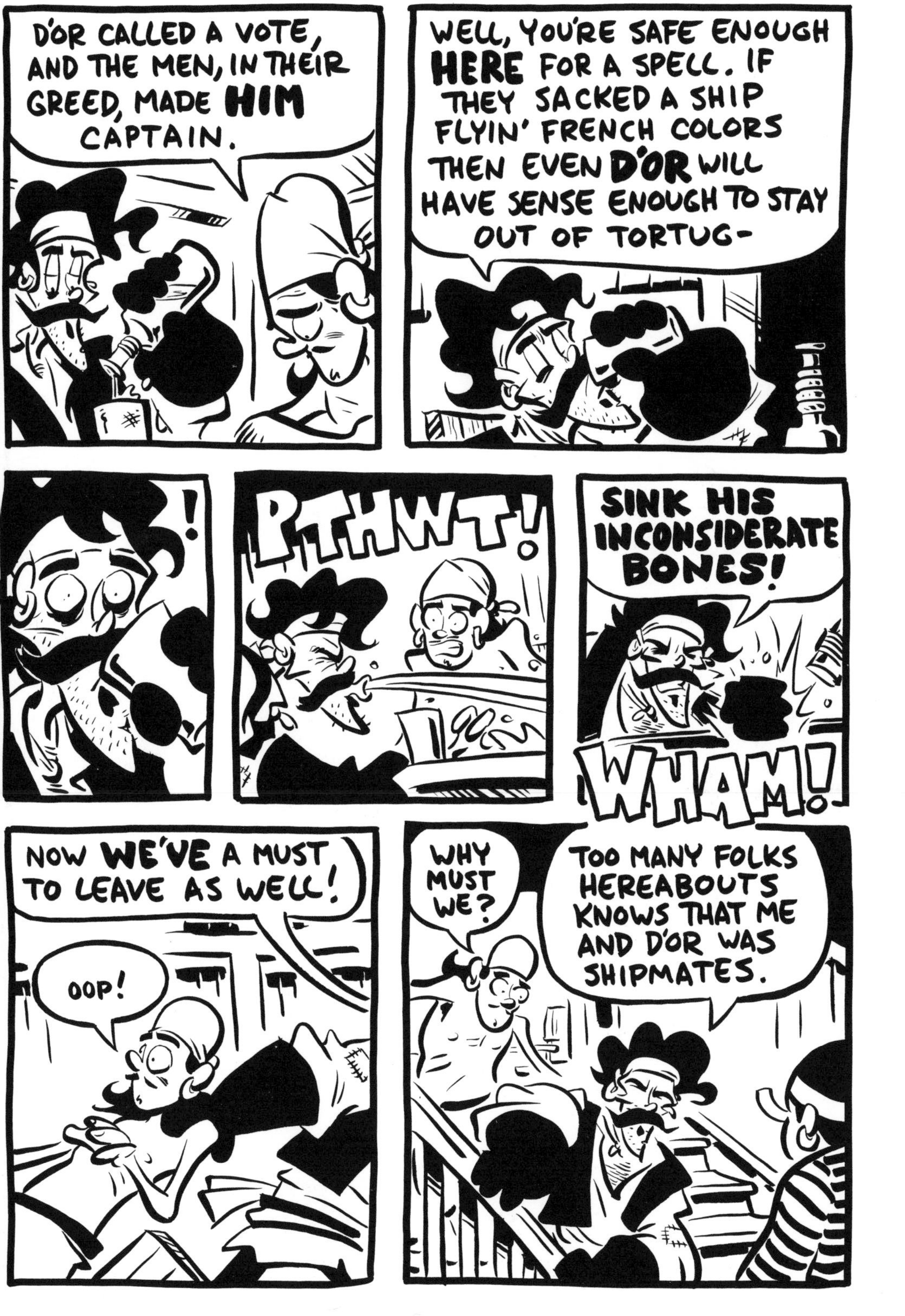
D'OR CALLED A VOTE, AND THE MEN, IN THEIR GREED, MADE HIM CAPTAIN.
WELL, YOU'RE SAFE ENOUGH HERE FOR A SPELL. IF THEY SACKED A SHIP FLYIN' FRENCH COLORS THEN EVEN D'OR WILL HAVE SENSE ENOUGH TO STAY OUT OF TORTUG-
!
PTHWT!
SINK HIS INCONSIDERATE BONES!
WHAM!
NOW WE'VE A MUST TO LEAVE AS WELL!
OOP!
WHY MUST WE?
TOO MANY FOLKS HEREABOUTS KNOWS THAT ME AND D'OR WAS SHIPMATES.

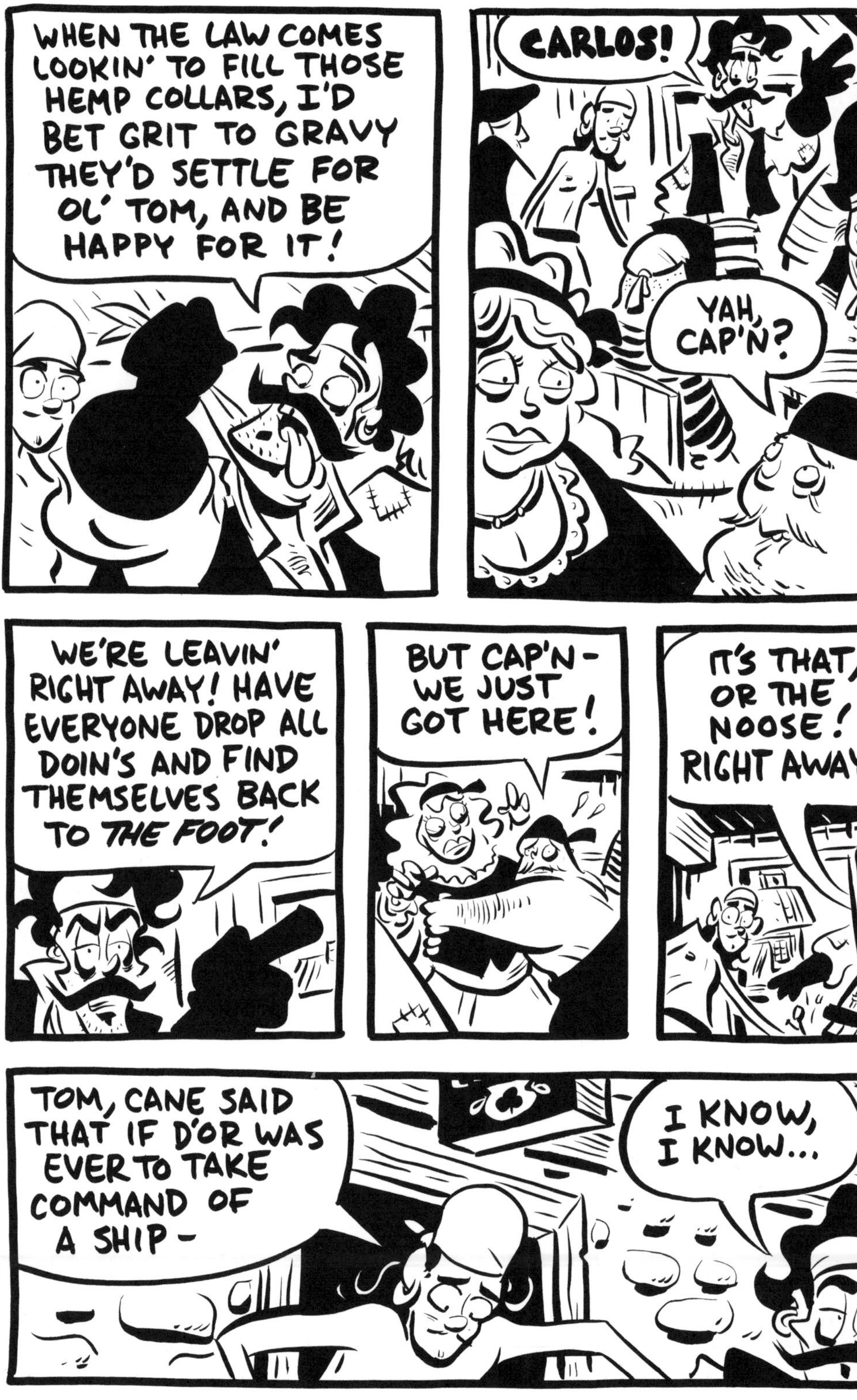
WHEN THE LAW COMES LOOKIN' TO FILL THOSE HEMP COLLARS, I'D BET GRIT TO GRAVY THEY'D SETTLE FOR OL' TOM, AND BE HAPPY FOR IT!
CARLOS!
YAH, CAP'N?
WE'RE LEAVIN' RIGHT AWAY! HAVE EVERYONE DROP ALL DOIN'S AND FIND THEMSELVES BACK TO *THE FOOT*!
BUT CAP'N- WE JUST GOT HERE!
IT'S THAT, OR THE NOOSE! RIGHT AWAY!
TOM, CANE SAID THAT IF D'OR WAS EVER TO TAKE COMMAND OF A SHIP-
I KNOW, I KNOW...

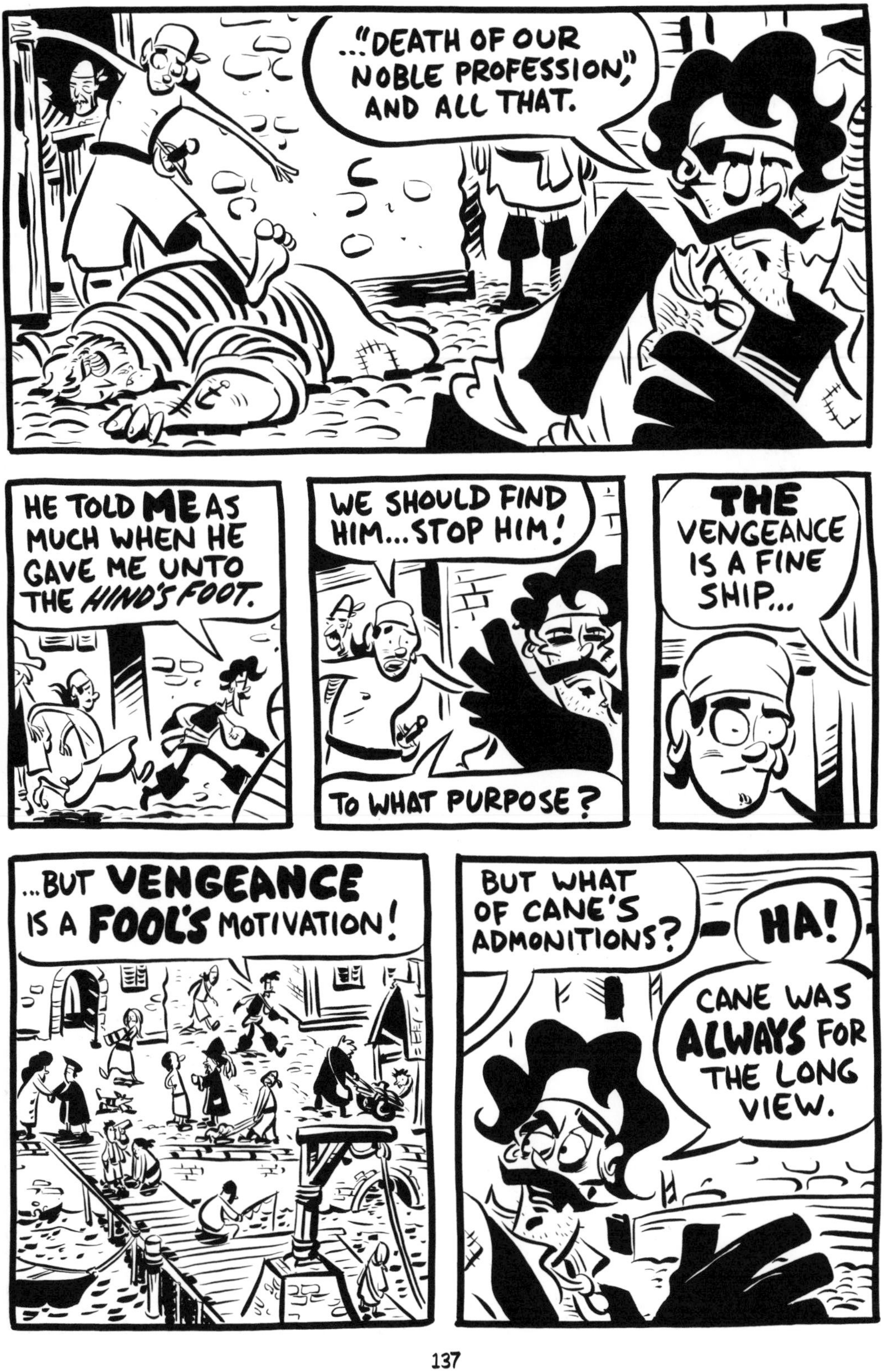
..."DEATH OF OUR NOBLE PROFESSION," AND ALL THAT.
HE TOLD ME AS MUCH WHEN HE GAVE ME UNTO THE HIND'S FOOT.
WE SHOULD FIND HIM...STOP HIM!
TO WHAT PURPOSE?
THE VENGEANCE IS A FINE SHIP...
...BUT VENGEANCE IS A FOOL'S MOTIVATION!
BUT WHAT OF CANE'S ADMONITIONS?
HA!
CANE WAS ALWAYS FOR THE LONG VIEW.

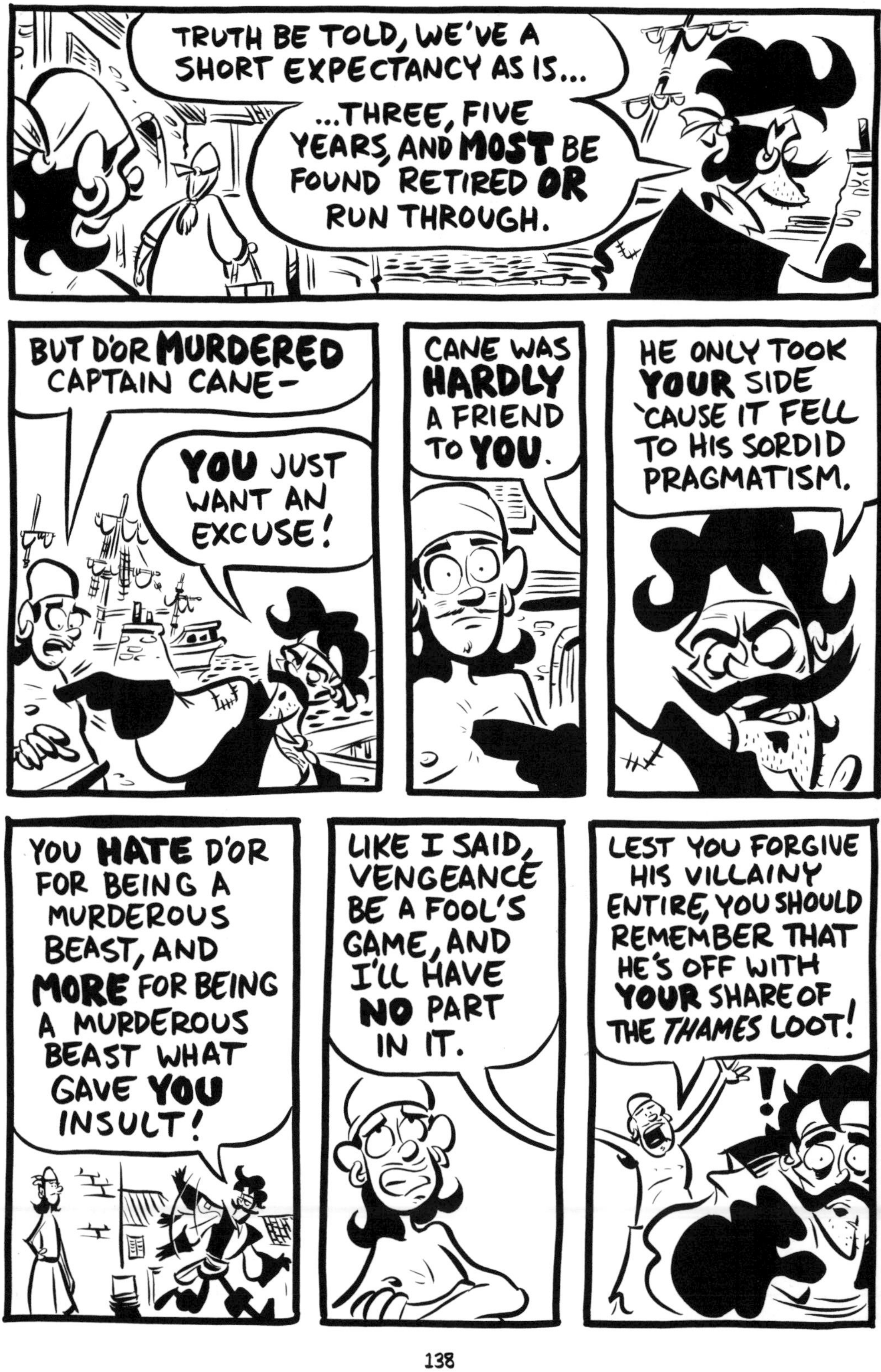
TRUTH BE TOLD, WE'VE A SHORT EXPECTANCY AS IS...
...THREE, FIVE YEARS, AND **MOST** BE FOUND RETIRED **OR** RUN THROUGH.
BUT D'OR **MURDERED** CAPTAIN CANE–
YOU JUST WANT AN EXCUSE!
CANE WAS **HARDLY** A FRIEND TO **YOU**.
HE ONLY TOOK **YOUR** SIDE 'CAUSE IT FELL TO HIS SORDID PRAGMATISM.
YOU **HATE** D'OR FOR BEING A MURDEROUS BEAST, AND **MORE** FOR BEING A MURDEROUS BEAST WHAT GAVE **YOU** INSULT!
LIKE I SAID, VENGEANCE BE A FOOL'S GAME, AND I'LL HAVE **NO** PART IN IT.
LEST YOU FORGIVE HIS VILLAINY ENTIRE, YOU SHOULD REMEMBER THAT HE'S OFF WITH **YOUR** SHARE OF THE *THAMES* LOOT!
!

NEPTUNE'S NAVEL, HE **DOES** HAVE MY SHARE!

...**AND** WHATEVER THAT TRADER HAD CARRY!

YOU COULD ROLL IN RICHES **AND** CONTENT THE FRENCH BY RIDDING THE SEAS OF HIM...

◎ξ☆!

SO WE'S CLEAR...

WE **AIN'T** GOIN' AFTER HIM TO SATISFY **YOUR** HONOR!

WE'RE GOIN' AFTER HIM FOR THE TREASURE **AND** TO INGRATIATE OURSELVES TO THOSE FLAGS WHAT WANT SEE HIM ENDED.

OF COURSE.

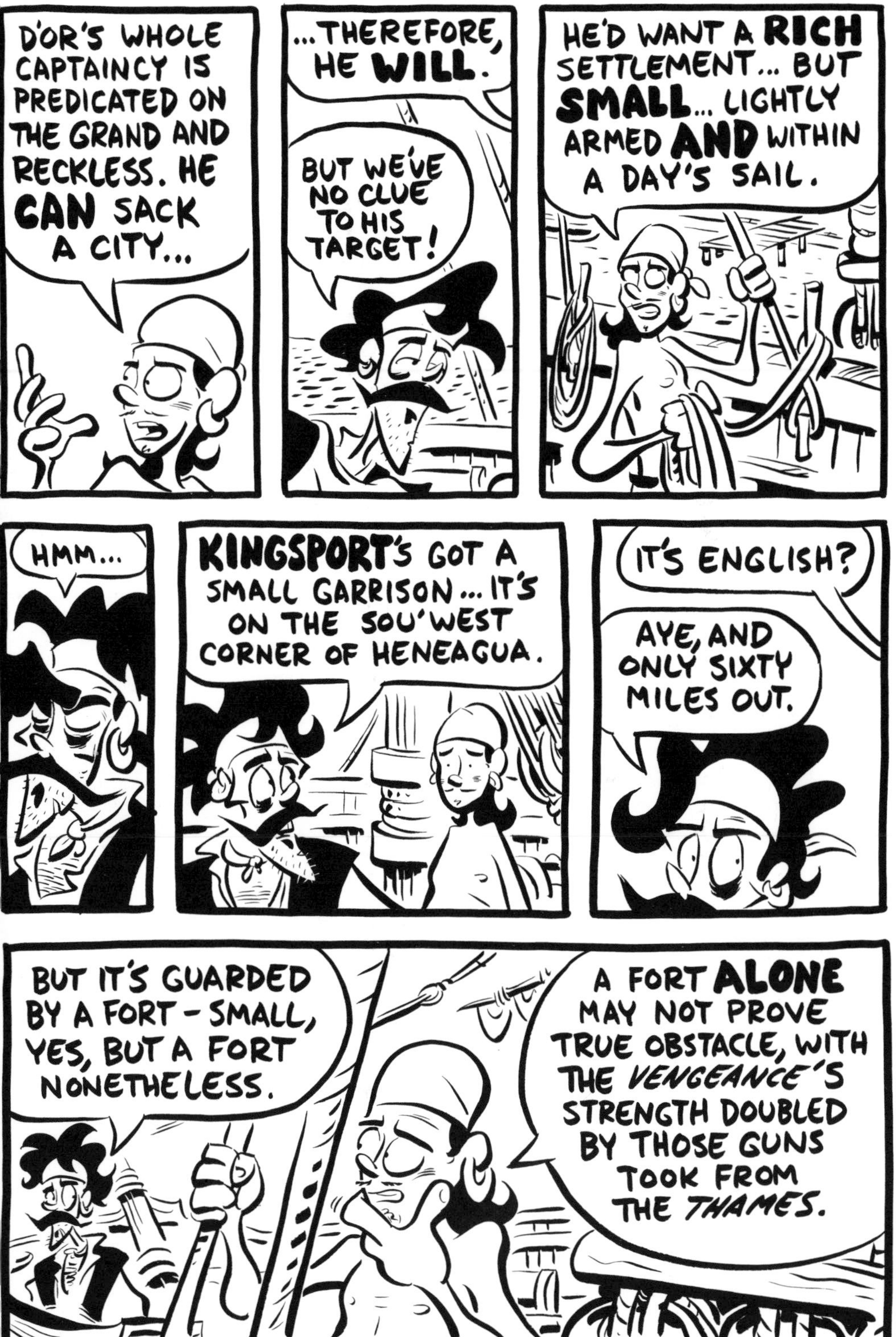
D'OR'S WHOLE CAPTAINCY IS PREDICATED ON THE GRAND AND RECKLESS. HE **CAN** SACK A CITY...
...THEREFORE, HE **WILL**.
BUT WE'VE NO CLUE TO HIS TARGET!
HE'D WANT A **RICH** SETTLEMENT... BUT **SMALL**... LIGHTLY ARMED **AND** WITHIN A DAY'S SAIL.
HMM...
KINGSPORT'S GOT A SMALL GARRISON... IT'S ON THE SOU'WEST CORNER OF HENEAGUA.
IT'S ENGLISH?
AYE, AND ONLY SIXTY MILES OUT.
BUT IT'S GUARDED BY A FORT - SMALL, YES, BUT A FORT NONETHELESS.
A FORT **ALONE** MAY NOT PROVE TRUE OBSTACLE, WITH THE *VENGEANCE*'S STRENGTH DOUBLED BY THOSE GUNS TOOK FROM THE *THAMES*.

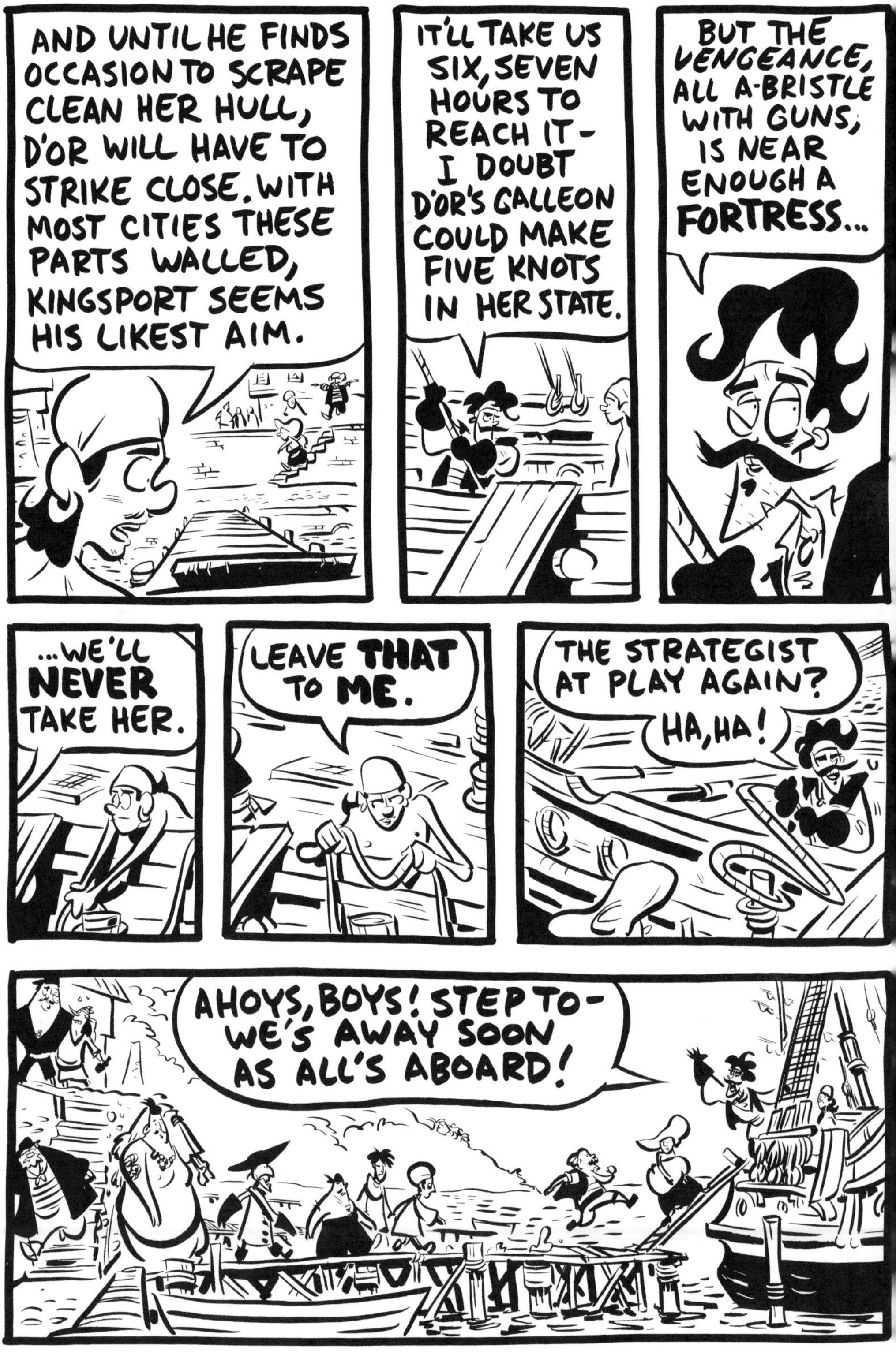
AND UNTIL HE FINDS OCCASION TO SCRAPE CLEAN HER HULL, D'OR WILL HAVE TO STRIKE CLOSE. WITH MOST CITIES THESE PARTS WALLED, KINGSPORT SEEMS HIS LIKEST AIM.
IT'LL TAKE US SIX, SEVEN HOURS TO REACH IT - I DOUBT D'OR'S GALLEON COULD MAKE FIVE KNOTS IN HER STATE.
BUT THE *VENGEANCE*, ALL A-BRISTLE WITH GUNS, IS NEAR ENOUGH A **FORTRESS**...
...WE'LL **NEVER** TAKE HER.
LEAVE **THAT** TO **ME**.
THE STRATEGIST AT PLAY AGAIN?
HA, HA!
AHOYS, BOYS! STEP TO - WE'S AWAY SOON AS ALL'S ABOARD!

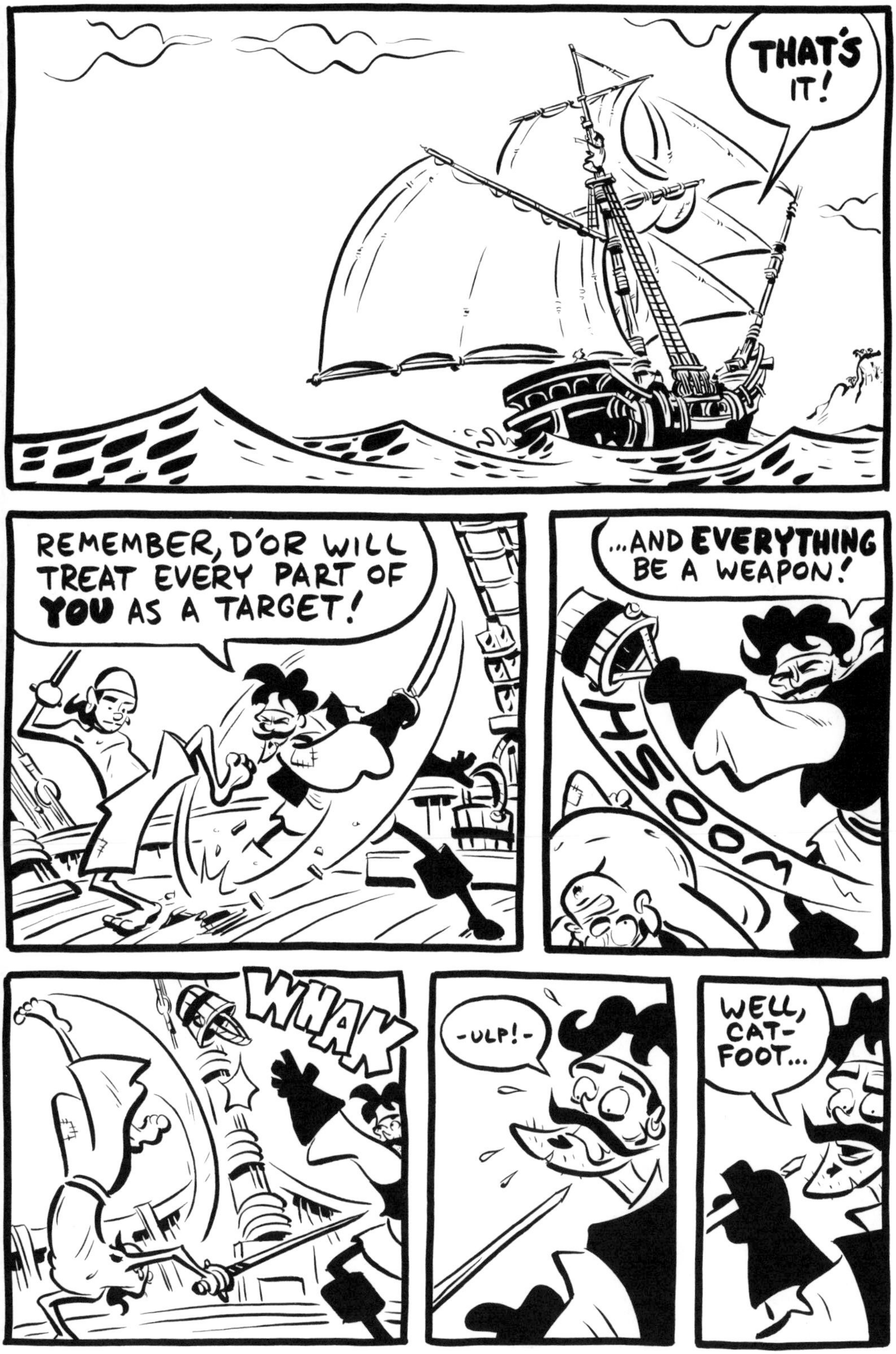
THAT'S IT!
REMEMBER, D'OR WILL TREAT EVERY PART OF YOU AS A TARGET!
...AND EVERYTHING BE A WEAPON!
SHOOOM
WHAK
-ULP!-
WELL, CAT-FOOT...

...SEEMS YOU'RE SET TO SET-TO!

HA!

CAP'N!

WE'S NEAR SIGHT O' THE FORT!

BRING HER IN NEAR THE SHOALS, MR. HUBER.

AYE, SIR!

HERE THEY BE...

...THE FINEST CLOTHES ABOARD, AS ASKED FER.

FUNNY... MOST TIMES IT'S **ME** ACCUSED OF VANITY.

IT'S NOT VANITY. THE GOVERNOR IS FAR MORE LIKE TO MEET A RICH BUSINESSMAN THAN HE IS A SEA ROGUE.

I **STILL** AIN'T KEEN ON TURNING TO THE CROWN'S MINIONS.

AS YOU SAID...

...**WE** CAN'T TAKE THE VENGEANCE, BUT WITH THE FORT, IN CONTROL OF THE ENGAGEMENT...

WELL? HOW DO I LOOK?

HMF!

HA! HEE HEE!

HOO HOO HAHA!

HA! HA!

HEH HEH HEH!

ONCE WE'VE ANCHORED, WE'LL CARRY A BOAT THROUGH THE TREELINE.

HEH, HEE! RIGHT.

WE'LL SEND YOU DOWN WITH A SMALL -HA!- CREW...

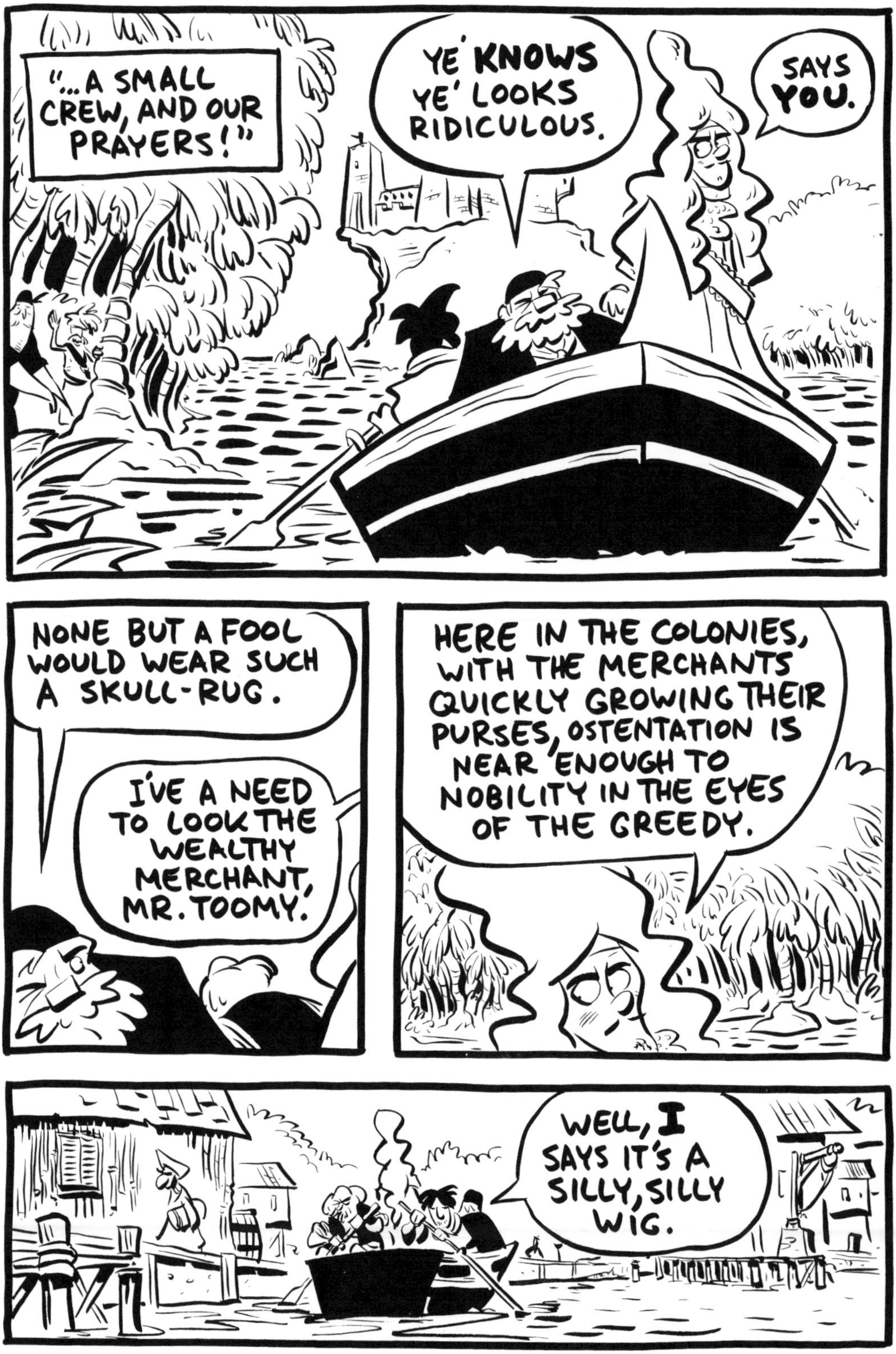
"...A SMALL CREW, AND OUR PRAYERS!"
YE' KNOWS YE' LOOKS RIDICULOUS.
SAYS YOU.
NONE BUT A FOOL WOULD WEAR SUCH A SKULL-RUG.
I'VE A NEED TO LOOK THE WEALTHY MERCHANT, MR. TOOMY.
HERE IN THE COLONIES, WITH THE MERCHANTS QUICKLY GROWING THEIR PURSES, OSTENTATION IS NEAR ENOUGH TO NOBILITY IN THE EYES OF THE GREEDY.
WELL, I SAYS IT'S A SILLY, SILLY WIG.

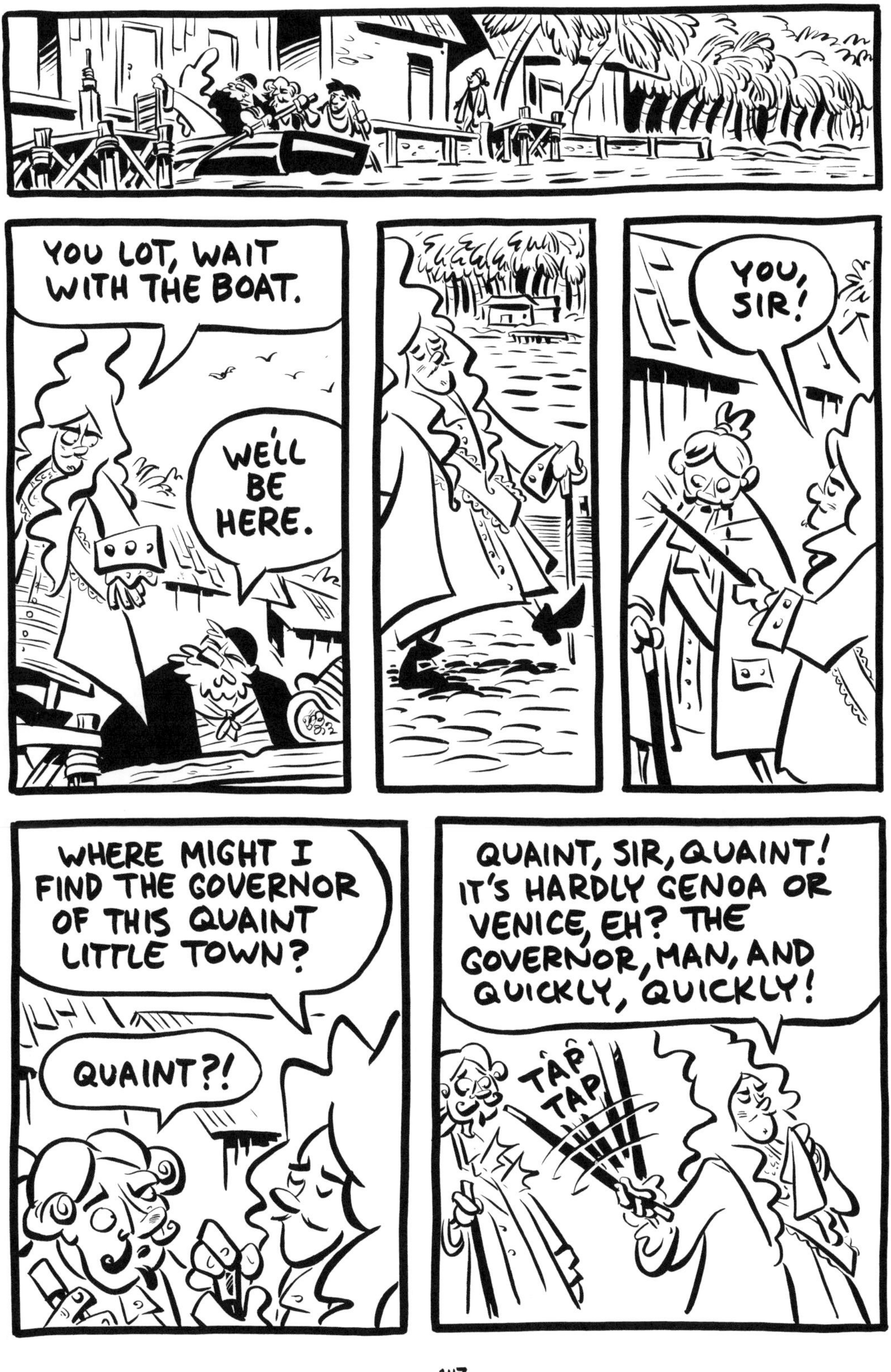
YOU LOT, WAIT WITH THE BOAT.
WE'LL BE HERE.
YOU, SIR!
WHERE MIGHT I FIND THE GOVERNOR OF THIS QUAINT LITTLE TOWN?
QUAINT?!
QUAINT, SIR, QUAINT! IT'S HARDLY GENOA OR VENICE, EH? THE GOVERNOR, MAN, AND QUICKLY, QUICKLY!
TAP TAP

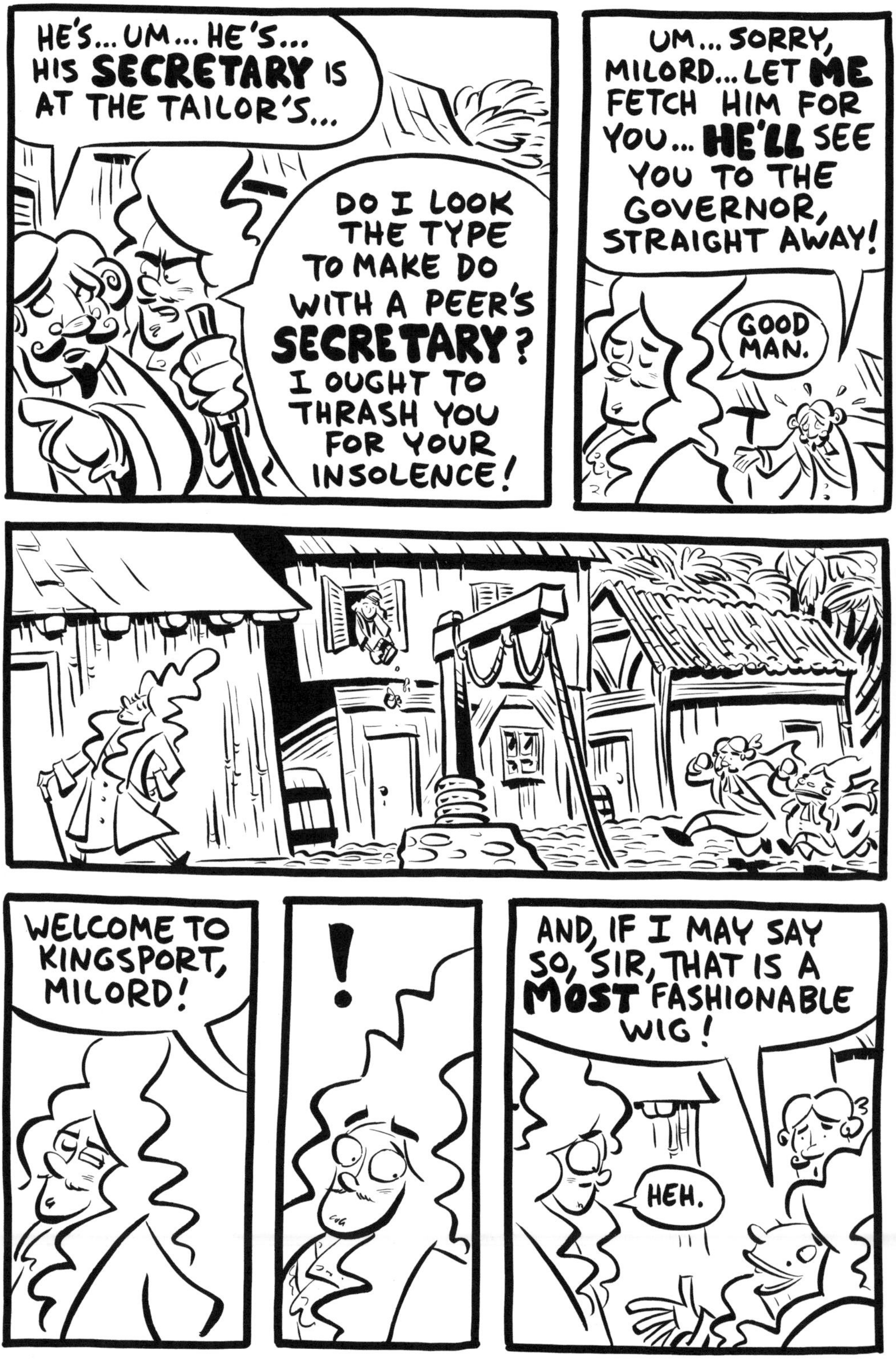
HE'S... UM... HE'S... HIS SECRETARY IS AT THE TAILOR'S...
DO I LOOK THE TYPE TO MAKE DO WITH A PEER'S SECRETARY? I OUGHT TO THRASH YOU FOR YOUR INSOLENCE!
UM... SORRY, MILORD... LET ME FETCH HIM FOR YOU... HE'LL SEE YOU TO THE GOVERNOR, STRAIGHT AWAY!
GOOD MAN.
WELCOME TO KINGSPORT, MILORD!
!
AND, IF I MAY SAY SO, SIR, THAT IS A MOST FASHIONABLE WIG!
HEH.

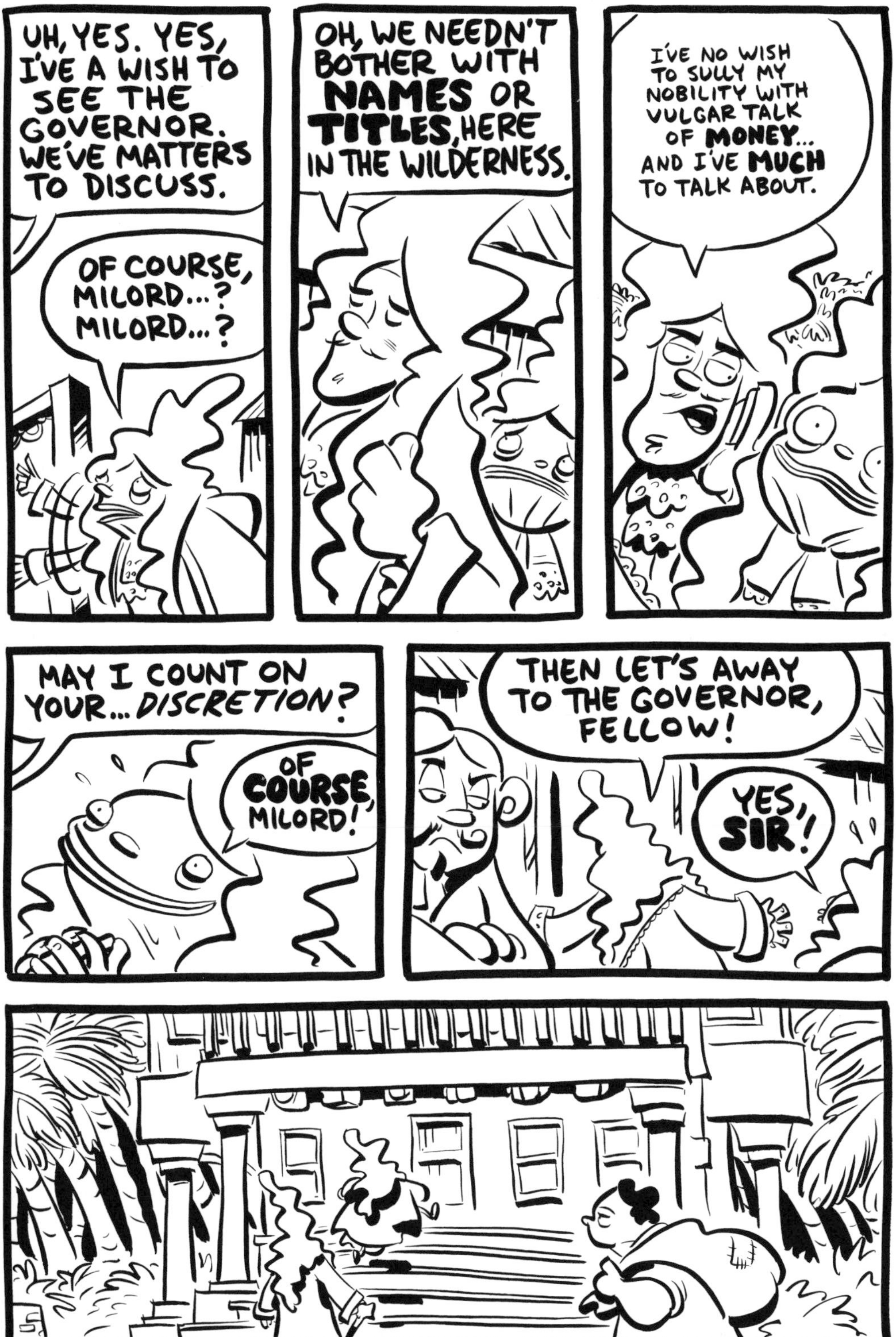
UH, YES. YES, I'VE A WISH TO SEE THE GOVERNOR. WE'VE MATTERS TO DISCUSS.
OF COURSE, MILORD...? MILORD...?
OH, WE NEEDN'T BOTHER WITH NAMES OR TITLES, HERE IN THE WILDERNESS.
I'VE NO WISH TO SULLY MY NOBILITY WITH VULGAR TALK OF MONEY... AND I'VE MUCH TO TALK ABOUT.
MAY I COUNT ON YOUR... DISCRETION?
OF COURSE, MILORD!
THEN LET'S AWAY TO THE GOVERNOR, FELLOW!
YES, SIR!

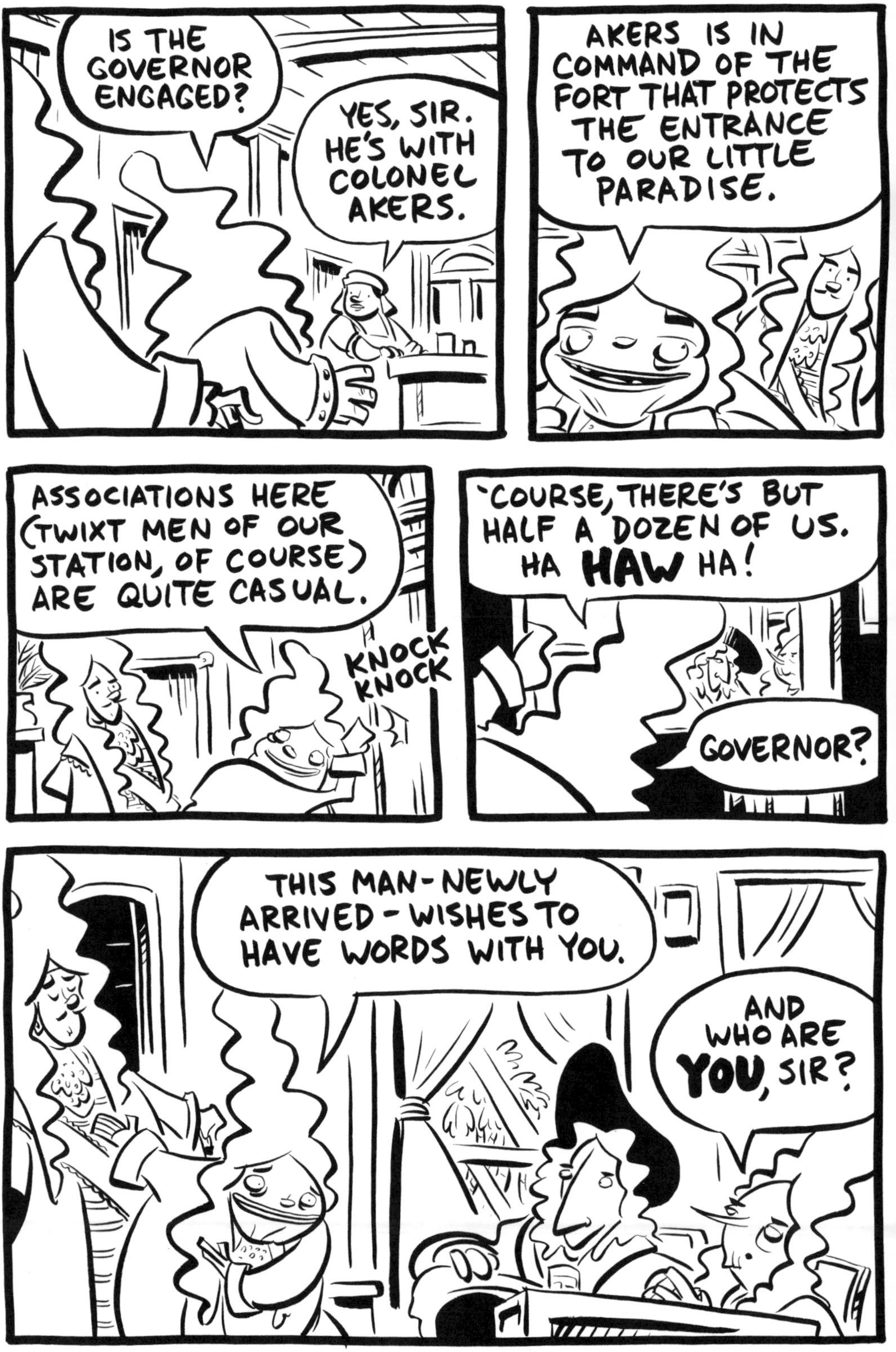
IS THE GOVERNOR ENGAGED?
YES, SIR. HE'S WITH COLONEL AKERS.
AKERS IS IN COMMAND OF THE FORT THAT PROTECTS THE ENTRANCE TO OUR LITTLE PARADISE.
ASSOCIATIONS HERE (TWIXT MEN OF OUR STATION, OF COURSE) ARE QUITE CASUAL.
KNOCK KNOCK
'COURSE, THERE'S BUT HALF A DOZEN OF US. HA HAW HA!
GOVERNOR?
THIS MAN-NEWLY ARRIVED-WISHES TO HAVE WORDS WITH YOU.
AND WHO ARE YOU, SIR?

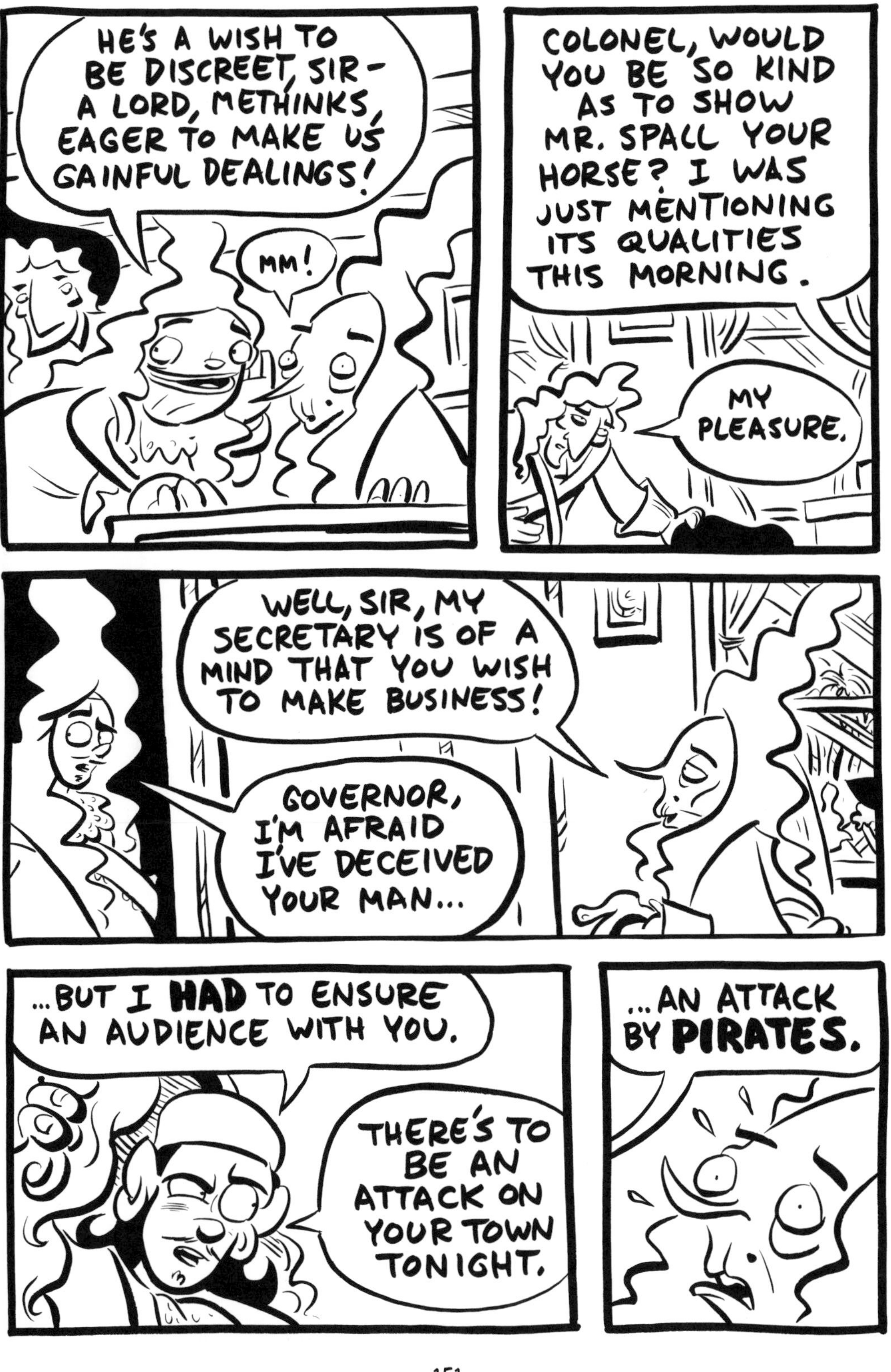
HE'S A WISH TO BE DISCREET, SIR- A LORD, METHINKS, EAGER TO MAKE US GAINFUL DEALINGS!
MM!
COLONEL, WOULD YOU BE SO KIND AS TO SHOW MR. SPALL YOUR HORSE? I WAS JUST MENTIONING ITS QUALITIES THIS MORNING.
MY PLEASURE.
WELL, SIR, MY SECRETARY IS OF A MIND THAT YOU WISH TO MAKE BUSINESS!
GOVERNOR, I'M AFRAID I'VE DECEIVED YOUR MAN...
...BUT I HAD TO ENSURE AN AUDIENCE WITH YOU.
THERE'S TO BE AN ATTACK ON YOUR TOWN TONIGHT.
...AN ATTACK BY PIRATES.

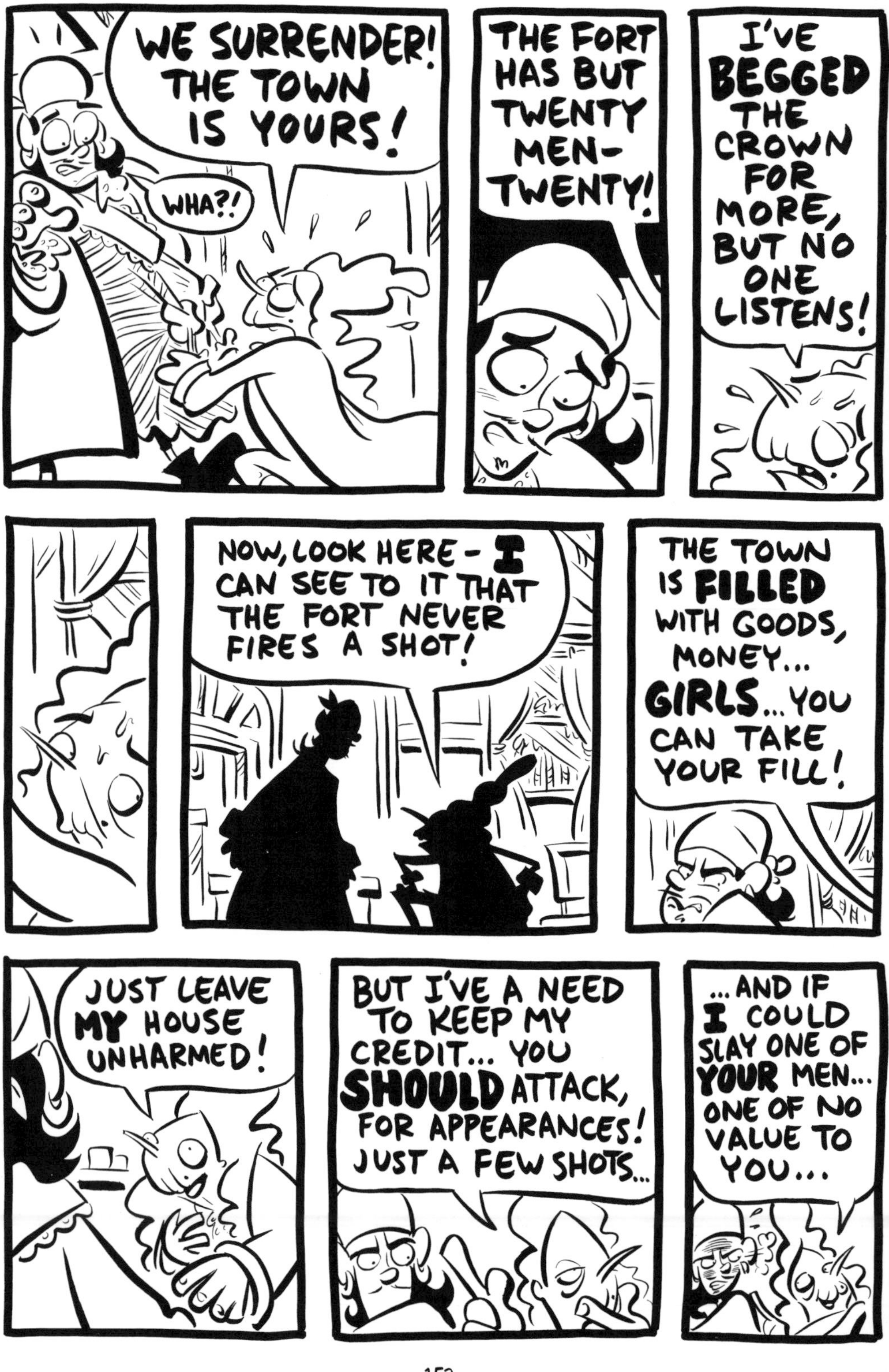
WE SURRENDER! THE TOWN IS YOURS!
WHA?!
THE FORT HAS BUT TWENTY MEN- TWENTY!
I'VE **BEGGED** THE CROWN FOR MORE, BUT NO ONE LISTENS!
NOW, LOOK HERE - **I** CAN SEE TO IT THAT THE FORT NEVER FIRES A SHOT!
THE TOWN IS **FILLED** WITH GOODS, MONEY... **GIRLS**... YOU CAN TAKE YOUR FILL!
JUST LEAVE **MY** HOUSE UNHARMED!
BUT I'VE A NEED TO KEEP MY CREDIT... YOU **SHOULD** ATTACK, FOR APPEARANCES! JUST A FEW SHOTS...
...AND IF **I** COULD SLAY ONE OF **YOUR** MEN... ONE OF NO VALUE TO YOU...

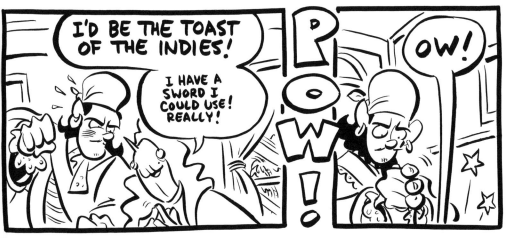

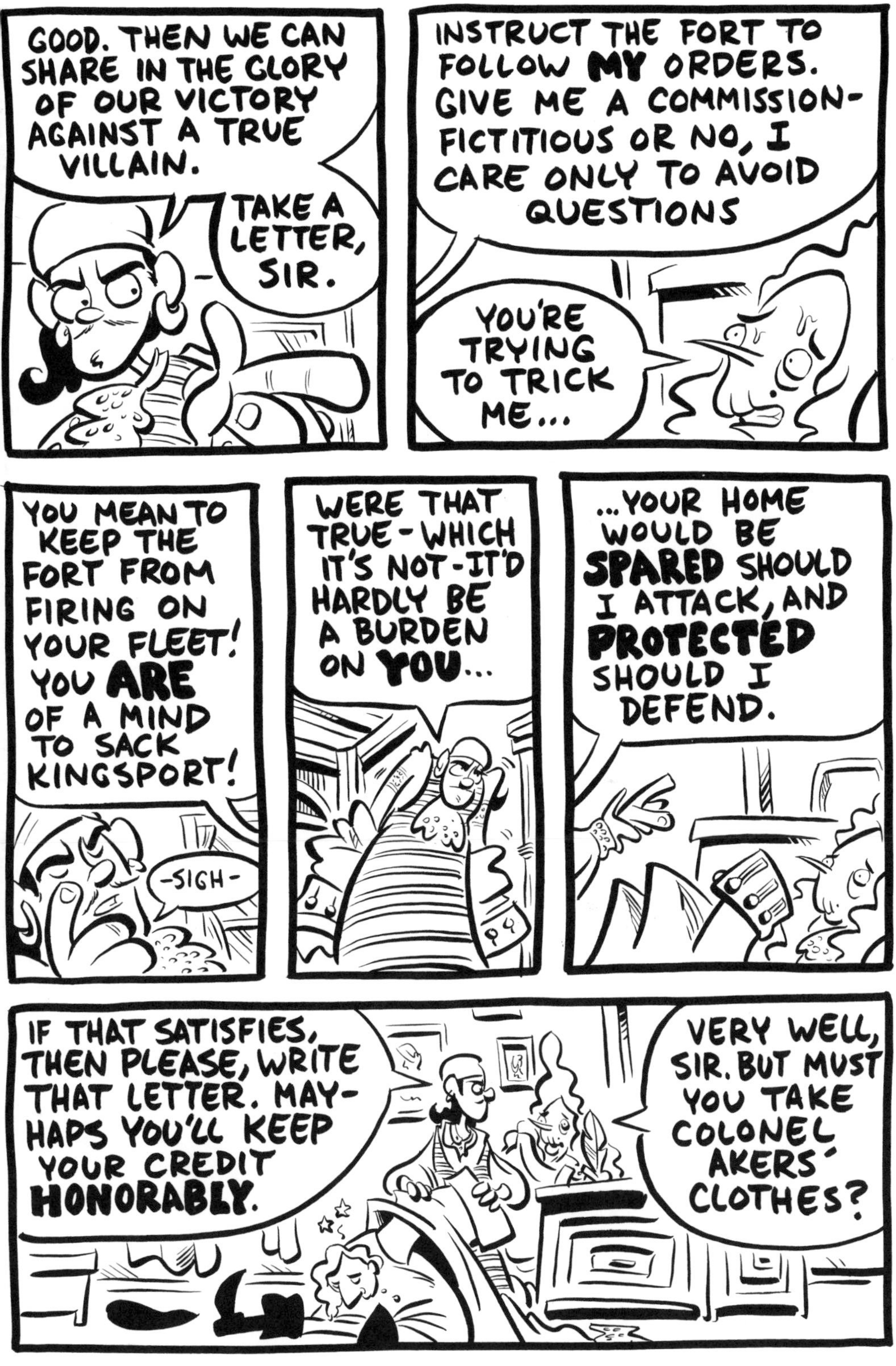
GOOD. THEN WE CAN SHARE IN THE GLORY OF OUR VICTORY AGAINST A TRUE VILLAIN.
TAKE A LETTER, SIR.
INSTRUCT THE FORT TO FOLLOW **MY** ORDERS. GIVE ME A COMMISSION- FICTITIOUS OR NO, I CARE ONLY TO AVOID QUESTIONS
YOU'RE TRYING TO TRICK ME...
YOU MEAN TO KEEP THE FORT FROM FIRING ON YOUR FLEET! YOU **ARE** OF A MIND TO SACK KINGSPORT!
-SIGH-
WERE THAT TRUE- WHICH IT'S NOT- IT'D HARDLY BE A BURDEN ON **YOU**...
...YOUR HOME WOULD BE **SPARED** SHOULD I ATTACK, AND **PROTECTED** SHOULD I DEFEND.
IF THAT SATISFIES, THEN PLEASE, WRITE THAT LETTER. MAY- HAPS YOU'LL KEEP YOUR CREDIT **HONORABLY**.
VERY WELL, SIR. BUT MUST YOU TAKE COLONEL AKERS' CLOTHES?

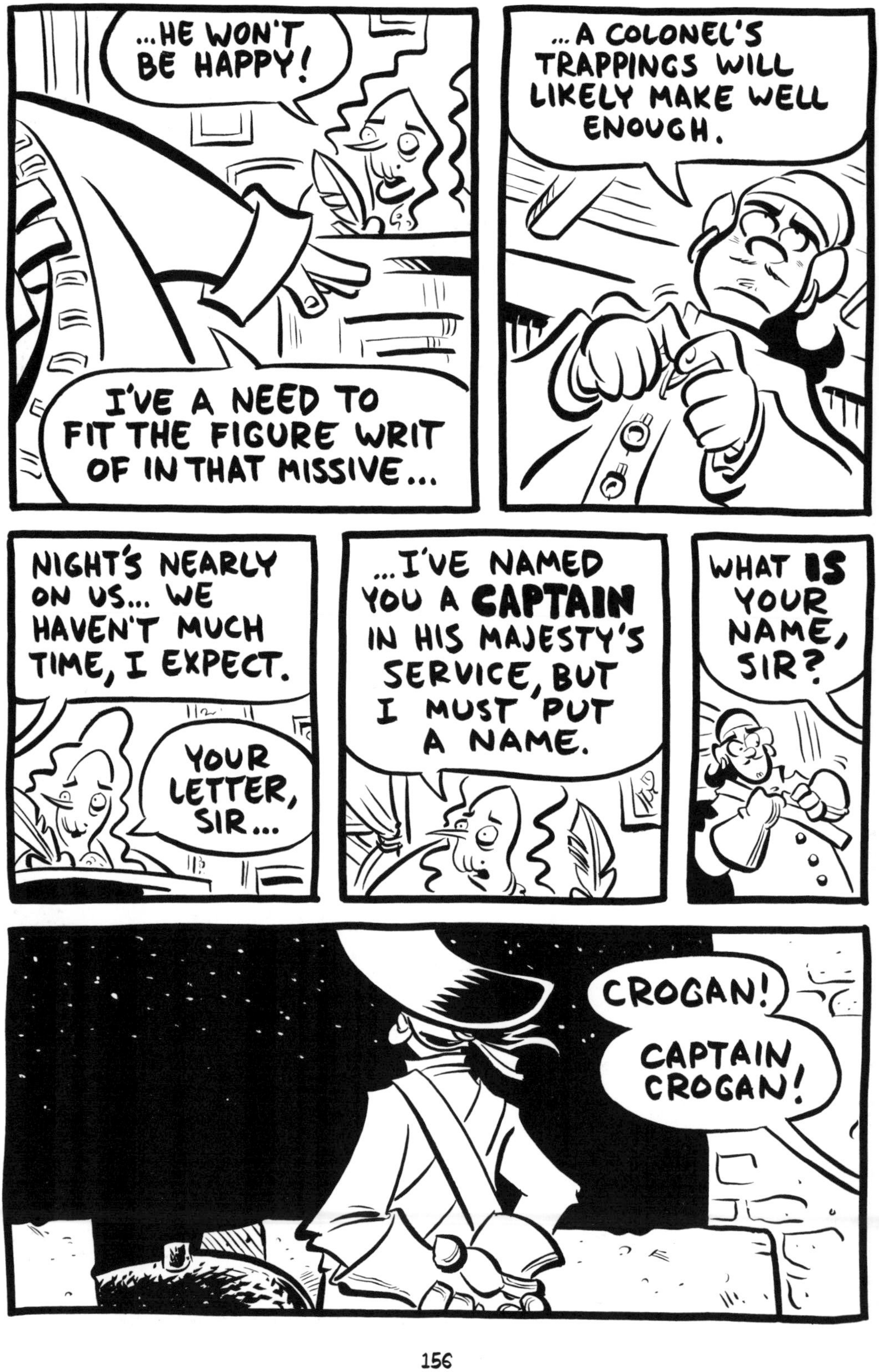
...HE WON'T BE HAPPY!
I'VE A NEED TO FIT THE FIGURE WRIT OF IN THAT MISSIVE...
...A COLONEL'S TRAPPINGS WILL LIKELY MAKE WELL ENOUGH.
NIGHT'S NEARLY ON US... WE HAVEN'T MUCH TIME, I EXPECT.
YOUR LETTER, SIR...
...I'VE NAMED YOU A **CAPTAIN** IN HIS MAJESTY'S SERVICE, BUT I MUST PUT A NAME.
WHAT **IS** YOUR NAME, SIR?
CROGAN!
CAPTAIN, CROGAN!

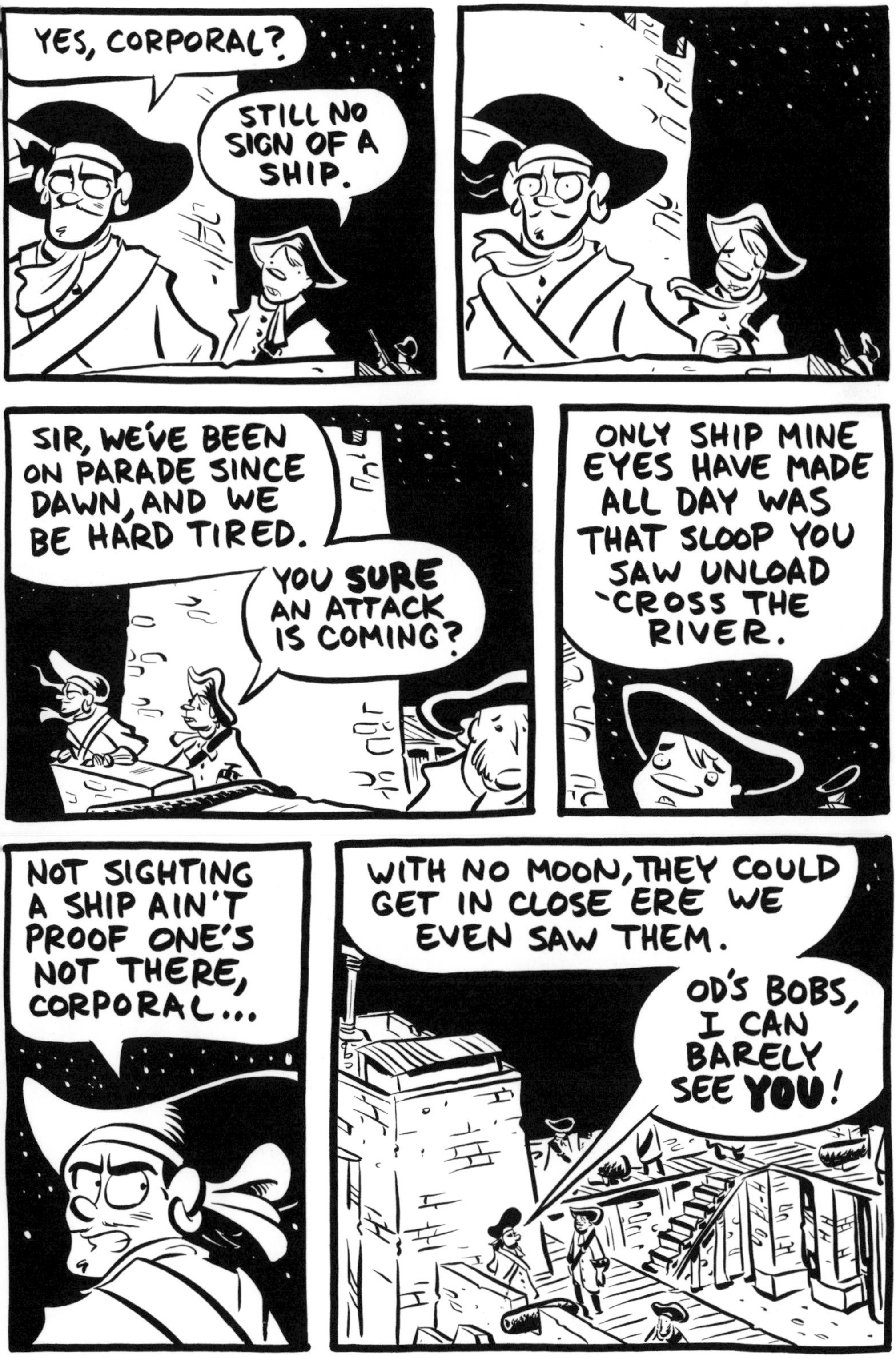
YES, CORPORAL?
STILL NO SIGN OF A SHIP.
SIR, WE'VE BEEN ON PARADE SINCE DAWN, AND WE BE HARD TIRED.
YOU **SURE** AN ATTACK IS COMING?
ONLY SHIP MINE EYES HAVE MADE ALL DAY WAS THAT SLOOP YOU SAW UNLOAD 'CROSS THE RIVER.
NOT SIGHTING A SHIP AIN'T PROOF ONE'S NOT THERE, CORPORAL...
WITH NO MOON, THEY COULD GET IN CLOSE ERE WE EVEN SAW THEM.
OD'S BOBS, I CAN BARELY SEE **YOU**!

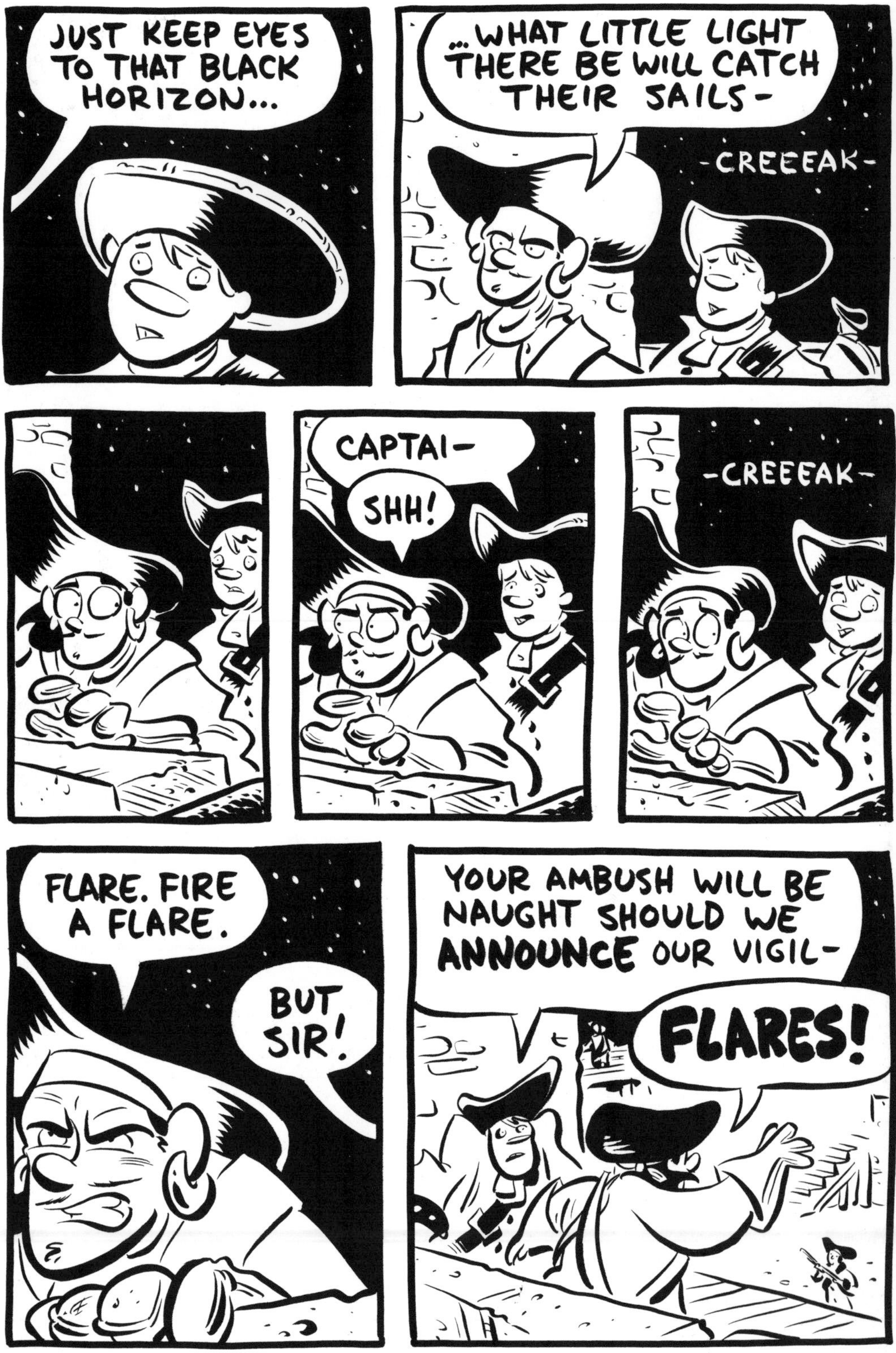
JUST KEEP EYES TO THAT BLACK HORIZON...
...WHAT LITTLE LIGHT THERE BE WILL CATCH THEIR SAILS-
-CREEEAK-
CAPTAI-
SHH!
-CREEEAK-
FLARE. FIRE A FLARE.
BUT, SIR!
YOUR AMBUSH WILL BE NAUGHT SHOULD WE ANNOUNCE OUR VIGIL-
FLARES!

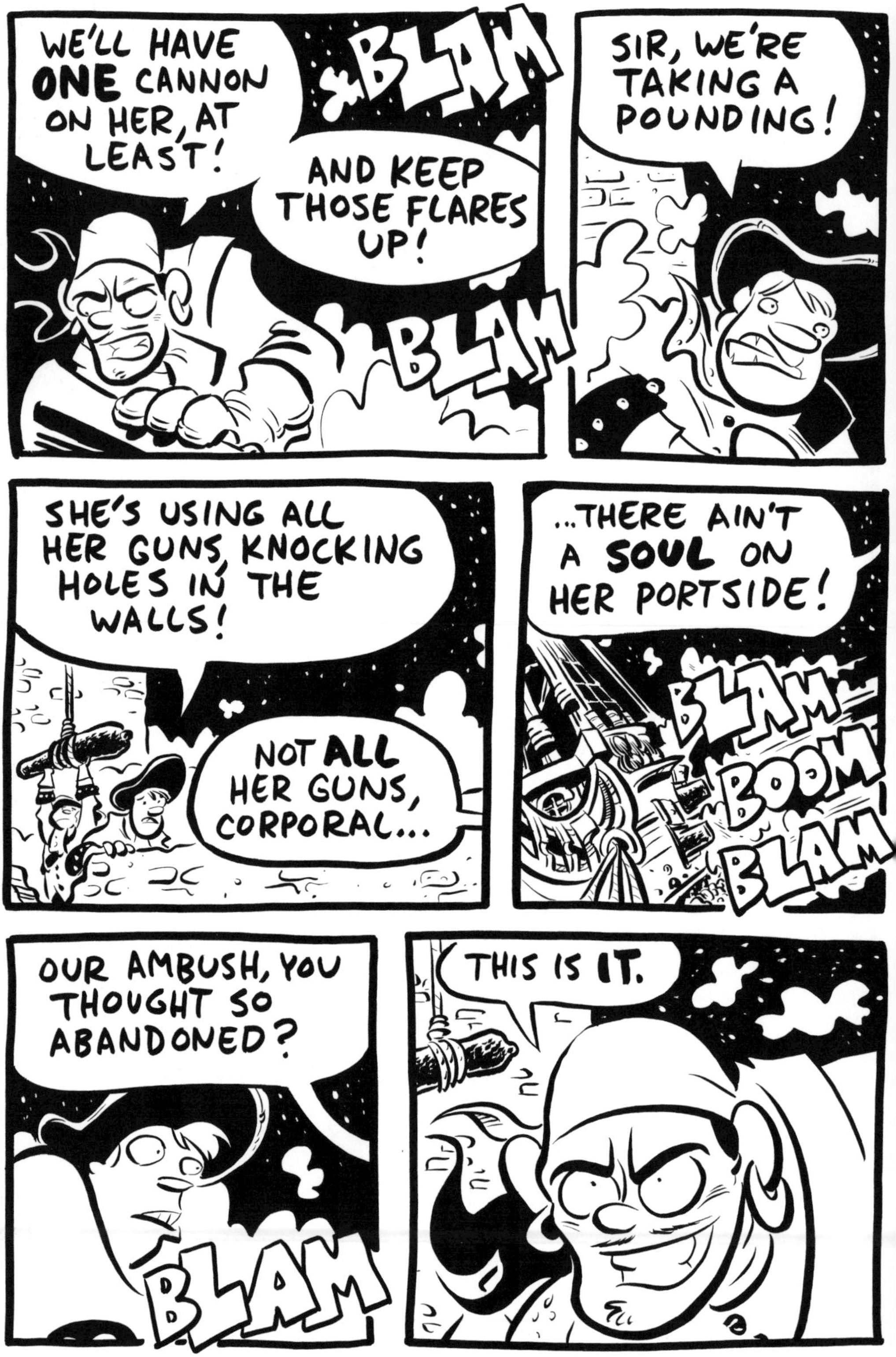
WE'LL HAVE ONE CANNON ON HER, AT LEAST!
BLAM
AND KEEP THOSE FLARES UP!
BLAM
SIR, WE'RE TAKING A POUNDING!
SHE'S USING ALL HER GUNS, KNOCKING HOLES IN THE WALLS!
NOT ALL HER GUNS, CORPORAL...
...THERE AIN'T A SOUL ON HER PORTSIDE!
BLAM
BOOM
BLAM
OUR AMBUSH, YOU THOUGHT SO ABANDONED?
BLAM
THIS IS IT.

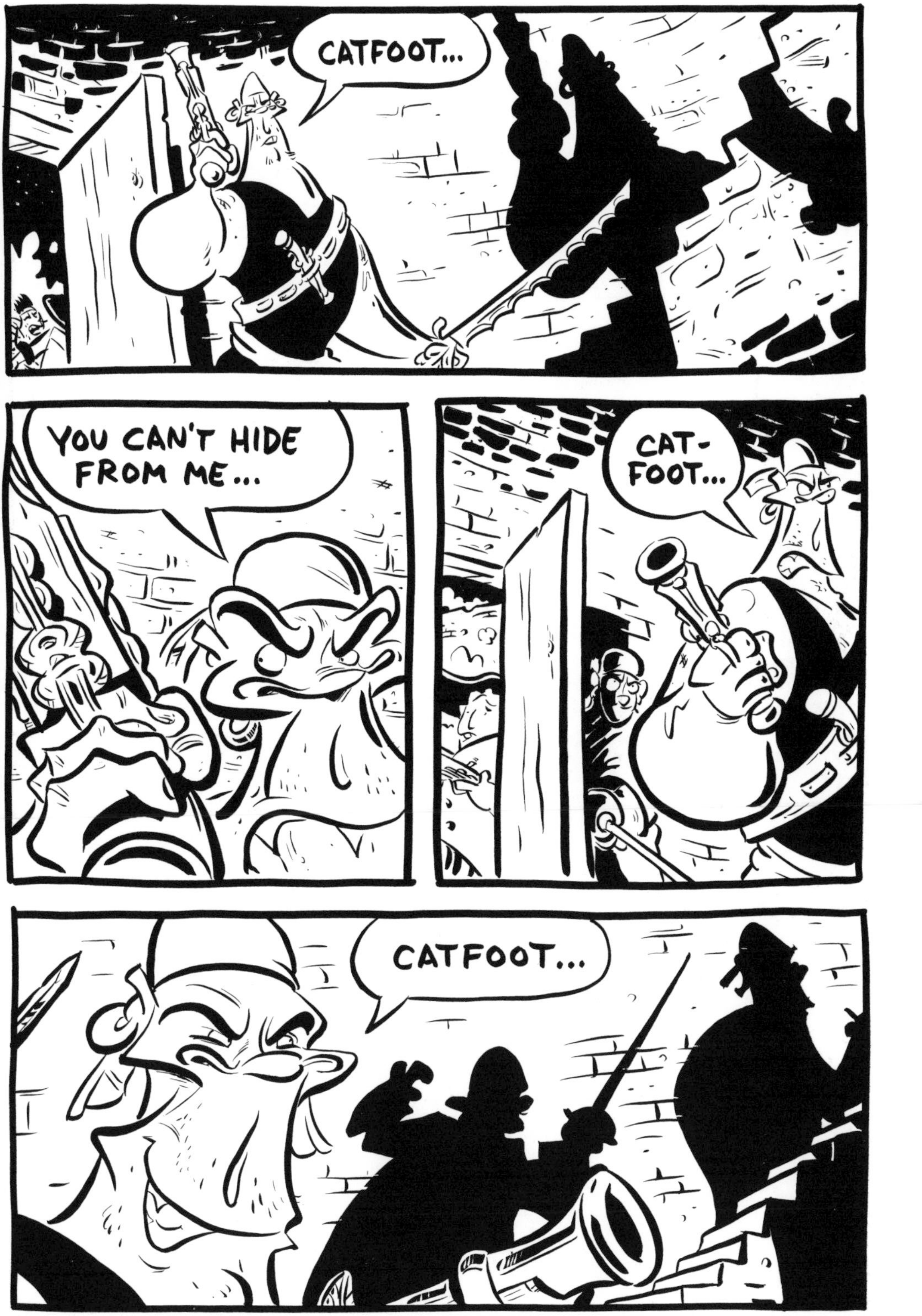
CATFOOT...
YOU CAN'T HIDE FROM ME...
CAT-FOOT...
CATFOOT...

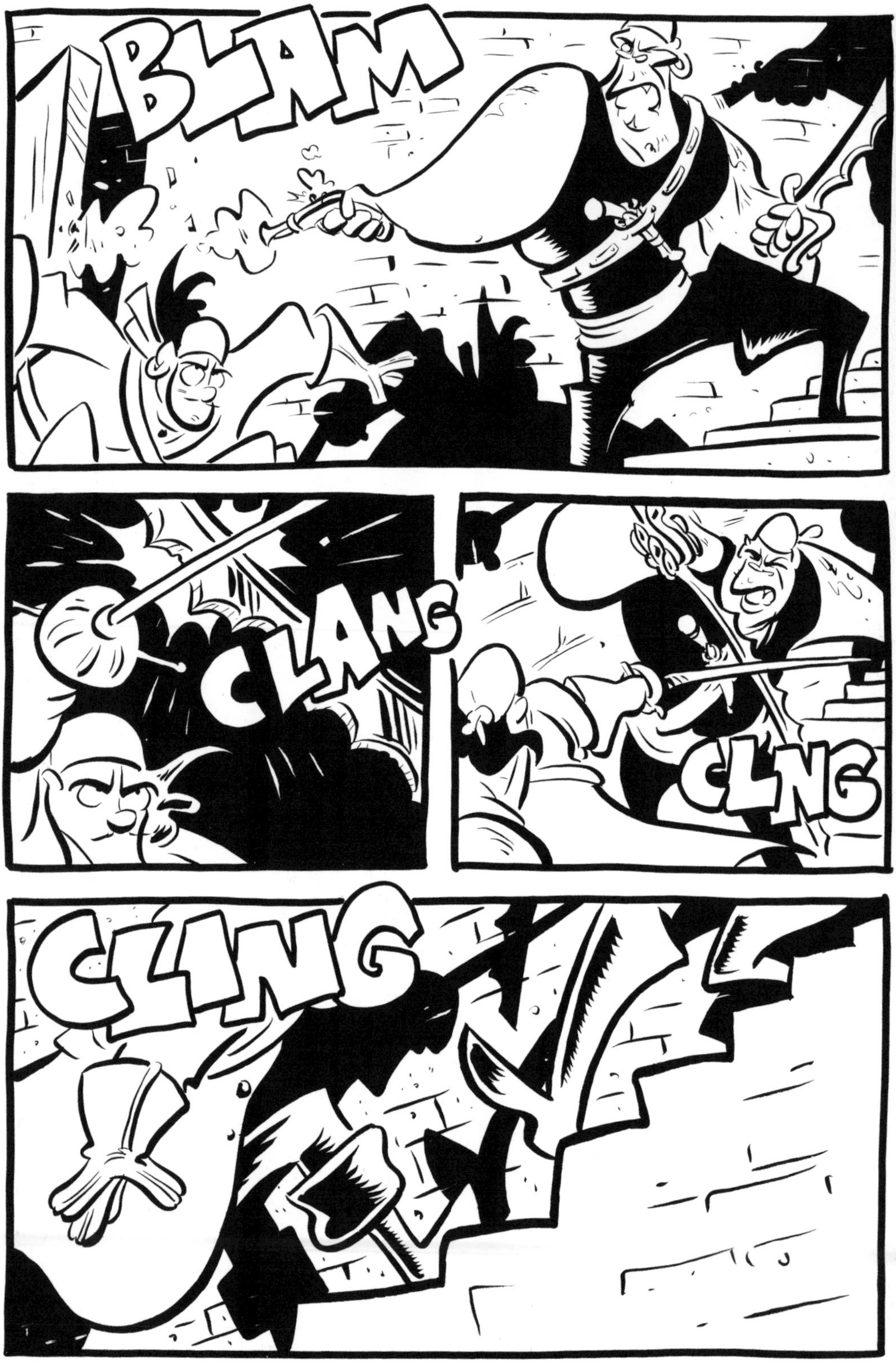
BLAM
CLANG
CLNG
CLING

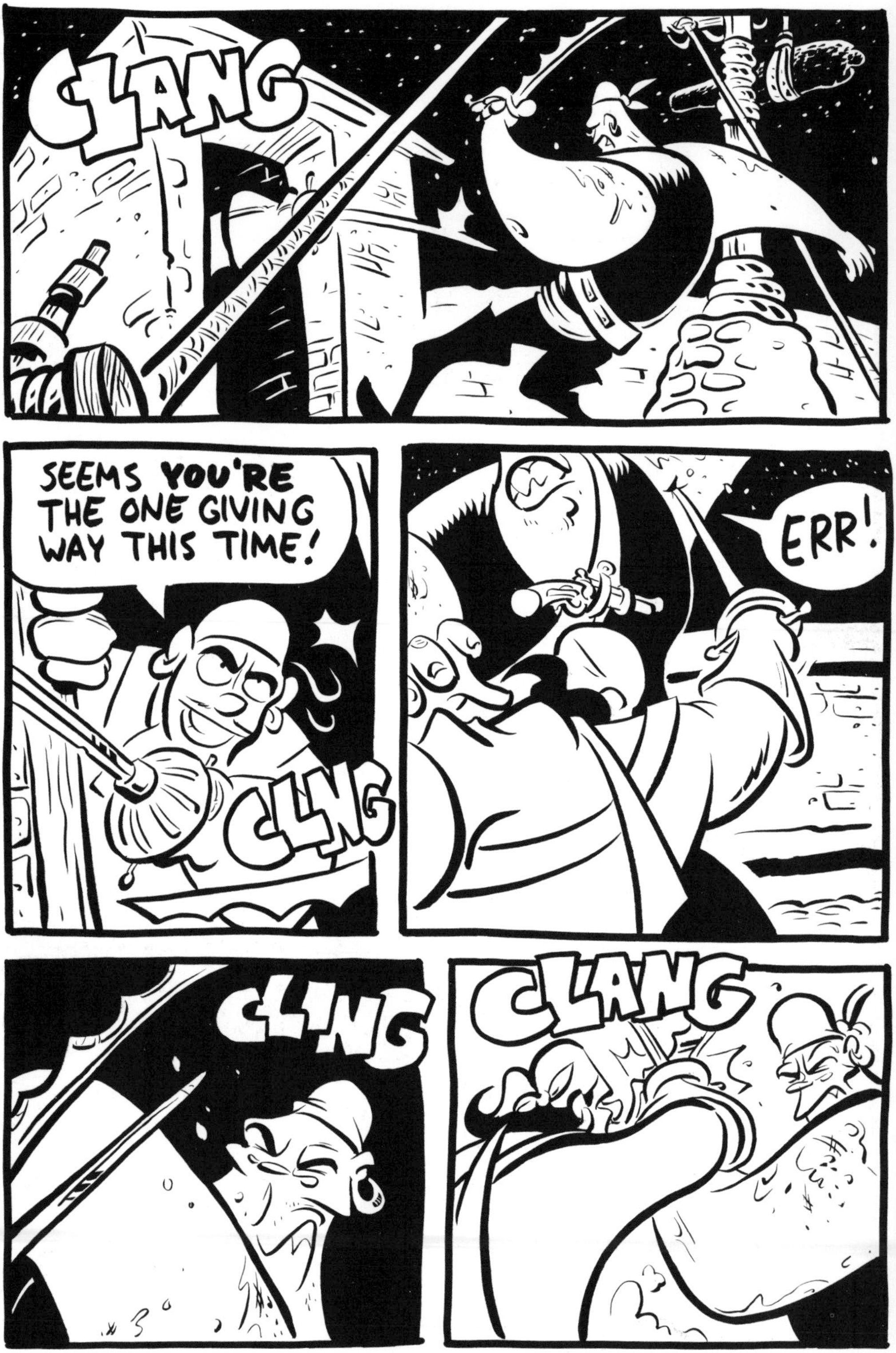
CLANG
SEEMS YOU'RE THE ONE GIVING WAY THIS TIME!
CLNG
ERR!
CLING
CLANG

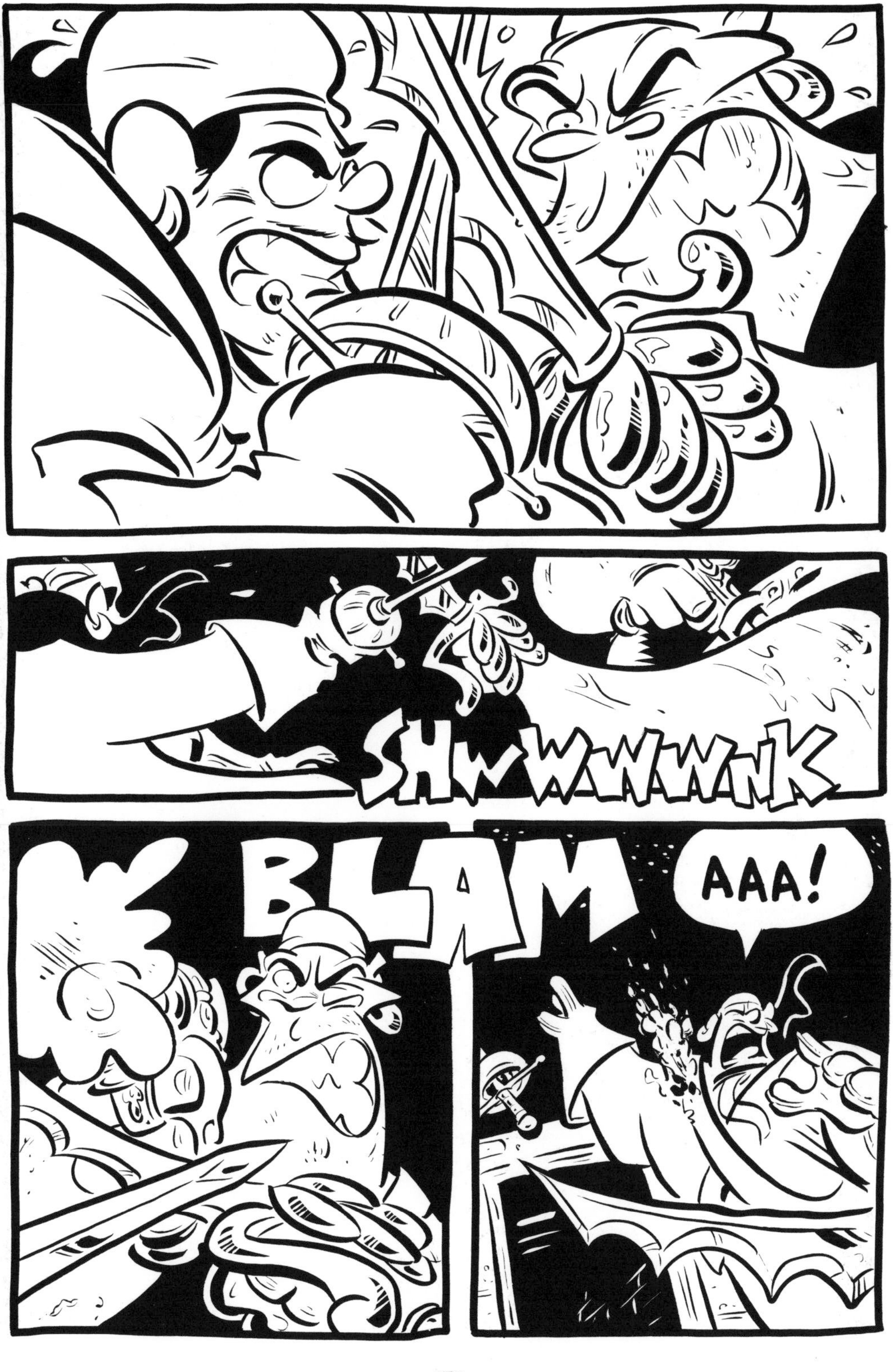
SHWWWWWNK
BLAM
AAA!

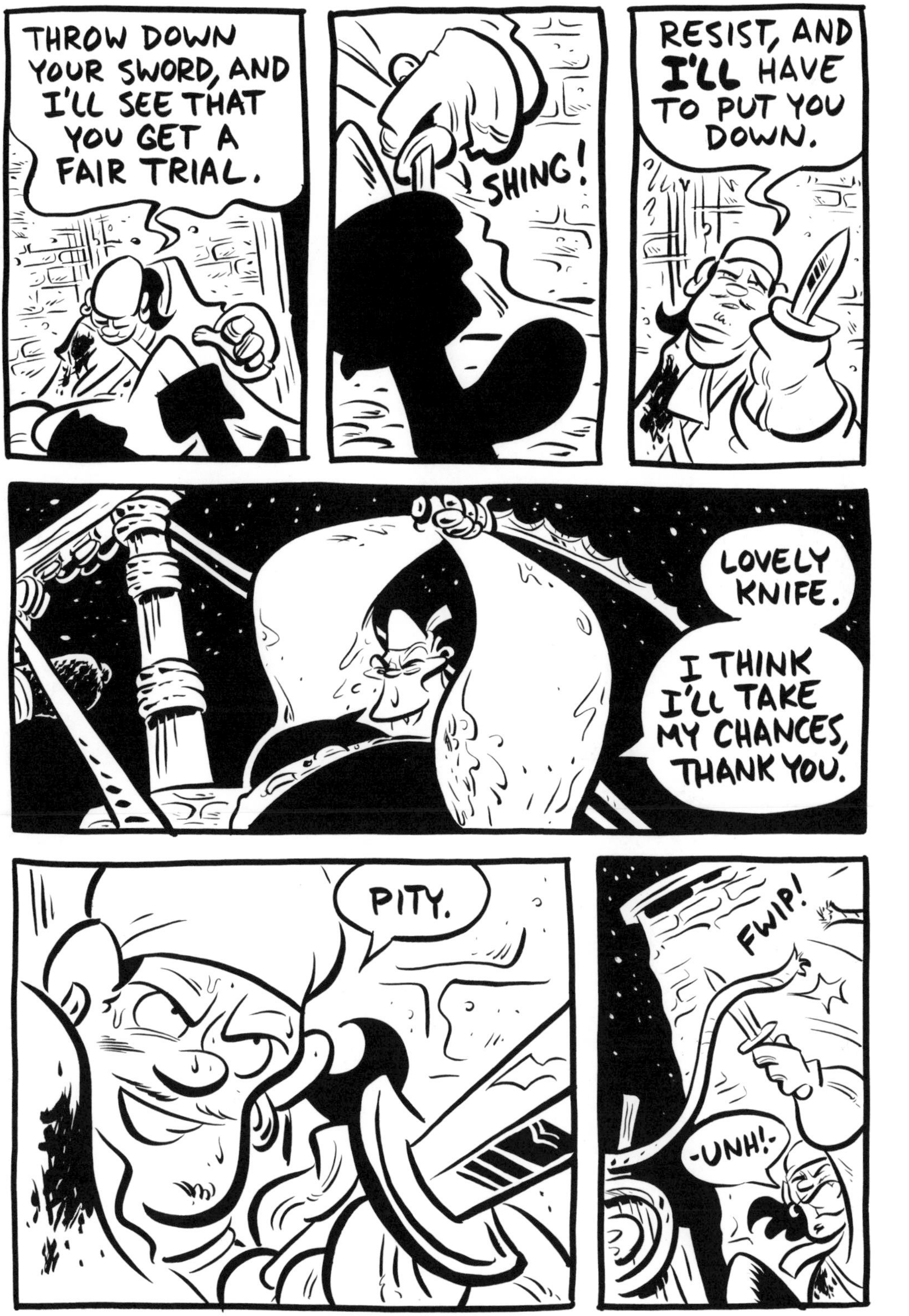
THROW DOWN YOUR SWORD, AND I'LL SEE THAT YOU GET A FAIR TRIAL.
SHING!
RESIST, AND I'LL HAVE TO PUT YOU DOWN.
LOVELY KNIFE.
I THINK I'LL TAKE MY CHANCES, THANK YOU.
PITY.
FWIP!
-UNH!-

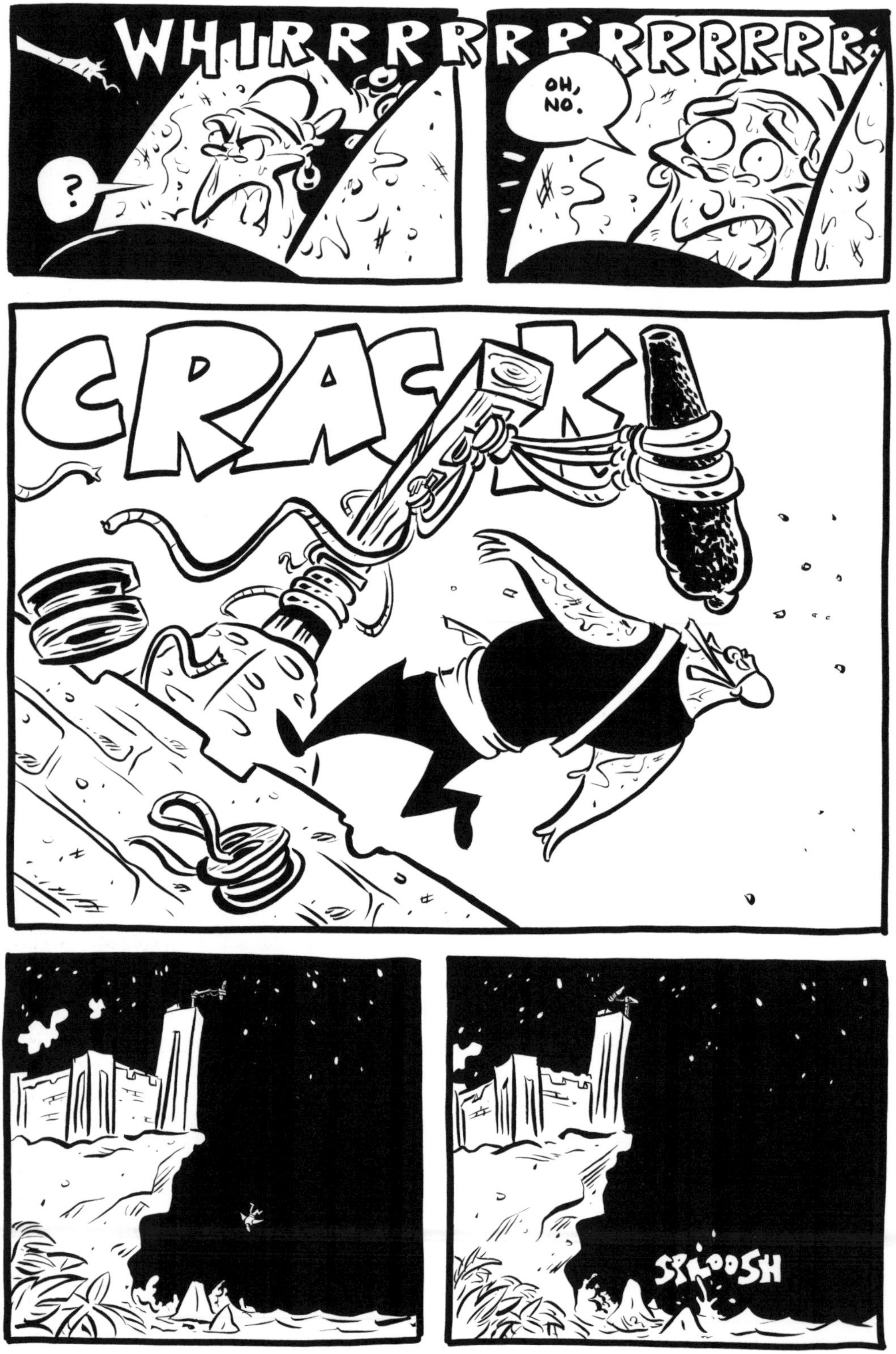
WHIRRRRRRRRRRRR
?
OH, NO.
CRACK
SPLOOSH

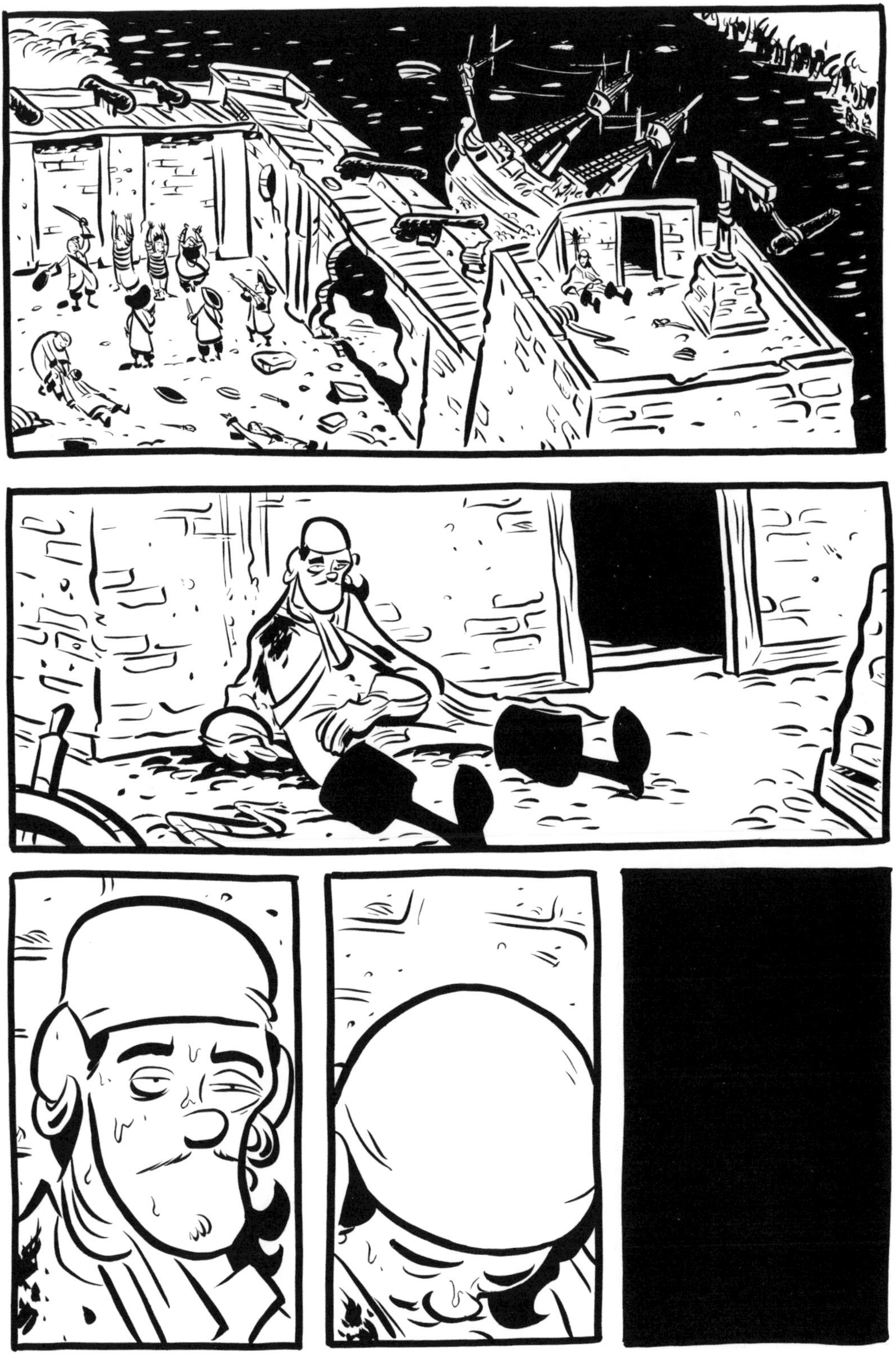

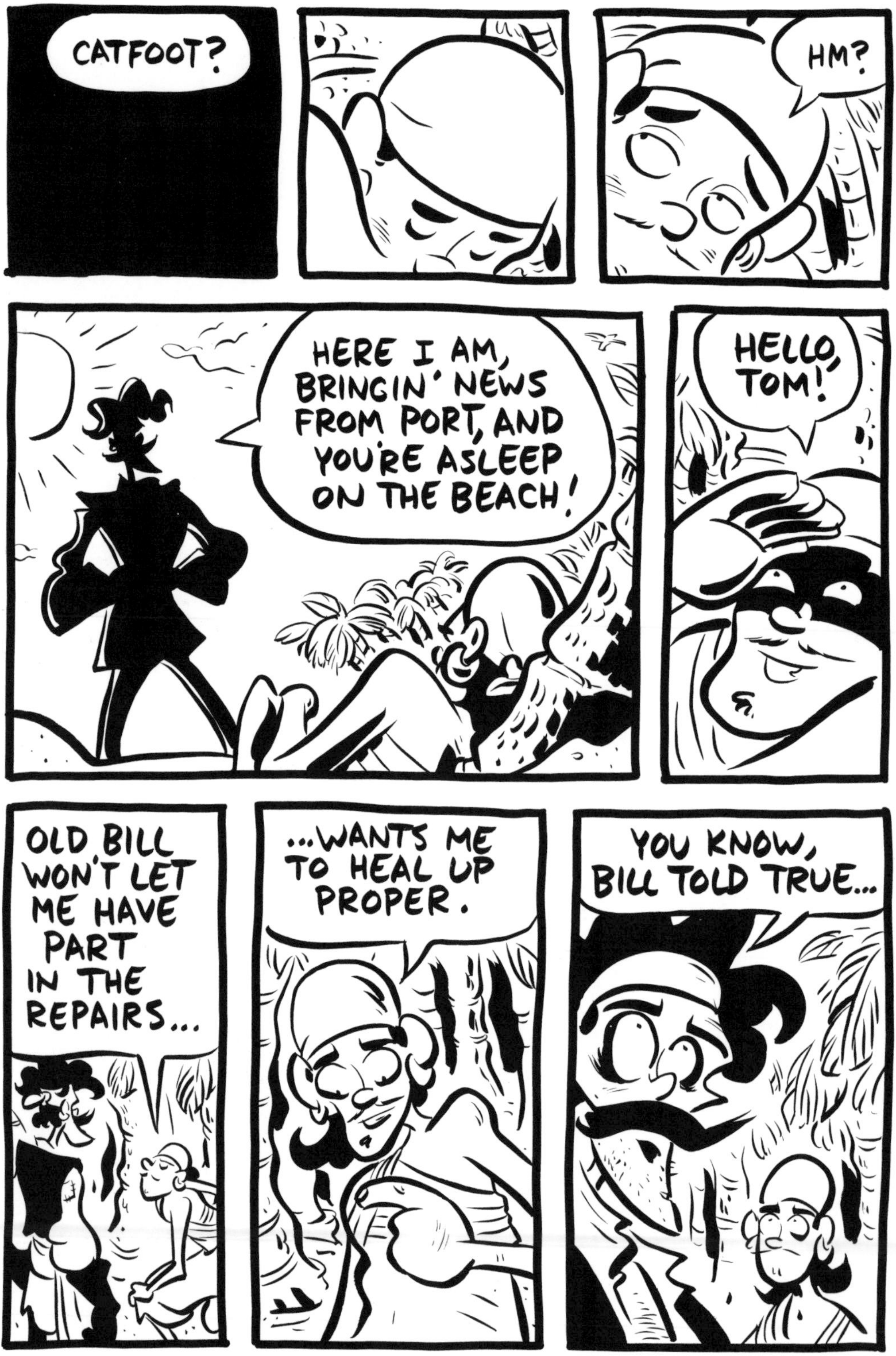
CATFOOT?
HM?
HERE I AM, BRINGIN' NEWS FROM PORT, AND YOU'RE ASLEEP ON THE BEACH!
HELLO, TOM!
OLD BILL WON'T LET ME HAVE PART IN THE REPAIRS...
...WANTS ME TO HEAL UP PROPER.
YOU KNOW, BILL TOLD TRUE...

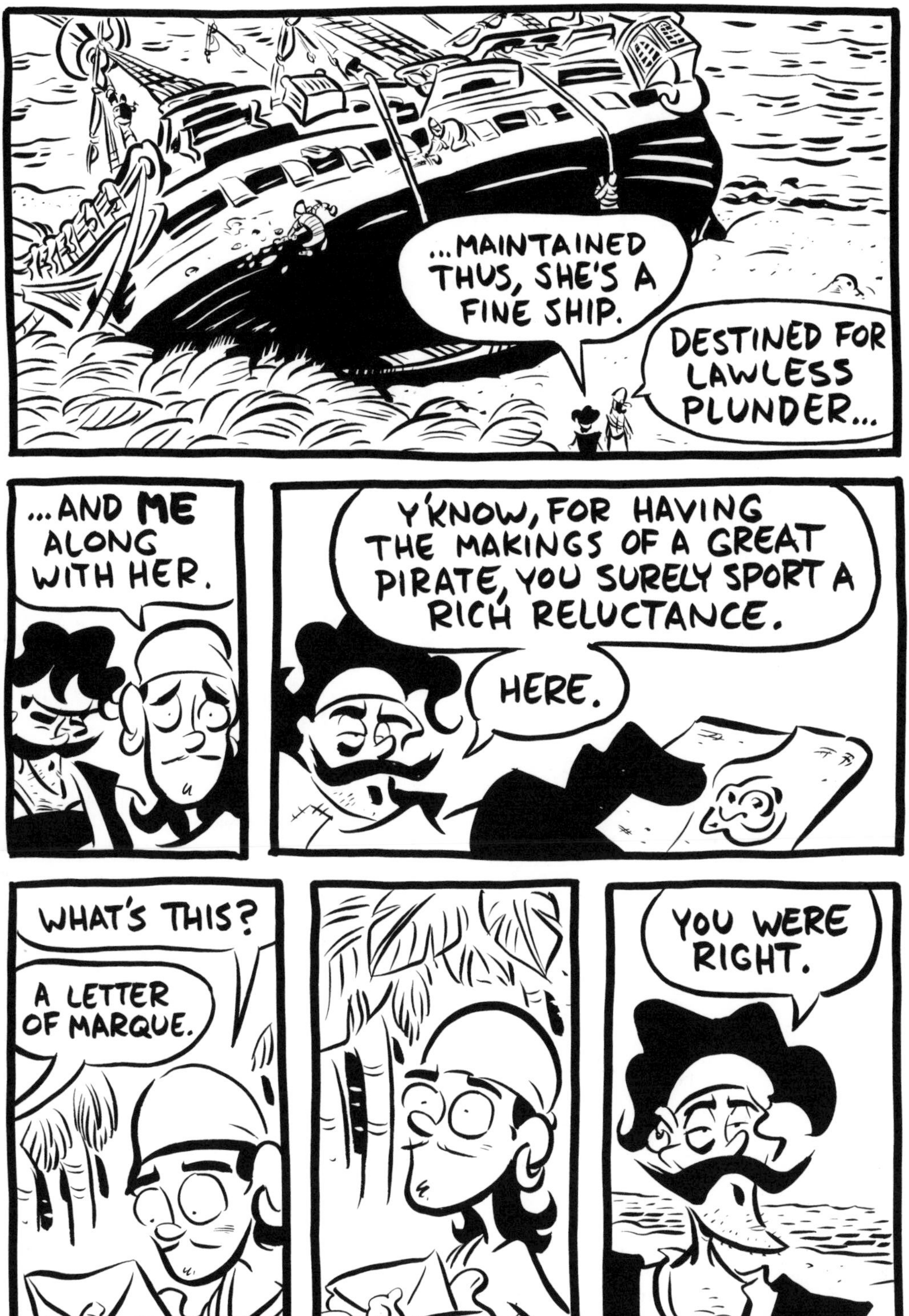
...MAINTAINED THUS, SHE'S A FINE SHIP.
DESTINED FOR LAWLESS PLUNDER...
...AND **ME** ALONG WITH HER.
Y'KNOW, FOR HAVING THE MAKINGS OF A GREAT PIRATE, YOU SURELY SPORT A RICH RELUCTANCE.
HERE.
WHAT'S THIS?
A LETTER OF MARQUE.
YOU WERE RIGHT.

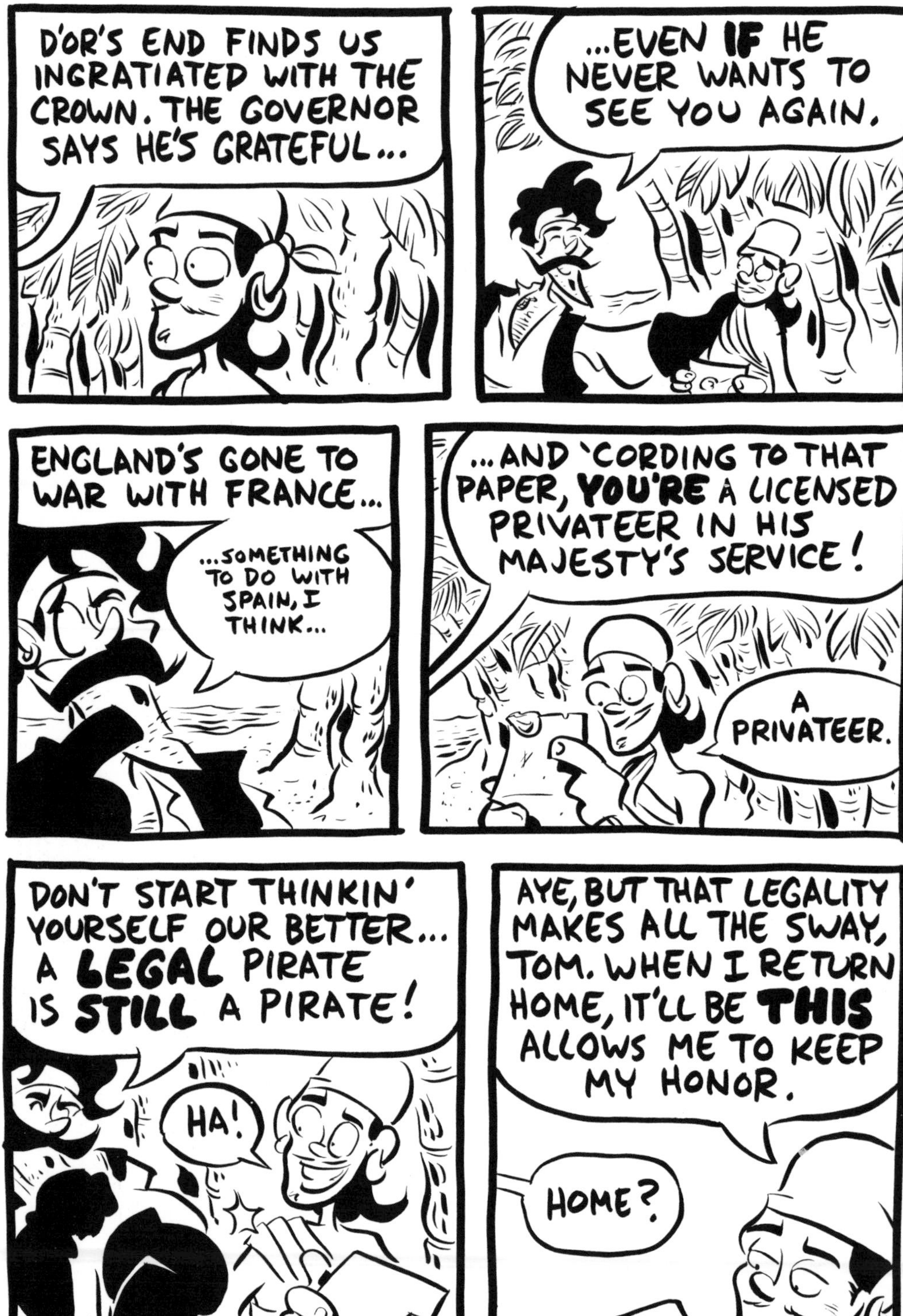
D'OR'S END FINDS US INGRATIATED WITH THE CROWN. THE GOVERNOR SAYS HE'S GRATEFUL...
...EVEN **IF** HE NEVER WANTS TO SEE YOU AGAIN.
ENGLAND'S GONE TO WAR WITH FRANCE...
...SOMETHING TO DO WITH SPAIN, I THINK...
...AND 'CORDING TO THAT PAPER, **YOU'RE** A LICENSED PRIVATEER IN HIS MAJESTY'S SERVICE!
A PRIVATEER.
DON'T START THINKIN' YOURSELF OUR BETTER... A **LEGAL** PIRATE IS **STILL** A PIRATE!
HA!
AYE, BUT THAT LEGALITY MAKES ALL THE SWAY, TOM. WHEN I RETURN HOME, IT'LL BE **THIS** ALLOWS ME TO KEEP MY HONOR.
HOME?

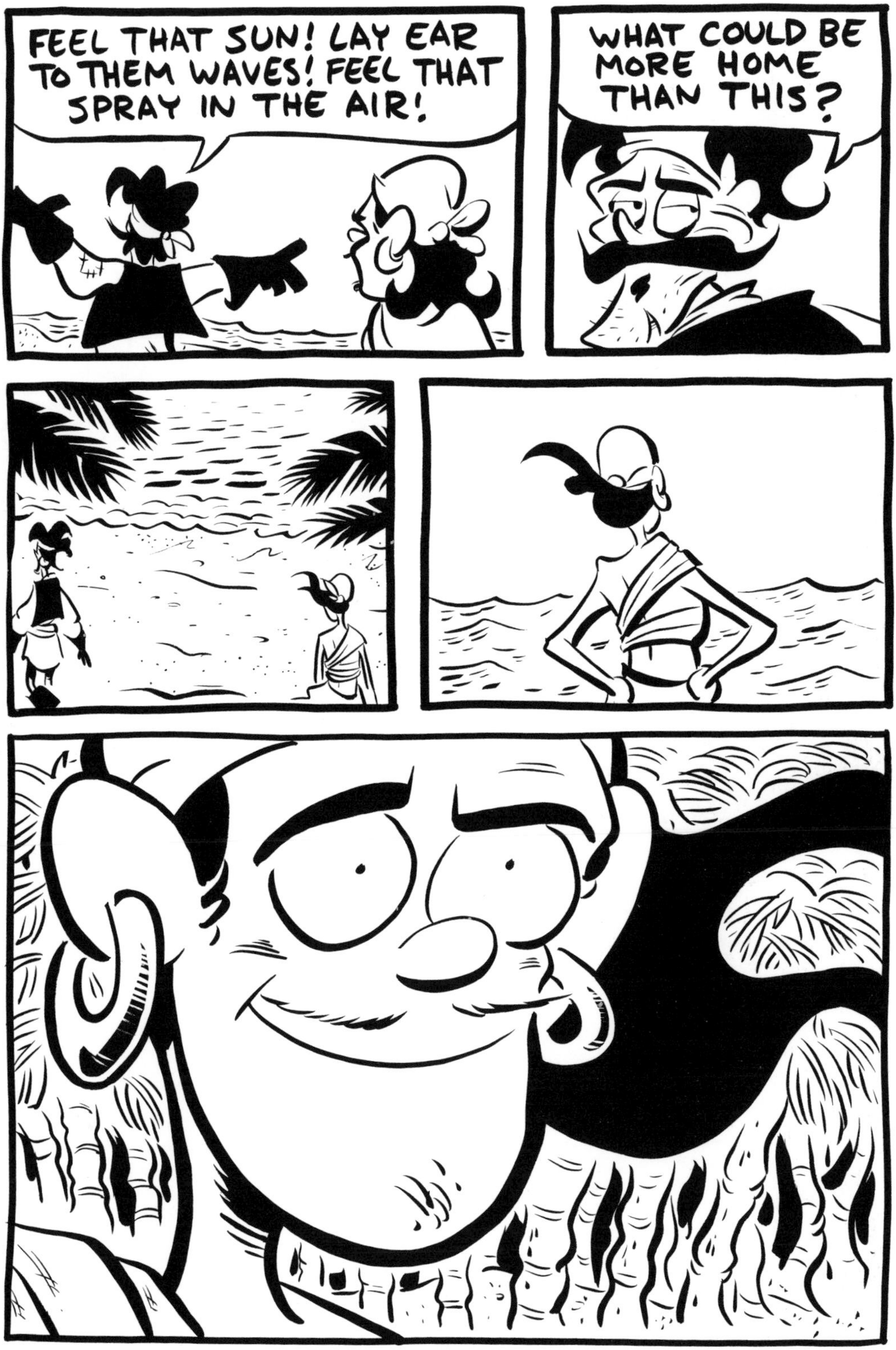
FEEL THAT SUN! LAY EAR TO THEM WAVES! FEEL THAT SPRAY IN THE AIR!
WHAT COULD BE MORE HOME THAN THIS?

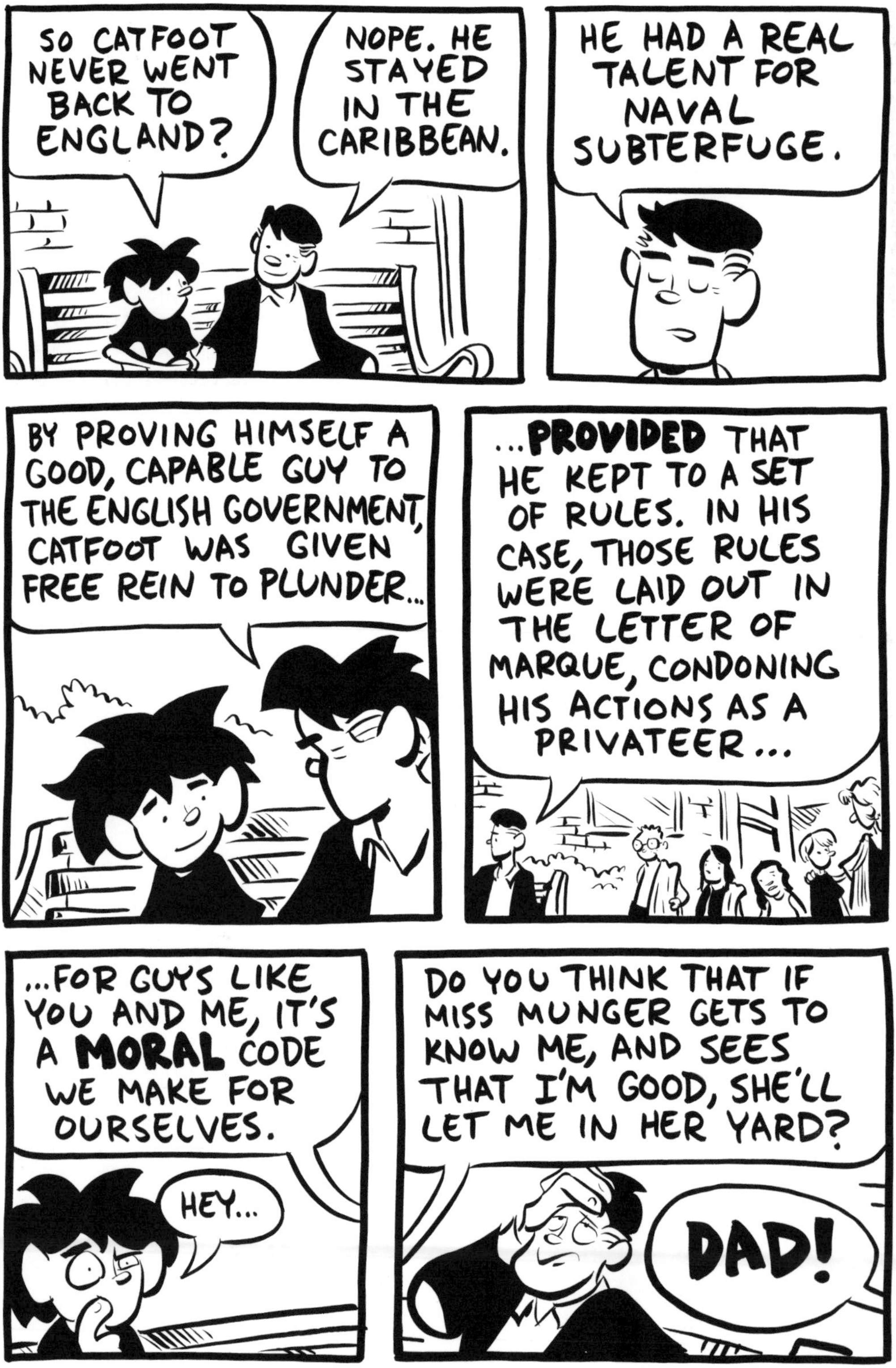
SO CATFOOT NEVER WENT BACK TO ENGLAND?
NOPE. HE STAYED IN THE CARIBBEAN.
HE HAD A REAL TALENT FOR NAVAL SUBTERFUGE.
BY PROVING HIMSELF A GOOD, CAPABLE GUY TO THE ENGLISH GOVERNMENT, CATFOOT WAS GIVEN FREE REIN TO PLUNDER...
...PROVIDED THAT HE KEPT TO A SET OF RULES. IN HIS CASE, THOSE RULES WERE LAID OUT IN THE LETTER OF MARQUE, CONDONING HIS ACTIONS AS A PRIVATEER...
...FOR GUYS LIKE YOU AND ME, IT'S A MORAL CODE WE MAKE FOR OURSELVES.
HEY...
DO YOU THINK THAT IF MISS MUNGER GETS TO KNOW ME, AND SEES THAT I'M GOOD, SHE'LL LET ME IN HER YARD?
DAD!

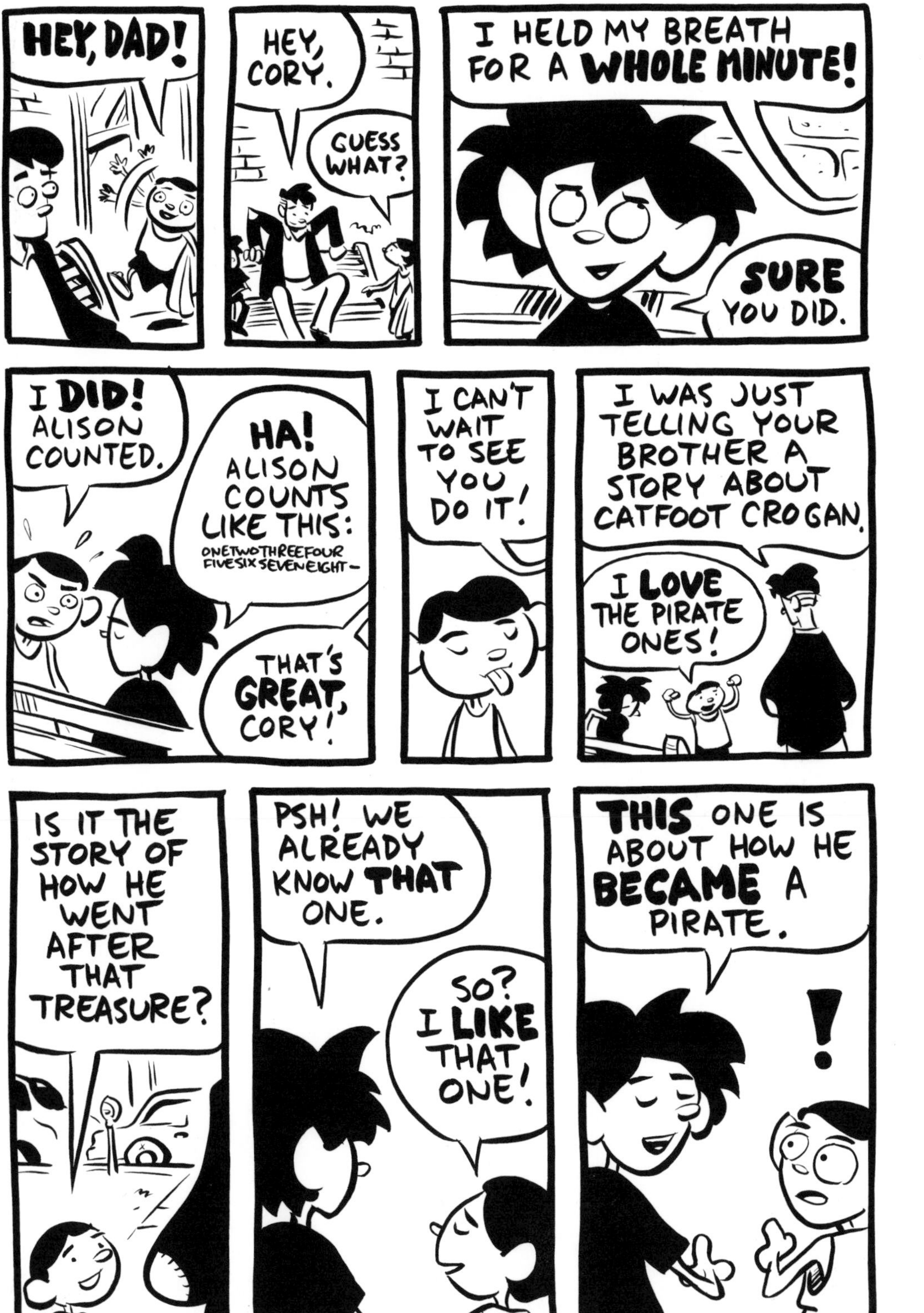
HEY, DAD!
HEY, CORY.
GUESS WHAT?
I HELD MY BREATH FOR A WHOLE MINUTE!
SURE YOU DID.
I DID! ALISON COUNTED.
HA! ALISON COUNTS LIKE THIS: ONETWOTHREEFOUR FIVESIX SEVENEIGHT–
THAT'S GREAT, CORY!
I CAN'T WAIT TO SEE YOU DO IT!
I WAS JUST TELLING YOUR BROTHER A STORY ABOUT CATFOOT CROGAN.
I LOVE THE PIRATE ONES!
IS IT THE STORY OF HOW HE WENT AFTER THAT TREASURE?
PSH! WE ALREADY KNOW THAT ONE.
SO? I LIKE THAT ONE!
THIS ONE IS ABOUT HOW HE BECAME A PIRATE.
!

About the author...

CHRIS SCHWEIZER was born in Tucson, AZ in 1980 to parents who are both classical musicians. He received his BFA in Graphic Design from Murray State University in 2004, and his MFA in Sequential Art from the Savannah College of Art and Design in Atlanta. He lives on the outskirts of Atlanta with his wife Liz and daughter Penelope.

Chris has, at various points, been a hotel manager, a movie theater projectionist, a guard at a mental institution, a martial arts instructor, a set builder, a process server, a window-painter, a church music leader, a life-drawing model, a bartender, a car wash attendant, a bagboy, a delivery boy, a choirboy, a lawn boy, a sixth-grade social studies teacher, a janitor, a speakeasy proprietor, a video store clerk, a puppeteer for a children's television show, a muralist, and a lineworker at a pancake mix factory. He now teaches comics at SCAD-Atlanta.

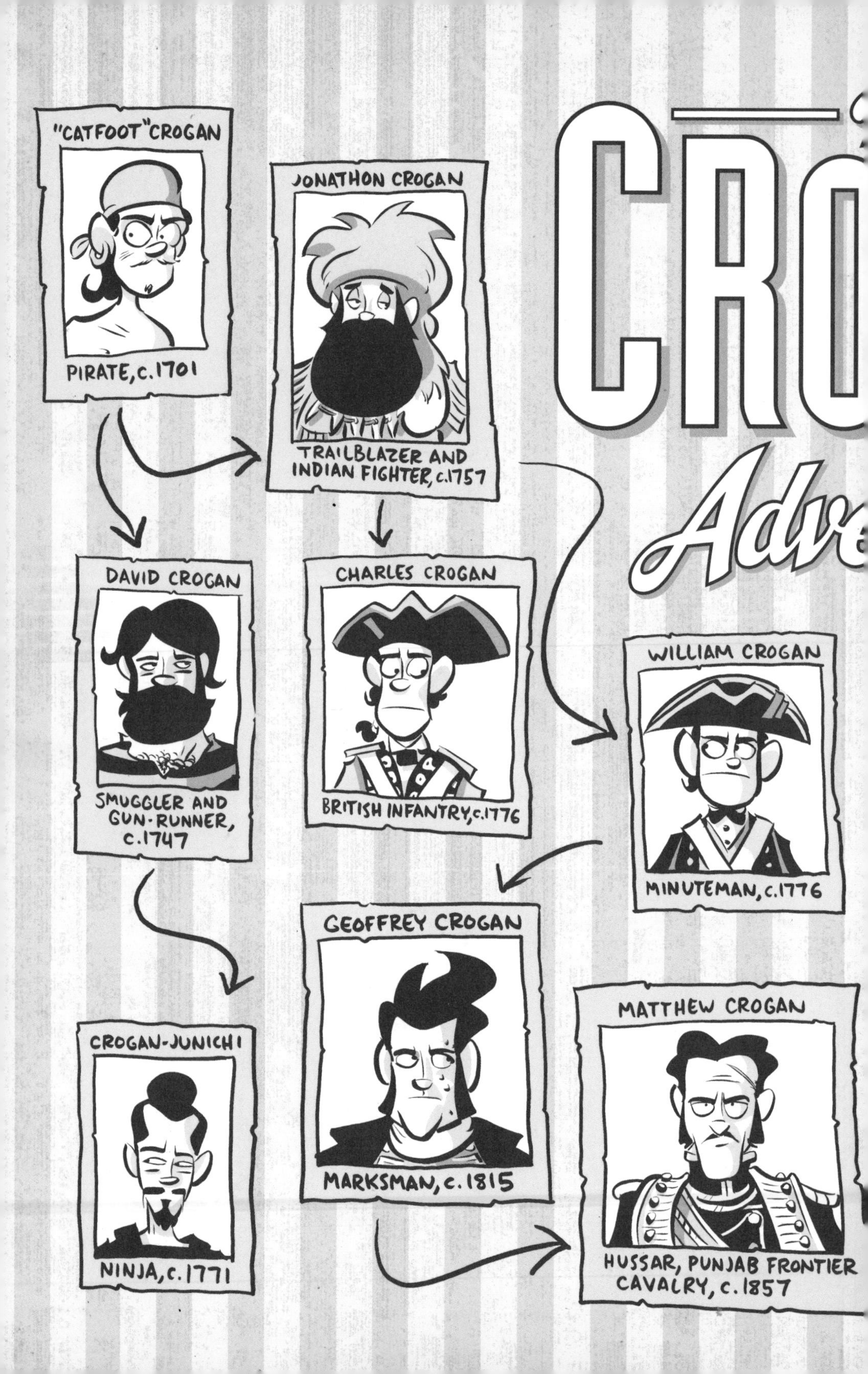

"CATFOOT" CROGAN
PIRATE, c.1701
JONATHON CROGAN
TRAILBLAZER AND INDIAN FIGHTER, c.1757
DAVID CROGAN
SMUGGLER AND GUN-RUNNER, c.1747
CHARLES CROGAN
BRITISH INFANTRY, c.1776
WILLIAM CROGAN
MINUTEMAN, c.1776
GEOFFREY CROGAN
MARKSMAN, c.1815
CROGAN-JUNICHI
NINJA, c.1771
MATTHEW CROGAN
HUSSAR, PUNJAB FRONTIER CAVALRY, c.1857